DAVID ASTLE

THE BABYLONIAN WOE

A Study of the Origin of Certain Banking Practices,
and of their effect on the events of Ancient History,
written in the light of the Present Day.

THE BABYLONIAN WOE

BY DAVID ASTLE

A Study of the Origin of Certain Banking Practices, and of their effect on the events of Ancient History, written in the light of the Present Day.

First Edition - 1975

Published by Omnia Veritas Ltd

www.omnia-veritas.com

The intellectual faculties however are not of themselves sufficient to produce external action; they require the aid of physical force, the direction and combination of which are wholly at the disposal of money, that mighty spring by which the total force of human energies is set in motion.

Augustus Boeckh; Translated;
The Public Economy of Athens, p. 7;
Book I. London, 1828.

THE BABYLONIAN WOE

TABLE OF CONTENTS

FOREWORD..9

IN THE BEGINNING WAS THE WORD.........................21

THE TEMPLE AND THE COUNTING HOUSE.................35

PER ME DEI REGNANT!..57

THE LEFT HAND OF DAWN..87

BLOOD, SORROW, AND SILVER.................................109

BABYLON, BANKING, AND BULLION..........................125

PHRYGIA, FINANCE, AND FRONT MAN......................135

TYRANT AND RAPEZITAE..147

POTSHERDS AND OTHER RAGMENTS........................169

PERGAMUM AND ITANE...190

VOICES FROM THE DUST..203

SPARTA, THE PELANORS, WEALTH, AND WOMEN.........233

MONEY CREATORS AND THE POLITICAL CONTROL......257

MAN PROPOSES BUT GOD DISPOSES.........................287

BIBLIOGRAPHY...297

FOREWORD

"For money has been the ruin of many and has misled the minds of Kings." —Ecclesiacticus 8, Verse 2.

When I originally approached my study as best as I might, dealing with the growth in pre-antiquity and antiquity of what is known as the International Money Power, and the particular derivative of the money creative activities of such International Money Power that might be defined as the Life Alternative Factor, I did so with some diffidence. Perhaps I was overly conscious of what seemed to be the inadequateness of my preliminary training in these matters and that in no way could I describe myself as deeply conversant with the languages of ancient times, or, in the case of Mesopotamia, their scripts.

However, in my preliminary studies involving checking through the indices of a number of those standard books of reference dealing with the ancient civilizations, I soon found that any feelings of inferiority in so far as the adequacy of my scholarship relative to my particular subject was concerned were unwarranted, and that qualms in these respects were by no means justified.

In almost all of such books of reference, except those that classified themselves as economic or monetary histories, was practically no clear approach to the subject of money and finance, or to those exchange systems that must have existed in order that the so-called civilizations might come to be. In the odd case where the translations of the texts might reveal some key clue, no more special emphasis was placed herein than might have been placed on the mention of a gold cup, a ring, a seal, or some exquisite piece of stone work.

In Jastrow's *Assyria* there was no reference to money at all; in Breasted's *History of Egypt* a volume of six hundred pages or so, only brief mention on pages 97-98. In *A History of Egypt* by Sir William M. Flinders-Petrie, in the records of Sir John Marshall and E.J.C. McKay in respect to the diggings at Mohenjo-Daro, and in the writings of Sir Charles L. Woolley and others on their findings from their studies of the exhumed archives of the city states of ancient Mesopotamia, little enough information exists on the matters referred to above. In Christopher Dawson who wrote widely on ancient times, particularly in the *Age of the Gods* which dealt with most cultures until the commencement of that period known as antiquity, there is only one reference to money, casual and not conveying much to the average reader; this reference to be found on page 131. In King's *History of Babylon* there was practically nothing on these matters.

Thus in almost all of the works of the great archaeologists and scholars specializing in the ancient civilizations, there is a virtual silence on that all important matter, the system of distribution of food surpluses, and surpluses of all those items needed towards the maintenance of a good and continuing life so far as were required by climate and custom.

In all the writings of these great and practical scholars, the workings of that mighty engine which injects the unit of exchange amongst the peoples, and without which no civilization as we know it can come to be, is only indicated by a profound silence. Of the systems of exchanges, of the unit of exchange and its issue by private individuals, as distinct from its issue as by the authority of sovereign rule, on this all important matter governing in such totality the conditions of progression into the future of these peoples, not a word to speak of.

While it is true that the average archaeologist, in being primarily concerned with the results of the forces that gave rise to the human accretions known as civilizations, has little enough time to meditate on these forces themselves, especially since so little evidence exists of what created them, or of how they provided guidance to men in the earlier days, the widespread character of this omission borders on the mystifying. Virtual failure to speculate on those most important matters of all: the structure of the machinery of the systems of exchanges which undoubtedly had given rise to the ancient city civilizations, and the true nature of the energy source by which such machinery was driven, whether by injections of *money* as known this last three thousand years or so, or by injections of an exchange medium of which little significant evidence or memory remains, is cause for concern. The truth of the lines as quoted herein from Boeckh's *Public Economy of Athens* (p.ii, present work) is immediately clear to all and that the physical force underlying all civilizations must have been the system whereby surpluses were allocated to the people according to their place in the pyramid of life and to their need; thus, when being controlled by the benevolent law of a dedicated ruler, maintaining at all times the true and natural order of life.

It must not be supposed, therefore, that there is lack of understanding of the importance of these matters; nor that there is any special conspiracy of silence, even though there might indeed be temptation to arrive at such a conclusion.[1] Rather it were better to accept things as they appear, and assume that these scholars merely present the fragments of fact as they unearth them; leaving speculation of the true significance of such fragments of fact in relation to the weft and warp of life, to those considered to be particularly specialized in the various fields represented. In the case of money and finance, the scholars concerned would be classified as economic or monetary historians.

---

[1] According to *Tragedy and Hope*, the important and compendious work of Dr. Carroll Quigley, an outstanding scholar of liberal outlook, (as interpreted by the reviewer, W. Cleon Skousen), such conspiracy certainly exists, and is vast in scope to say the least.

Thus little enough seems to be available on the subject of money and finance in ancient days. Nor seems to exist examination of the significance of such money and finance relative to the progress about which so much has been written in modern times. Apart from that of Alexander Del Mar who wrote in relatively recent days, and apart from that of the philosophers of antiquity such as Plato, Aristotle, Socrates, Zeno, etc., almost no speculation seems to be available from scholarly sources in regards to the unprejudiced *PHILOSOPHY* of money, in ancient times. On the all important subject of the consequences of the creation and issuance of money by private persons as opposed to its creation and issuance according to the will of a benevolent, instructed and dedicated ruler, almost no speculation seems to exist in ancient or in modern times. Of those forces that sought throughout history to undermine any ruler who may have been firmly in the saddle because of his exercise of that prerogative which is the foundation of the State Power or God-Will of which he is the living evincement, insomuch as he maintained firm control of the original issuance of money and its injection into circulation amongst the people as against State expenditures, almost nothing seems to be known. Very little information is available of the means those forces employed towards this purpose through injection into circulation amongst the peoples of silver and gold, and of instruments indicating possession of the same.

Practically no information seems to exist of the growth of private money creation in the days of the ancient city states of Mesopotamia, of which, because of their records being preserved on fire-baked clay, more is known than of more recent civilizations; and the gap must necessarily be filled by a certain amount of speculation. Little is known of the beginnings of the fraudulent issuance by private persons of the unit of exchange, as in opposition to the law of the gods from whom kings in ancient times claimed to derive their divine origin; nor is there any information on the significance of such practice relative to the continued stability of the natural order of life in which obtained that system wherein the fount of all power was the God; such power descending to man by way of king and priesthood and directing him as he proceeded about his everyday affairs, content that God's in His Heaven and all's right with the world.

The use of tools of hardened iron in the mining industry about the beginning of the first millennium B.C., together with a changed attitude towards slave labour in which the slave, so far as mining was concerned, was assessed at cost per life, must have brought relatively a very flood of silver into the circulation of the cities of the Near East.

Such flood of silver injected into the circulation largely by private business houses who no doubt controlled the mines, however distant, especially after the institution of coinage in which a piece of silver of known weight and fineness passed from hand to hand, must finally and forever have broken that control of exchanges previously exercised by the god of the city through priest king, and priest.

Thus all, priest-kings and priests, came to forget that the foundations of the power given to them from on High towards the maintenance of the right living and tranquil procession through life, of their peoples, were the laws of distribution of surpluses as written on the scribes tablet; laws instituted by the god himself each ordering a specified dispensation from the surpluses in his warehouses in the Ziggurat, to the holder of the tablet. They too fell into the error of believing that silver with value created as a result of its being used as a balancing factor in international exchange could become a perpetual storehouse of value. They themselves became consumed in the scramble for this gleaming metal, so conceding it, through its controllers the power to set itself up in opposition to the law of the gods; to raise itself up in its own right, god in itself.

In its exercise, the fiat of the internationally minded group of merchants or bullion brokers that arbitrarily dictated the exchange value of such silver, being in actuality determination internationally of the value of money, placed such groups controlling silver exchanges above and beyond local law and the law of the local god, and indeed conferred on them the power to influence kingly appointment. It made of them the servants of a one god, a god above all gods; thereby somewhat relegating the god whose order on the state warehouses as inscribed on clay by scribe or priest, had been the law governing exchanges, to the place of their servant, the instrument.

"I have however, kept before me as a guiding principle, in this as other historical works I have written, the maxim that the complexity of life should never be forgotten, and that no single feature should be regarded as basic and decisive,"[2] wrote Professor Rostovtsev, scholar and Economic Historian of renown.

It is true that while no single feature in the progression of history might be regarded as basic and decisive, it is certain that neither money nor treasure will protect the weak and disarmed in the face of a brutal and determined conqueror beyond whose successful achievements, can be no decision more final. It is also certain that the money accumulation mania injected by fame into the minds of the people as a replacement to their concern with those natural qualities endeavouring to colour the current of human life through time, amongst which are numbered virtue, honour, and godliness, destroys equally as any other debilitating disease, and will surely and speedily drag any people down to degeneracy and decay. A great army could not be more efficient in its power of destruction.

---

[2] Mikhail I. Rostovtsev: *A Social and Economic History of the Hellenistic World*, p. viii, Vol. I. (Oxford; 1941).

The main discussion of the *Artha-Sastra* of Kautilya, Hindu classic instructing kings and rulers as to their proper conduct towards good government, was as to whether financial or military organization came first of all as the root of strength and power in any organized state.³ Clearly in that day no less than in this day, financial organization preceded military organization; therefore there is not much point really in discussion of so obvious a fact and truth.

While an effete people, though *money* as it is known, is in their hands, soon give way to vigour; nevertheless vigour, without strict organization of its finances, which, while constituting strict organization of its labour, also enables it to create, or to obtain by purchase from elsewhere the finest of weapons, will not much avail. Thus, and it has been demonstrated through history over and over again, it is clear there is one feature basic and decisive in the progression of human life; certainly during the latter years of which memory exists. That feature, particularly in relatively modern societies from the bronze age onwards, and during that period of the rapid perfection of the mass production of weapons, is monetary organization, and what precious metals are available for purposes of international exchange as against the purchase of those finest of weapons and essential materials of war only obtainable abroad, and as wages for the most skilled men at arms from wherever obtainable, abroad or otherwise.

The gates of Egypt stand fast like Inmutet
They open not to the Westerners,
They open not to the Easterners,
They open not to the Northerners,
They open not to the Southerners,

---

³ Sarvepalli Radhakrishnan and Charles Moore: *A Source Book in Indian Philosophy*, pp 219-220. Princeton; 1957.

They open not to the enemy who dwells within.[4]

Much of history as we know it is the record of civilizations to counter and evade destruction of themselves from without or within, or is the record of their efforts to destroy other seemingly competing civilizations or peoples attacking them from without or within.

War is as inevitable as is peace as the result of the exhaustion of war, and there are few peoples that escape; but wars of the last three thousand years have not been relatively infrequent occurrences, and have been an incessantly recurring evil. It is no chance that; the growth of warfare into a very cancer eating into the vitals of mankind, and more particularly the white races is parallel to the growth of that other cancer which is private, and therefore irresponsible, money creation and emission.

It seems that almost none of the scholars make any serious effort to throw light on the real meaning of this matter of private monetary emission, and the disastrous effects that it has had, and in finality, will have, towards the defining of the remaining period of time of man upon this earth, as being brief and uncertain.

Those strange decisions of kings signalling the opening of wars as frightful and disastrous to the European peoples, as the last two so-called "World Wars," decisions so abnegatory of self, but more than that, abnegatory of the best interests of the peoples they represented before God, far from being the directives of benevolent force, are the directives of a force

---

[4] Ancient Egyptian Poem; Christopher Dawson: *The Age of the Gods*, p. 148.

which cannot but be described in any way but as being wholly malevolent.[5]

The great engine which is the international control of monetary emission and regulation, driven as it was until recently by the catalytic fuel of gold alone, is now almost world embracing in the scope of its operations. It seems there is no change in the attitude of those its guides, nor any admission of the folly of their misuse of this God-Power which they direct towards the good of themselves and their friends. Their obsession, despite ruin for all looming on every horizon, seems to remain the same narrow vision of the day of their own world supremacy wherein they will rule as absolute lords over all; although by now it should be apparent to them, no less than to all thinking people, that if this madness concealed within the much talked about conception known as *progress* is not brought to a complete arrestment, nothing remains but an end wherein shall be silence and no song, for indeed there will be no singer, nor any to sing to.

As it looks today, it may be the end for the Indo-European peoples whose diligent labours made so much of this world of today. It may be the end, final and absolute for all men for that matter. it may be the end for this our Earth, our only place and home and hope in the awful endlessness of space and time.

It should be more than apparent that in the relatively recent day when kingship and god-ship were one, so far as the simple souls were concerned, and the god and his viceroy on earth, the priest-king, were creators and controllers of the economic

---

[5] For example, the folly of Britain in letting itself and the Empire be stamped into these last two so-called "Great" wars, may be compared to that of the man described by the Emperor Augustus who goes fishing with a golden hook; he has everything lose and little to gain. (Suetonius: *the Twelve Caesars* II, 25)

good, exchanges were created in order that the people might live a fuller life, and not so much to benefit any secret society or interlocked group standing aside from the main paths of mankind, but to benefit all who kneeled humbly before the Almighty, each fully in acceptance of himself as part of the god-wish, eternal and infinite; each one in his time an integral unit carefully placed in the pyramid of life itself.

History over these last three thousand years particularly, has largely been the interweaving of both a witting, and an unwitting distortion of the truth, with all the inevitable consequences which have been expected[6] and now are but a little way ahead. Kings largely became the mouthpiece and sword arm of those semi-secret societies that controlled the material of money as its outward and visible symbols came to be restricted to gold, silver, and copper. The fiat of the god in heaven which had been the decisive force behind that which brought about an equitable exchange, was replaced by the will of those classes controlling the undertones of civilization, leaders of the world of slave drivers, caravaneers, outcasts, and criminals generally, such as was to be discerned on the edges of the ancient city civilizations, and followed the trade routes between them. The instrument of this will was precious metal, whose supply was controlled by the leaders of these classes through their control of the slave trade, since mining was rarely profitable in the case of the precious metals, except with slave labour, even after the development of hardened iron tools and efficient methods of smelting.

The power of these men, indifferent and alien to most cities as they were, relative to that power it was replacing, which was the will of the benevolent god of the city, had been made absolute by sowing in the minds of men over the thousands of years, the idea of such metals having a specially high value relative to

---

[6] Much of this was foretold in the *Revelation of St. John the Divine*.

other goods and services being offered for exchange; indeed that they were veritable store house of value.

The law of the ruler previously exercised towards the well being of the people in that they might live a good and honourable life accordingly became corrupted. It became merely a symbol raised before their gaze, in order that they might not look down and see the evil gnawing away at the roots of the Tree of Life itself, destroying all peace and goodness. Nor could those semi-secret groups of persons be seen who so often were the sources of such evil. In their contemptuous indifference to the men of the state who found meaningfulness and tranquillity through life lived in natural order under the law of the King, they constituted hidden force deeply inimical to the best interests of mankind.

Through stealthy issue of precious metal commodity money into circulation amongst the peoples, replacing that money which represented the fiat or will of the god of the city and which was merely an order on the state warehouses through his scribes, this internationally minded group from the secrecy of their chambers were able to make a mockery of the faith and belief of simple people. The line of communication from god to man through priest-king and priest was cut, being replaced by their own twisted purposes such as they were; not however guiding mankind into the heaven that could have been and where all would be life, and light, and hope, but into such a hell as to escape from which men might gladly come to accept the idea of Mass Suicide.

My sincere acknowledgements are due to:

    1. Professor Fritz Heichelheim, and Sijthoff International Publishing Company, Leyden, for their very kind permission to use the short extracts from Professor Heichelheim's work: *An Ancient Economic History*.

2. Professor W.F. Albright, and Cambridge University Press for their very kind permission to use the short extracts from Professor Albright's work *The Amarna Letters from Palestine*; the same being found in Volume II of the *Cambridge Ancient History*.

3. G.R. Driver and John C. Miles, and the Clarendon Press, Oxford, for their very kind permission to use the rendering of Hammurabai's Law No. 7, as given by G.R. Driver and John C. Miles in their joint work: *Ancient Codes and Laws of the Near East*.

4. Dr. T.B.L. Webster and Messrs. Methuen Publications for their very kind permission to use the short extracts from Dr. Webster's work: *From Mycenae to Homer*.

5. Sir Charles Leonard Woolley and Messrs. Faber & Faber Ltd. for their very kind permission to use the short extracts from Sir Charles Leonard Woolley's work: *Abraham*.

6. Sir Charles Leonard Woolley and Messrs. Ernest Benn for their very kind permission to use the short extracts from Sir Charles Leonard Woolley's work: *Excavations at Ur*.

7. Christopher Dawson & John Murray Publishing House for their kind permission to use an extract from Christopher Dawson's work: *The Age of the Gods*.

8. Dr William Langer and The Houghton Mifflin Company for their very kin permission to use the short extracts from the *Encyclopaedia of World History*.

9. Dr. Charles Seltsman and the Associated Book Publishers for their very kind permission to use the short extracts from *Greek Coins*.

My sincere acknowledgements are also due to all those friends and acquaintances who in any way have assisted me in the present work.

IN THE BEGINNING WAS THE WORD

Every conclusion arrived at as a result of study of the fragments of information available in respect to money and its creators in the world of the Ancient Civilizations, indicates the existence of a far reaching conspiracy in respect to monetary issuance influencing the progression of man's history in the earliest times of which written record exists. It is also outstandingly clear that it was parent to that acknowledged and most obvious conspiracy such as exists today.[7]

The whole notion of the institution of precious metals by weight as common denominator of exchanges, internationally and nationally, cannot but have been disseminated by a conspiratorial organization fully aware of the extent of the power to which it would accede, could it but maintain control over bullion supplies and the mining which brought them into being in the first place. Clearly such notion had originally come into being during that historically distant period when first of all free silver began to be extensively used as a convenient and highly portable commodity in settlement of balances outstanding in foreign trade; certainly as far back as Neolithic times. This fact was indicated by the evidence existing that values (and by inference money) were already expressed in terms of silver by weight at the time of the Azag-Bau Dynasty at Kish in Mesopotamia (3268-2897 B.C.); although in a sense perhaps narrow and strictly national.

---

[7] According to the review of *Tragedy and Hope* by Dr. Carroll Quigley; (New York, 1966.), as contained in the *Naked Capitalist* published by W. Cleon Skousen, Salt Lake City, 1970.

According to tablets unearthed recording a sale of land, the sellers were known as "The eaters of the silver of the field."[8] This expression clearly showed a connection between the conception of money as an abstract unit in circulation, and silver, the tangible material on which the symbols of this money were later recorded. Such silver would then be valued according to the ancient customs of the international trade routes which were manifested in the rules of the travelling merchants who controlled these routes; these rules being established towards the better regulation of exchanges between themselves.

In other words, as a result of the establishment of the custom of settlement of balances in external trade by silver bullion by weight, it seems that a system of values had grown up in the cities of Mesopotamia, over what period of time it would be impossible to say for sure, in terms of those accepted values of definite weights of silver bullion in such external trade, relative to the staples of life: barley, dates, etc.

That sales are recorded in the 4th Millennium B.C. means that even at that time there was a clear conception of the significance of the abstract monetary unit, which is in itself an integral part of the law structure of any state, for such sales were in terms of *money*. The true meaning of such a concept

---

[8] *Cambridge Ancient History*; Vol. I; p. 371. On first reading this unusual expression, there is temptation to think that an error has been made in the translation of the tablet. However, according to the correspondent in Zaire for the magazine known as *Awake*, chiefs of the natives of this country in pre-Europeanized times announced the copper mining season with the words *Tuye Tukadie, Tuye Tukadie mukuba*, which literally translates as "Let us go eat copper; in effect meaning "Let us go enrich ourselves to provide for our life." (Awake, p. 25; July 8th, 1974.).

Similarly the expression describing the sellers of land as "eaters of the silver of the field," derives from the same root idea and implies that they enriched themselves to provide for the essentials of life by the sale of their land for silver.

being largely incomprehensible to most even as in this day, except they were the truly initiated, those controlling the internal exchanges, namely the priesthood and scribes, might well be excused if they early fell into the error of expressing values in terms of the standard of values in international trade. This serious error brought about finally, not only the collapse of that power through whose medium the god kings were best able to serve their peoples, but also as a further consequence, the collapse and fading of the meaning and benevolent purpose of the god kings themselves.

With silver bullion controlled by an international and conspiratorial minded group, as indeed it is obvious it must have been, considering the main sources of silver supply as being far away from those centres of civilization whose money depended on it and yet with people coming to equate money, in actuality the law of the ruler, with value according to the law created in the exchanges by the custom of the use of that same privately controlled commodity, then it becomes quite clear that scarcity or plenty in money, whatever way it was evinced in the circulation, depended on the manipulations internationally of that group controlling the distribution of precious metal bullion, and the plenty or scarcity they created, as was convenient to them.

If there was no silver, why then! there was no money, and prices fell. Substitute gold for silver, and history seeming to fast repeat itself, we have the condition of the European world of the last 2000 years. If there was no gold, Why then again! There was no money!

Hence was able to develop that conspiracy against mankind most exemplified by a continuous propaganda of hate against all authority: in pre-antiquity and antiquity against the many city gods, and in relatively modern times against the kings that rose out of the ruins of that which had been Rome.

As those controlling totally the economic life of a state through monetary creation and emission, must have felt that kings and gods were more of a nuisance than anything else, the instigators of this conspiracy in whatever place and era, obviously were those who first did the business of bankers; the controllers of values, and consequently the economic life of the states wherever the precious metal standard was used.

According to Sir Charles L. Woolley, excavator of the city of Ur in Southern Mesopotamia, the unit of exchange in the days of the great city states of Mesopotamia of the third and fourth Millennium B.C., and which served, therefore, as common denominator of the value of goods and services, was the measure of barley. While however pointing out that gold and silver came to pass from hand to hand, with a value dictated by their value with reference to the constant value of a measure of barley, he asserts that the salaries of government officials at the time of Hammurabai (about the beginning of the second millennium B.C.) were assessed in barley but paid in silver, such silver having neither stamp nor government guarantee.[9]

The notion therefore herein implied, of the numerous officials and labourers of Hammurabai of Babylon waiting in line to have silver cut off from the bullion bar, and weighed as against pay for the day, or the week, or the month, as the case might have been, although offered with sincerity, patently is as erroneous as that conception of the every day use in the exchanges of the *aes rude* in a similar way, in which the classical scholars and numismatists would have us believe; and which implied that the foreman and his labourers in ancient Rome of the days of the kings also waited in line after their day's labour, say, on the Circus Maximus, to have a fragment of copper cut

---

[9] Sir Charles L. Woolley: *Abraham*, p. 123.

off and weighed in order that their wives might be able to go to the market to purchase the evening meal.¹⁰

Clearly the word silver in the texts means no more than the word *Plata* in modern day Spanish, or *Argent* in modern day French. These words literally translate as silver, but as money which they are most used to indicate, they may be anything from grimy tattered paper note, to a silver peso, or to the brass coin which may function as divisible thereof. Similarly the word from the texts denoting silver may be safely said to have meant that which passed for money, perhaps exchangeable in the temple or the money shops for silver, but being in itself anything which circulated, denoting multiple or divisible of the unit o exchange; be it clay or wood or glass[11] or leather or papyrus or stone.

Thus, as was the case in Sumeria indeed, long, long before the time of the great Hammurabai once money had come to be more of an abstract unit of account based for its value in desirable goods and services, on the barter power of a certain weight of silver bullion related to the constant value of barley,[12] it was no major advance for those who benefited most from

---

[10] With all due deference to an otherwise most eminent scholar.

[11] Very little is known of the former relatively extensive use of glass as material to record definite numbers of the unit of exchange, or, more simply put, as *money*. On this subject François Lenormant commented in his book: La Monnaie dans l'Antiquité (p. 214; Tome I, Book II):

"Nous possédons des preuves irréfragables da l'usage de monnaie de verre en Egypte des la temps du Haut-Empire (1) usage que se continua dans le même pays sous les Byzantins (2) puis sous les Arabes (3). C'est principalement de temps des Khalifes Fatimite que l'Egypte vit fabriquer le plu grand nombre de ces assignats le verre, portant l'indication d'une valeur da monnaie. Les Arabes de Sicile en firent aussi a l'imitation de ceux d'Egypte."

[12] Sir Charles Woolley: *Abraham*, p. 123; London; 1936.

this conception, namely the bullion brokers and their satellites, the money changers or barkers, to find a weak king and a corruptible priesthood, who could be brought to lose sight of the total control of the city which was the right of the god they served; and who might turn a blind eye to those other more sinister activities by which the power of the Ziggurat was further undermined.

Of those time Dawson in the *Age of the Gods* remarks:

"Originally the state and the temple corporations were the only bodies which possessed the necessary stability and resources for establishing widespread commercial relations. Temple servants were sent on distant missions, provided with letters of credit which enabled them to obtain supplies in other cities. Moreover the temple was the bank of the community through which money could be lent at interest and advances made to the farmer on the security of his crop. Thus in the course of the 3rd millennium there grew up in Mesopotamia a regular money economy based on precious metals as standards of exchange, which stimulated private wealth and enterprise and led to real capitalist development. The temple and the palace remained the centres of the economic life of the community but by their side and under their shelter there developed a many sided activity which found expression in the guilds of the free craftsmen and the merchants, and the private enterprise of the individual capitalist."[13]

This information from Christopher Dawson with the translation of the tablets before him, and every assistance no doubt from those students in that particular field, is most illuminating; but of the undertones of those highly significant years in man's period upon this earth, he seems to see little, or he just does not choose to speculate as to their nature.

---

[13] Christopher Dawson: *Age of the Gods*, p. 130. (London; 1928.)

Principal amongst those undertones, and quite possibly the force that brought these changes about, may safely be assumed to be the secret and private expansion of the total money supply effected primarily by the issuance into circulation of false receipts for silver and other valuables supposedly being held on deposit in thief proof vaults, or otherwise, for safe custody.

Such receipts would be accepted by merchants instead of the actual metal, and would function as money, and would be an addition to the total money supply, though not understood as such by the rulers who would thus easily be inveigled into lending their sanction to seemingly harmless practices; or at least into turning a blind eye; especially if priesthood and scribes so advised.

With that growth of the conception of private wealth which would automatically follow on the acceptance of the idea of buying and selling, or perhaps better put, preceded such idea of buying and selling as according to a silver standard internationally accepted, such involvement of priesthood and scribe would not be hard to achieve. According to Sir Charles Woolley, trade seemed to extend from the city of Ur, particularly during the so-called IIIrd. Dynasty, over the whole known world which certainly reached as far afield as Europe[14] being carried on by means of letters of credit, bills of exchange, and "promises to pay" (cheques), made out in terms of staple necessities; of life expressed in terms of silver at valuation of barley (probably at a given season of the year).[15]

---

[14] Actually evidence exists of Sumerian culture extending as far as the Caspian Sea even before the Dynastic Period. Reference to this subject is to be found on page 47 of *The Sumerians*.

[15] On pages 124-125 of his book *Abraham* (London, 1936.) comment is made by Sir Charles Woolley: "a trade which involved the greater part of the

There also is no doubt that the merchant as representative of the god of the city from which he journeyed, loaned money by which his customers were able to make their purchases, such money merely being an abstraction indicated by the figures on the clay tablet; in earlier days being backed by the will-force of the god of the city, and in latter days by the promises of silver issued by one who at that time would be the equivalent of today's banker, and who, should such need arise, such as would be occasioned by the temple withdrawing its sanction or permissiveness towards his activities would be able to partially back his self-created abstract money which was the reality of such promises, with actual silver.

Thus the caravaneer or travelling merchant gave credit. Whether his own or that of the merchant for whom he was agent, or direct; from the Ziggurat itself, dwelling place of the god, it functioned as a form of foreign aid similar to the foreign aid of today.

---

then known world was carried on with remarkable smoothness by means of what we should call a paper currency based on commodity values. The fluctuations of currency values which are the bugbear of modern commerce were virtually overcome by a currency which depended ultimately on the staple necessity of life but was qualified by the use of a medium possessed of intrinsic value; the commercial traveller had to use his wits and exercise his judgement as to the form in which he cashed his credit notes."

Further comment was made by Sir Charles Woolley and Jacquetta Hawkes in *Prehistory and the Beginnings of Civilization* (pp. 615-616; London; 1963): The difficulty was solved by what might be called Letters of Credit facilitated by the existence of established agents on the trade routes. The traveller started with a consignment of grain, might sell it in some town on his road, receiving a signed tablet with the value expressed in copper, possibly, or in silver with which he could buy there or elsewhere something to the same value which he could sell at a profit farther along on his journey. his tablets payable on demand by the agents to whom he was accredited were the ancient equivalent of a Paper currency."

Considering that the merchant in earlier times operated solely with the credit of the temple that raised him up, while the temple remained supreme, such foreign aid was instrument of state policy, maintaining the servility of lesser states, while at the same time maintaining the steady working capacity of the home manufactures, and contented people in consequence. The classes of the dominant power were content that the manufacturies gave them daily labour, and the classes of the subordinate power were able to buy the luxuries they craved, and the necessities they needed as against money deducted from the credits loaned by the dominant power. Repayment of these credits, as in today, was made by way of return shipment of raw materials such as were needed for the manufacturies of the dominant state. That such raw materials were assessed in value as according to the international value of silver related to the national value of barley in the dominant state seems most likely.

However it is clear that with the growth of silver in circulation between private persons, and between private persons and states, as now would become an inevitability, that which had been total economic control from the gods through his servants in the Ziggurat, was bypassed, and merchants were now able to deal privately using their own credit, or powers of abstract money creation. They were also able, through their control of distant mining operations, to afflict a previously dedicated priesthood with thought of personal possession; and through the control of the manufacture of weapons in distant places, they were able to arm warlike peoples towards the destruction of whosoever they might choose.

Those merchants of whatever race they may have been, who voyaged to the cities of Sumeria from places as far distant as the great cities of the Indus valley civilization known today as Mohenjo-Daro and Harrapa, as is clearly demonstrated by the

Sumerian seals found at Mohenjo-Daro[16] and the seals from Mohenjo-Daro found at Ur,[17] and who were without a doubt one of the main sources of precious metal supply in Sumeria,[18] came to realize that they could actually create that which functioned as money with but the record incised by the stylus on the clay tablet promising metal or money. Obviously, as a result of this discovery which depended on the confidence they were able to create in the minds of the peoples of their integrity, provided they banded themselves together with an absolute secrecy that excluded all other than their proven and chosen brethren, they could replace the god of the city himself as the giver of all. If so be they could institute a conception of a one god, *their* god, a special god of the world, a god above all gods, then not merely the city, be it Ur or Kish or Lagash or Uruk, but the world itself could be theirs, and all that in it was. A strange dream! One whose fulfilment they never really expected!

Some evidence of the knowledge and previous existence of such practice of issuance of false receipts as against supposed valuables on deposit for safe-keeping clearly exists in the Law No. 7 of the great Hammurabai, which same law was undoubtedly intended as a preventative to this sickness in society, which, even at that day, may very well have been the cancer that destroyed much that has been before.

---

[16] E.J.C. McKay: *Further Excavations at Mohenjo-Daro* p 582. (Govt. India. Delhi; 1938.)

[17] Sir Charles Woolley: *Excavations at Ur,* p. 112.

[18] In the words of Sir Charles L. Woolley on page 193 of *Excavations at Ur.* " Raw materials were imported sometimes from over the sea, to be worked up in the Ur factories; the Bill of Lading of a merchant ship which came up the canal from the Persian Gulf to discharge its cargo on the wharves of Ur details gold, copper ore, hardwood, ivory, pearls, and precious stones."

According to Professor Bright, the Code of Hammurabai was but a revision of two legal codes promulgated in Sumerian by Lipit-Ishtar of Isin, and in Akkadian by the King of Eshnummua during the period of the breakup of that power formerly wielded by the God at Ur, that is, at about the same time that Ur was sacked by the Elamites in 1950 B.C., and Amorite and Elamite political power was established over Northern and Southern Mesopotamia.[19] Both of these codes are well before the Code of Hammurabai, and are evidence of the latter being but a revision of law codes existing in the days of UR-NAMMU, or before, UR-NAMMU being that most outstanding ruler who reigned from 2278 B.C. to 2260 B.C. during the third dynasty at Ur.[20]

The severity of the penalty and the placing of the law so high in the code leaves little doubt that it was directed against an evil that was by no means new, and, who knows, may have been one of the deep seated causes of the invasions that devastated Ur, both from the Gutim,[21] the Elamites, the Amorites, and the Hittites; for no doubt of old, just as today, Money Power was as busy arming the enemies of the people amongst whom it sojourned, as that people themselves.

While the scholars do not appear to have paid any special attention to this particular law, or to have attached to it any special significance, its true intent and purpose is clear to anyone conversant with the origins of private money issuance in modern times, as indicated by the familiar story of the goldsmith's multiple receipts.[22]

---

[19] John Bright: *A History of Israel*, p. 44; London; 1960.

[20] Sir Charles Leonard Woolley; *The Sumerians*, p. 25 New York; 1965.

[21] *The Goyim of Genesis*, Chapter XIV; verse I.

[22] A. Andreades: *History of the Bank of England*, p. 23; London; 1966.

If a man buys silver or gold or slave, or slave girl, or ox or sheep or ass or anything else whatsoever from a [free] man's son or a free man's slave or has received them for safe custody without witness or contract, that man is a thief: he shall be put to death.[23]

The requisite of witnesses and contract attesting to the true facts of valuables on deposit, would to some extent obviate the danger of the goldsmiths, silversmiths or traders, involved in a transaction, creating receipts for valuables that did not exist, in safe custody or otherwise. It was equally possible in ancient times as much as in modern times to circulate such receipts as money lawfully instituted.

Provided a corrupted priesthood turned a blind eye to this practice and loaned their sanction thereto, such fraudulent money or, in the misleading euphemism of a corrupted world, "credit," would be equally effective in foreign markets as in the home markets, if not more so because of the greater danger of exposure of the criminal nature of this activity that would undoubtedly exist in the home market.

The severity of the penalty required by this Law Number 7 of the Code of Hammurabai, exercised by a strong and dedicated ruler, would have been an absolute deterrent to such practice that since that time, and more especially in modern times since the 16th Century A.D., has become so indurated to a fixture. Its results are to be seen on every hand, not to speak of the final result which though not yet arrived, else this book would not be in existence, is clear.

The Laws of Hammurabai, King of Babylon, just the same as those more ancient codes of which they were revision, were directed towards the regulation of life of nobleman, as well as

---

[23] *The Laws of Hammurabai*; No. 7; (G.R. Driver & John C. Miles: *Ancient Codes and Laws of the Near East*, Vol. II, p. 15. Oxford, 1952.).

freeman, merchant, or slave, and no special concessions were given to either of these stations in life, even if such stations in life were accepted as integral part of the structure of the state life. Euphemistic and misleading words such as "businessman" or "financier" had not yet, it seems, been planted in the vocabulary. By and large, the king still ruled in absolute, and his law giving justice to all was carved in stone, and placed in the market place for the highest or the lowest to understand clearly the rules by which he must live. Merchants were unequivocally described as such, and law ruthlessly prescribed severe penalties for their corrupt conduct. They were kept in place as a caste, not of the highest order, and, it would appear, somewhat similar to the Hindu system, they served the priesthood and nobility, and were conceded a place in life as an instrument whereby the people generally might live a better life.

The Code of Hammurabai, revision of more ancient codes as it was, does not reveal any particular regard towards this caste of persons. However, as by the time of its promulgation, both privet property and privately issued money seem to have been well established, it is to be assumed that the ignorant of noble caste or otherwise, were already deferring to that magic known as money, in much the same manner as they did at all times through latter history when faced with the necessity of compromise with privet money creative power, whose activities had been permitted by foolish kings, and to whom such kings had even committed the finances of the realm. Such was most clearly illustrated during the last four hundred years in England; perhaps more so than at any other time in recorded history.

In the time of Hammurabai, King of Babylon, matters were by no means as desperate as they are today. Merchandising was by no means regarded as an end in itself, and a means whereby it was the right of ignoble men to proffer any corruption to the people so long as it made "profit" for them, and "interest" for the so-called barker who supplied the original "finances" out of his secret and costless money-creative processes. Money lending and merchandising as it is known, still had not come to be a means whereby man-hating and therefore corrupt secret societies might seek to overturn the tree of life itself by way of sowing the seeds of decay in that true and natural order of life which had been ordained from time immemorial.

Private money creators and the merchants their satellites, had at that time by no means arrived at that point when they might conspire to present complete defiance to the gods and their appointed, and as a small matter in the way of their business, install jackasses, or whatever might be, in the places of the mighty, as too often was the case in the latter days.

THE TEMPLE AND THE COUNTING HOUSE

Out of those vague shadows of war and power and peace and settlement of ancient strife that drifted out of the faded memory of man's former abiding on the Anatolian plateaus and throughout the Near East as it is so described by us, emerged that force known as Classical Greece; a force which may be said to principally derive from the union of the essential forward thrust of the re-vitalized energies of the god-ruled city, and the political structure by which the cattle raising men of the Indo-European warrior nations had been governed.

Much of the revitalization of such energies derived from increasing availability of silver as a result of the expansion of the mining industry due to the increasing use of tools of hardened iron, and the consequent expansion of the volume of money in circulation amongst the peoples, abstract, or as now obtained, of actual pieces of silver of known weight and fineness carrying the identifying mark of the emitter.

This flood of the precious metals to which the new methods of mining gave rise, with the consequent strengthening of the shift of money creative, or total power center, from the god and the temple, to what some might describe as the devil and the counting house, enabled those conspiratorial groups who undoubtedly controlled precious metal bullion supplies, perhaps at this stage alliance between the priesthood of certain cities whose god was not getting fair acknowledgment, and those mysterious people, the Apiru, who, concerned with the carrying trade between the cities as is clear,[24] seemingly

---

[24] According to professor W.F. Albright (*The Amarna Letters from Palestine. Cambridge Ancient History* Vol. 11; pp. 14-17.): "There was also a large and

belonged to no city, yet were to be found in them all, to set up a supra-national god as the fount of their secret power. He

apparently increasing class of stateless and reputedly lawless people in Palestine and Syria to whom the appellation Apiru was given, it has now become certain that they were a class of heterogenous ethnic origin, and that they spoke different languages, often alien to the people in whose documents they appear."

Further on in the same work, after pointing out the distinct differences between the desert tribes (Bedawin), the grooms, and the SA.GAZ troops ('Apiru'), using an old text relative to the Hittite armed forces as the source of his information (about 1500 B.C.), professor Albright further points out that the word Apiru must mean dusty ones in N. West Semitic, and that it still appears in Syriac conveying the same meaning. "Characteristic of all these terms is the common fact that the bearer of the designation trudges in the dust behind donkeys, mules or chariots. In 1961 I collected the then available archaeological and documentary material bearing on the caravan trade of the twentieth to nineteenth centuries B.C., and the organization of donkey caravans; I found far-reaching correlations with early patriarchal tradition in Genesis." (p. 17). The complex problem of the significance of the *'Apiru'* (or *Habiru*) is not rendered less so by the fact that it recurs in cuneiform texts from different parts of Mesopotamia, Syria, Egypt, and Asia Minor; all of which date from between the dynasty of Agade, and the 11th century B.C. Thus it would appear that the restless *'Apiru'* of later times, mercenary soldier, bandit, or smuggler, was the descendant of the donkey caravaneers who maintained the trade between the cities of the known world previous to the collapse of the main cities in Babylonia before the arms of the Gutim, the Hittites, and the Elamites at different times, and which resulted in the extinction of a great deal of the donkey caravan trade by the 18th century B.C., and left the followers of that trade uncertain of where to settle or what occupation to follow.

In the *Tel Amarna Tablets*, Vol II, Samuel A.B. Mercer refers to the use of the name Habiru at Babylon in the time of Hammurabai, (p.840); he further records that a list of Hittite gods, headed *List of the Gods of the Habiru*, was found at Bog-Haz Koi by Winckler, (p. 841). The secret societies of a group known as the *Haburah* seem to have existed beyond the time of the destruction of Jerusalem by Titus. According to Jost (I. *History of the Jews*; p. 210) Vespasian appointed a Rabbi John Ben Zakkai, chief of the Haburah as ruler of Jamnia. As *Haburah* derives from *habor*. to join, there may not be significant connection between *Habiru* or *'Apiru'* and the more modern *Haburah*.

would be a god who should be contemptuous of all other gods; living in no idols, he would be in all, and over all; unseen, but all pervading.

If the god of such secret society or confederacy controlled movements of silver bullion internationally, he well might be contemptuous of all city gods other than himself, for when money values were based on the exchange value of his silver in such international exchanges, then he and his acolytes, whoever they were, knew that all prosperity in the kingdoms of those most ancient times depended on him, and whether he ordained through his servants that silver should be plentiful or otherwise; whether indeed there should be no money and hardship, or plenty of money and prosperity.

Also it may be assumed in the latter days of the declining temple power, prosperity or otherwise would also depend on whether rulers of such kingdoms and cities turned a blind eye, as it were, to that privately created ledger credit page entry money whose use the international money changers were undoubtedly promoting as a facilitation to exchanges between select and secret groups of persons. It would be completely external to the money creative power of the temple even if clandestinely linked thereto, and so would strengthen themselves and their one-God, all-powerful, all omnipotent.

The ruthless and stern edicts of such princes as Hammurabai of Babylon, previously quoted, while perhaps effective in Babylon, would not avail in all those cities or states to which the money changers undoubtedly carried their arts, especially if they were not subject to the rule of Babylon. Who knows to what extent the seizure of Ur by Hammurabai was the result of his determination to totally extirpate the source of this attack on kingly power, undoubtedly sanctioned, if not connived at by a cynical priesthood who were largely the rulers, in this most ancient city. That close to the throne and therefore the god himself, were those who secretly held in contempt the god-king, and to whom the utter devotion of the people, even unto death, was of no meaning, is clear from the following excerpt from Sir Charles L. Woolley in respect to his discovery of the tombs of the kings of the IIIrd dynasty at Ur:

"When we dug away the filling we found that in the upper part of the blocking of the door of each of the tomb chambers, there had been made a small breach just large enough for a man to get through; the dislodged bricks were lying in front of the door covered by the clean earth imported for the filling. The tomb had been robbed, and obviously just as the earth was about to be put in; nobody would have dared to rob them when the pit was still in use, nor, if such sacrilege had been done, would the bricks have been left scattered on the floor and the breach unfilled; the robbers must have chosen their moment when the inviolable earth would at once hide all traces of their crime and they could afford to be careless."[25]

According to the description of the burial scene by Charles L. Woolley on page 72 of *Excavations at Ur*, on the ramp leading down to the king's tomb, would have lain the bodies of those who had elected to accompany their Lord into the regions beyond, in the order in which they had lain down to die; for death was obviously their wish and intention. It would have been almost impossible for such carefully timed robbery to have taken place over the bodies of those who would be amongst the first ladies of the court and certain officials, military and otherwise, without there having been a well planned conspiracy; for it was clear, dressed as they were in their finest clothing of crimson and gold, they had gladly and voluntarily offered themselves as company and comfort to their god-king at the commencement of that eternal journey which was his heavenly home. Testimony of their willingness existed

---

[25] Sir Charles Woolley: *Excavations at Ur*, p. 158.

in the lethal cup still clutched in their long decayed hands[26] as they lay before his tomb in their last poisoned sleep.

As, when the robbery was effected, it is clear they were already dead, there had to be the connivance of certain persons in high places to whom this great devotion was without meaning. Additionally, such gold and silver would have been a useless and dangerous possession[27] except to those whose lives so far as ordinary men were concerned were secret from first to last; such as to whom it meant money and power internationally, and by whom it could be melted and rapidly transferred abroad.

Speculating on the functions of the famous temple of Solomon, similar to the temples of Egypt and the Sumerian city states, although according to professor Paul Einzig little information exists as to how the evolution of the monetary system of the Jews, prior to the adoption of coinage, affected the Hebrew economic system or its price levels, it seems that this temple in the earlier days was not only used as a treasury, but, as in Babylonia, as a bank. Thus it received money on deposit (for safe keeping).

Professor Einzig informs us that the gold lavishly adorning the temple for decorative purposes, existed at the same time, as a monetary reserve. When Hezekiah had paid a tribute of three hundred talents of silver and thirty talents of gold to the king of Assyria (around 700 B.C.), he "cut the gold from the doors of

---

[26] *Ibid.*, p. 72.

[27] "Mes-Kalan-Dug, 'the good Hero of the Land,' Prince of Ur, buried probably as early as 3500 B.C., took with him to the next world a wealth of golden vessels and weapons such as no commoner would have ventured to posses.": Charles Seltsman, in *Creek Coins* (p. 2.).

the Temple of the Lord and from the Pillars;" (II *Kings*; 18, 16).[28]

The arts of banking were, however, in no way as developed as they were in Babylonia and Assyria. Amongst the '*Apiru*,' undoubtedly confederates of the Israelites in later times, were clearly many refugees[29] from the cruel debt slavery existing in Babylonia and its outposts during the 2nd Millennium B.C., and later. Apart from the firm laws in respect to the taking of interest, the Jubilee of the 50th year (*Leviticus* 25.II), if fully enforced, would render any effort to create monopoly ineffective.

Thus it can be seen that the God in his holy shrine ruled in the same way in that ancient Hebrew kingdom, so much better known to most than perhaps the temple cities of ancient Sumeria; many of which, until relatively recently, were not even names, and were no more than faintly discernible mounds on the desert.

The Greek sanctuary owed existence to similar forces that had given rise to the temples of Mesopotamia and to the temple of Solomon above mentioned. Functioning in like manner, in modified form, clearly it originated from those distant days when the shrine of the mother goddess of the cities of the Anatolian plateau and the Persian highlands such as Catal Huyuk,[30] Hacilar, Dorak, Susa, etc., was the point from which

---

[28] Paul Einzig: *Primitive Money*, p. 214. Oxford; 1949.

[29] In the *Amarna Letters from Palestine*, (p. 16), Professor W.F. Albright records that one of the letters from the Tel Amarna archives reports that Zemredda of Lachish had been killed by slaves who had become '*Apiru*.' Further Professor Albright records that "in thirteen century documents from Ugarit, we hear of men of Ugarit, including slaves, who had escaped to the '*Apiru*' in Hittite territory."

[30] James Mellaart: *Catal Huyuk*; London; 1967.

the people drew spiritual guidance, and the nucleus around which these human accretions gathered in ancient times. These shrines gave force to those mysteries whose existence and purpose towards the continuity and good in life, drew the devotion of all. The Temple of Artemis at Ephesus, the Temple of Aphrodite at Corinth, the Temple of Athene at Athens, all obviously owed their origin to the ancient worship of the Mother Goddess who, through the wonder and urge in her body, consumed the whole life force of man. The controllers of the healthy continuance of life in these cities were a priesthood who considered themselves as the direct representatives of the goddess on earth, the shepherds appointed to the flock.

The temple states that existed to a relatively late date such as those of Cappadocia, were indeed the direct projection forward into time of this tradition of government of the city by the goddess in her holy shrine, as much as were those of the city states of early Sumeria. In Greece too, in earlier times, such rule existed beyond much doubt, and during that period when Cretan civilization extended to the mainland, and when power stemmed from the halls of Cnossus, and the mystic place of mythology where once upon a time lived the Minotaur, it would be an absolute certainty. It would not bear much difference to those systems of god control by which all those rulers of the Ancient Orient[31] had governed, and which had guided the calm and blessed procession of the peoples through time and under the sun.

The temple of each small city state in Greece during the earlier days of Greek industry may have functioned to some extent as did the great temples or ziggurat of the powerful city states of

---

[31] These words "the Ancient Orient" so aptly supplying loose definition to that world that lived under the political system that governed most of the cities of the Ancient Near East, derive from professor Heichelheim's *Ancient Economic History*.

Sumeria of much earlier days, and money, that is the law controlling exchanges as to a common denominator of values, may have come into existence as entry in the temple ledger, although how represented in the circulation does not seem to be clearly known. The notion of exchanges being conducted in terms of cattle, one animal representing the unit, even if having existed in large scale business in ancient times of the wandering Indo-European cattle raising tribes of the Scythian plains, cannot be accepted as that which created an exchange amongst the common people of the city civilizations. True, the word for cattle may have continued in some areas to have been used to indicate money, but, as previously pointed out, certainly bearing no more reference to cattle than does the French word *Argent*, or the Spanish word *Plata* bear reference to silver in a context where money is definitely referred to.

It is clear that local tribes, such as the Bushmen of South Africa,[32] the natives of Melanesia and Micronesia,[33] whose way of life obviously derives, with little change, from the way of life of the races that once occupied South China, Annam,[34] India, and Ceylon, in the very ancient times of the tertiary ages previous to the ice ages, long since have been conversant, with the basic principle of money. In their case money was an abstract unit circulating amongst the people with tangibility evinced by pieces of certain shell, cut according as tradition demanded; and of value deriving from custom, which, in such societies, is law.

---

[32] Kingston-Higgins: *Survey of Primitive Money*, p. 189. London; 1949.

[33] Paul Einzig: *Primitive Money*, p. 29-81. Also Kingston-Higgins.

[34] Kingston-Higgins also refers to shell money in the Neolithic caves of Annam (p. 139). Also at Mohenjo-Daro. (p. 1). For shell money at Mohenjo-Daro see E.J.C. McKay; p. 582. *Further Excavations at Mohenjo-Daro*.

Therefore it may reasonably be expected that the intelligent Indo-Europeans from whom stemmed the Greeks, were equally conversant with such principles; even if later they came to forget them. According to the Cambridge Ancient History: "Ivory beads in country now devoid of elephants suggest either wide range of movement or some form of exchange."[35]

When the Cambridge Ancient History speculated as above that the ivory beads of the Solutrean deposits of Northern France represented some form of exchange medium, the graves of Sungir which reveal similar mammoth ivory beads, proven to be 23,000 years old or more, had not been opened[36]. During the Old Kingdom in Egypt and during the earliest years of the cities of Babylonia, when "numberings" of all accepted as wealth and possession, were taken every two years, and therefore books kept,[37] a most refined system of distribution of surpluses and therefore creation of exchanges, must have existed. The connection between such system and the scarabs[38] in the case of Egypt, and the seals in the case of Mesopotamia, seems to have been generally dismissed. The fact that the scarabs have been found in their hundreds in places far removed from Egypt, from Palestine, to Crete, to Etruria, indicates significance far removed from their use as ornaments.

The agents of the Babylonian Money Power as it existed previous to the extensive growth of coined money as a base for that circulation, seen or abstract, which drove the trade and

---

[35] *Cambridge Ancient History*. p. 51; Vol. I.

[36] London Illustrated News. p. 24, March 7th, 1970; *The Boys of Sungir*, Dr. Otto Bader.

[37] James Henry Breasted: *A History of Egypt*, p. 44.

[38] According to Flinders-Petrie, scarabs first appear in Egypt during the fourth Dynasty and continue right through to the end (of Pharaonic rule) with no important break. *History of Egypt*. p. 52; Vol. I; London, 1897.

industry of the Greek industrial revolution, would themselves have promoted and encouraged the establishment of the temple nucleus to the city state. It was the form of government they understood best and whose essential powers they knew, from experience now grown ancient, how to control and subvert if necessary. Just as the similar secret money creative force heads directly for the seat of government itself in this day and age, and once it becomes fully lodged and acknowledged, in the same way as with the establishment of the Bank of England in 1694 and the establishment of the Federal Reserve Bank of the United States in 1913, two instances with which we are most familiar, it penetrates right into the heart of the treasury,[39] so it was in that day. In the little cities of early Greek industrial revolution, perhaps no less sly amongst this sturdy people, but clearly discernible it was.

As amongst the original aristocracy of Greece owing its origin to those heroic days of the Homeric Sagas, would be little enough sympathy for the smooth subtleties of those newcomers originating from the counting houses of the Phoenician, Aramean, or Babylonian Cities, it would not be to the natural political leaders that these newcomers would address themselves in the first place, but to the priesthood, those who controlled shrine and temple, the advisors and guides to such rulers. Just as in today such priesthood is too often composed of men of little understanding of the realities of financial life, and who will lend themselves almost eagerly to any power that may approach them with sufficient front to convince them that they are being offered more than the god they represent is already possessed of, so it was in that day. This village priesthood, conducting the simple rites such as may

---

[39] A Andreades: *History of The Bank of England*, p. 389-401. See also *The Federal Reserve System*, a pamphlet originally published by the Board of governors of the Federal Reserve System, 1939, and republished by Omni Publications of Hawthorne, California.

have been during the period known as the dark ages, and before the advent of the city states of historical record, when was breathed into their ears the possibilities of magnificent temples such as were to be found in Egypt, and the extent of the control they would exercise through the oracles, whose wisdom would be spread by fame across the whole world, would easily be gained.

Thus the cities that rose out of the industrial awakening of Greece had all the appurtenances of the sacred city state of more ancient days. However, just as sacred kingship existing as the projection of the guiding will of the Almighty on to this earth, too often during the last three hundred years has become little more than a front giving legality to such money as circulates bearing as it does, the profile of the ruler who so often has been unwitting co-conspirator, if only as essential instrument, with that money power, totally international in character, which has nowadays largely replaced kingly power as the true ruler, so it was that the temple that should owe fealty to the gods alone, became a front for the international money creative force of that day and age; connected closely with the trade in precious metals and slaves as it must have been.

The temple of the Sumerian city state had been palace, temple, warehouse, government offices and central bank in one, and its servants[40] had administered it in these capacities certainly until the end of what is known as the Dynastic period (in the case of the city of Ur), and with declining strength for long afterwards; and the king of the city state had been sufficiently as god on

---

[40] According to N.K. Sandars in the introduction to his translation of the *Epic of Gilgamish* (p. 14.): "The temples were served by a perpetual priesthood in whose hands, at one time, was almost the whole wealth of the state; and amongst whom were the archivists and teachers, the scholars and mathematicians. In very early times the whole temporal power was theirs, as servants of the god whose estates they managed."

earth, that, as previously has been described, there were those of his wives and concubines and officials who gladly went down to the grave with him.[41]

Thus, as the distant heir, in some degree, to this temple of ancient days, the temple of the Greek city state in the 1st Millennium

B.C. was still a place looked up to as the abode of the gods, and wherein the sacred rites were conducted; even if that economic power, by which, as the expression of the benevolent will of the god, it had controlled the total existence of men, and their comings and goings, was now exercised by an external and indifferent force, alien to Greece in thought and character, and with whom it connived against its own adherents.

In the same way the priesthood or laymen that promote, wittingly or unwittingly, the elements of decay penetrating the church of today, connive blindly or otherwise with those whose stated and clear plan has never been other than the disintegration of this selfsame church, and who have always had in mind no more than its ultimate destruction.

In a latter period it is true, but still within the first millennium B.C., the situation at the Temple of Apollo at Delos, and of which some proof exists, clearly illustrates this condition of the temple: still as controller of the mysteries, and the recipient of the bounty of devoted souls, but no longer the centre and control point of the god owned state. It had become merely a front for the economic purposes of a secret fraternity whose concern was money changing, silver bullion, the grain trade, and the slave trade. These persons had conducted their business in the shade of the temple courtyards from ancient

---

[41] Sir Charles L. Woolley: *Further Excavations at Ur*, p. 158.

days as, and if they could, in order that the power or mystery as locally was held in awe, might give sanctity to their activities which so often were exercised against the well being of the people who sheltered them. Such activities were frequently concerned with movements of bullion, the factor most of all giving rise to instability of prices, and movements of labour which then was slaves, hardly less a factor in such instability of prices, and therefore so necessary to the full exploitation of a given people.

The island of Delos, although virtually infertile and without special advantages such as natural harbours of any particular excellence, due to the contributions and gifts of the pilgrims visiting the Temple of Apollo, and the deposits of the cities, *trapezitae* and leading citizens, in precious metals and money, for such were esteemed to be safe in the Temple of the God, became very rich; a centre of trade and banking, and above all, a centre for the area slave trade from which almost none were safe.[42]

Of the commercial activities of the great sanctuaries, Oskar Seffert, the German antiquarian of the last century had to say, (*A Dictionary of Classical Antiquities*, p. 91.):

"We hear in isolated cases of State Banks, but this business was carried on in the vast majority of cases, by the Great Sanctuaries, such as those of Delphi, Delos, Ephesus, and Samos, which were much used as banks for loans and deposits both by individuals and governments."

In other words, therefore, the great sanctuary functioned very much the same way, from the economic standpoint, as the central bank in this day. The agents of International Money

---

[42] Plato was reputed to have been sold as a slave by Dionysus, ruler of Syracuse, for 20 minae. *Diodorus*: xv.7; Plutarch: *Dionysos*, 5.

Power, as used by the priesthood of the Temple of Apollo to take care of the fiscal or financial dealings of the temple, and to whom undoubtedly was farmed out the credit of the temple, must have fully understood that the priesthood had betrayed their high calling, and thereby had betrayed those devoted souls who continued to believe the sole concern of the temple was, as formerly, for their spiritual guidance and that they should live good, virtuous and pious lives.

These agents would have lurked as only faintly discernible shadows behind the temple facade, although they instigated much of what came to pass in those days, if themselves so little seen. Of first concern to them would have been the reputation of their masters, the priesthood, for piety, probity, and godliness, in so far as appearance went. For by maintaining the position of the priesthood, they maintained themselves and their secret power; yet for whatever they brought about, especially if of evil, it may safely be assumed, a nevertheless inviolate priesthood would be held responsible.

Hence the people never questioned the existence of the temple but as the place where the will of the god was exercised through his servants. That it had come to function more as instrument in the capacity of sanctifying front for an international power concerned largely with money creation and the control of the slave trade, itself mainly of criminal antecedents, was something they never came to fully understand; nor that this whole thing of prayer, worship, and devotion was dangerously near to becoming a cruel hoax manipulated by a handful of aliens, who looked at them and their fervour and belief with dead eyes. No more in this day do those who toil on through the few years of their lives realize that the governments that they so naively believe are theirs, are but a wavering shadow. The absolute reality of sovereign power only obtainable through total control over monetary creation and emission and cancellation, is not theirs. They but function as standards by which international money creative forces create the worlds money in a given area; places wherein exponents of the "Law" and talkative and by no means wise or learned men foregather to discuss road minding etc. and too often little things that occupy them, but matter not too much; never looking too closely at the direction from which they came, nor toward that direction in which they go; nor, above all, towards the place of the hand that feeds them.

Therefore this economic power apparently centering in the Temple of Apollo would not only derive from those loans in precious metals that it was able to grant, but also from the fact that those very secret fraternities understanding fully the principles of Ledger Credit Page Entry Money, operated under its patronage. There can be no doubt that the principles of monetary inflation, or, better put, abstract money creation, were well understood to the *trapezitae* or professional bankers to whom the Temple at Delos apparently delegated these functions;[43] and equally well known was how easily merchants could be trained to make payments by cheque drawn on account consisting of supposed deposits with a recognized banker either by signed and witnessed document, by signed document, even by no more than verbal instructions. Thus, provided the payee also had account at Delos or agency thereof, no transfer of actual silver need have been involved, and what is now euphemistically described as the fractional reserve system, (a swindle indurated in a system!) was operated. The enormous volume of exchanges a business that could be carried on without the movement of one drachma of silver, and consequently the monopolization of trade and industry and subsequent control over the whole world and its affairs that could be brought about at literally no real cost, provided those dealing in money changing and financial matters maintained close solidarity, was known to the bankers.

---

[43] Rostovtsev: *A Social and Economic History of the Hellenistic World*, Vol. I, p. 233.

The tremendous entre-pôt trade of Delos, especially in slaves,[44] could not derive from anything else other than the acceptance of the "Credit" of the Temple from the hands of these aliens. These men would be skilled money changers bred and trained in the ancient financial sophistication of the cities of Babylonia, Aram, a Phoenicia, etc. They would be fully conversant with the possibilities inherent in such ledger credit page entry money, and whose successful functioning as an abstract inflation of the number of units of silver they claimed to control, depended on secrecy, and solidarity amongst themselves, and above all, on the patronage of the corrupted temples.

Professor Rostovtsev relates at length the commercial dealings of Apollonius, manager of the economic affairs of the Ptolemic Pharaoh, Philadelphus.[45] If the true name of Apollonius or others of that necessarily interlocked money power was known, and substituted for that of Antigonus and Demetrius and Soter and, indeed of Philadelphus and all those rulers that succeeded Alexander, then the glass through which this tale is read, showing but dark and inscrutable figures incomprehensibly moving on the screen of time, becomes clear and meaningful. For instance it is unthinkable that those soldiers who were the successors to Alexander, probably by no means as instructed as their commander, should have understood the undercurrents that still supported enthroned kings, and upheld them before the gaze of those that yearned towards them as to the Lord's anointed.

When Antigonus Gonatus took over the patronage formerly extended by the Ptolemies to Delos, he made it an entre-pôt

---

[44] William L. Westerman: *The Slave Systems of Greek and Roman Antiquity*, p. 65.

[45] Mikhail Ivanovitch Rostovtsev: *A Social and Economic History of the Hellenistic World*; Vol. I; p. 227.

centre for the Northern Aegean trade in those materials so necessary in the building of ships; and more significantly again for silver; no doubt from the mines of Thrace and beyond.

This flow of silver to Delos from the North is of equal interest to the rest of the entre-pôt trade. It would have contributed to the augmentation of the temple reserves of silver that would have enabled Delos to partially replace Athens during the 3rd Century B.C. as the new centre from which international money power came to control the finances of the Eastern Mediterranean as formerly, in the days of the Athenian Empire; and therefore above all, that grain trade so essential to Athens[46] and mainland Greece. A document mentioned by Professor M. Rostovtsev refers to a purchase of grain in Delos by a *Sitones* of Histicaea, a subject city of Macedonia in which he observes that the purchase was made out of money advanced by a Rhodian banker. This particular case might suggest that the banking of Rhodes was interlocked with that of Delos and that those silver reserves of the Temple of Apollo functioned also as reserve to Rhodian banking. Delos, because of its sanctity would constitute a much safer store house for precious metal hoards than ever Rhodes might be.

Previous references to banking in the Grecian centres and sanctuaries as being conducted by aliens,[47] are also verified by Professor M. Rostovtsev.[48] The question therefore arises "What aliens?" Would they be members of the same fraternity as the Aramean, Apollonius above mentioned, manager for the economic affairs for Ptolemy Philadelphus; men who were

---

[46] Mikhail Ivanovitch Rostovtsev: *A Social and Economic History of the Hellenistic World*; pp. 218, Vol. I.

[47] Oskar Seffert: *A Dictionary of Classical Antiquities*, p. 91.

[48] Mikhail I. Rostovtsev: *A Social and Economic History of the Hellenistic World*, Vol. I. p.227.

standing almost above and beyond mankind in their manipulation of powers that not so long previously had been reserved solely to the gods and which had been exercised only by that dedicated priesthood surrounding the king, son of god, on earth? Such power being lost to kings forever when in the first place they permitted the institution of accounting to a silver standard in ancient times in the Lands of Sumer and Akkad.

The latter days of Delos and the Temple of Apollo when 10,000 slaves were shipped abroad in one day alone,[49] would certainly suggest the existence at Delos as controllers of its economic affairs, a class of persons internationally minded, and utterly callous to the sufferings of the mixture of broken races that passed before it the way to the slave stockades. Although slavery previous to the 4th century B.C. had been more in the nature of a benign custom similar to the custom of the bonded servant or apprentice of the 18th and 19th Centuries in Northern Europe, after the Macedonian conquests it became a custom in no way so benign,[50] and herding all kinds of persons formerly free, day in and day out, on to the ships of the day, could not have been accomplished but with whip and chain and families being torn apart without compunction or compassion, and little children defenseless against the abuse of monsters.

While the facts of the Temple of Apollo at Delos are relatively clear, supposition of the existence of the Temple of Athene, at Athens as being under the secret control of the bankers, while not being so clear, is logical.

---

[49] Strabo: XIV, v. 570, (Napoleon III: *Julius Caesar* Vol. I, p. 241; London; 1865).

[50] William L. Westerman: *The Slave Systems of Greek and Roman Antiquity*; American Philosophical Society; Philadelphia.

The reserve of 6000 talents of coined silver supposed to have been stored in the Acropolis at the beginning of the Peloponnesian War[51] would certainly seem to indicate that the Temple loaned itself to that major activity of so-called bankers, the creation of abstract money, and shielded them in their very carefully guarded secret that most money circulating as between Athenian merchants and those with whom they did business within, or without the Athenian Empire, was that which was created as by ledger credit page entry. The silver reserve would have been the banker's window dressing and would have served to take care of smaller day to day expenses and payments to foreign states where no other form of payment was possible or acceptable.

The Peloponnesian War ended no more than a little over a hundred years before the time of Alexander. According to A. Andreades in his essay on the war finances of Alexander the Great, total expenditures per annum of Alexander at the time of the crossing of the Hellespont were 5000 - 7000 talents[52]. This was the expenses of an army far from home, and to which, until the Battle of Issus and the certainty of Macedonian total victory, little enough credit would have been available, and most of the disbursements of which army would have been in solid metal. Of such metal, fortunately for the Macedonian Royal House, the mines of Phillipi had certainly made substantial contribution.

It is therefore out of the question to consider whether 6000 talents of silver were adequate for the total finances of the Peloponnesian War over ten years, so far as Athens was concerned. If all disbursements to traders etc. had been in

---

[51] The siege of Potidaea, a relatively minor engagement of a long war, cost the Athenians 2000 of these talents. (Thucydides: *The Peloponnesian War*, Book II, Ch. 7.).

[52] Andreades: *Annales d'Histoire Economique et Sociale*, p. 350, Paris, 1929.

silver, it is doubtful if such so-called reserve could have lasted six months.

This silver was merely the foundation of that illusion which was no doubt spread across the Athenian Empire, that those baked clay facsimiles of Greek coinages which circulated so well between merchants and governments, were redeemable in silver coin; just as for the last three hundred years in the British Empire all the Queen's loyal subjects have believed that every bank note in circulation was redeemable in gold!

On the subject of such fiduciary currencies in ancient times, particularly the Athenian, François Lenormant, eminent 19th Century Numismatist wrote:[53]

"Cedrenus claims that the Romans had wooden money in very ancient times. But this tradition can probably be relegated to the domain of fables with the Roman money of clay of which Suidas writes. However it could be that this last information is

---

[53] According to François Lenormant in his book *La Monnaie dans l'Antiquité*, pp. 215-216, Book II, Tome I: "Cedrenus prétend que les Romaines a une époque très ancienne auraient en des monnaies de bois; mais cette tradition doit très probablement être relegnée dans la domaine des fables avec la monnaie Romains de terre cuite dont parle Suidas. Pourtant ils se pourrait que cette dernier indication se rapportait a quelques espèce d'assignat momentamente en usage et qui n'aurait ermané des autorités publiques. On trouve fréquemment a Athènes des moulages en terre cuites de monnaies d argent ou d'or de diverses contrées, appartenant principalement a la période, qui s'étend du milieu de V siècle avant J.C. entres outres de statères de Cyzique. Le savant Numismatist Sicilien, M. Antonio Salinas pendant son séjour en Grèce, a recueilli un grand nombres de ces monuments, soit en originaux, soit en moulage, et soit en dessins. La destination de cette classe spéciale d'objets qui se rattachent forcement a la numismatique, est très obscure. Mais on peut conjecturer que de telles pseudo-monnaies de terre cuites, moulées sur des espèces existantes, ont du avoir une circulation fiduciaire, mais d'une caractère tout prive comme celles des billets de crédit. dont la loi autorise dans certains pays l'émission par des institutions particulière."

connected with several types of assignat briefly used at the time and which could not have been emitted by public authority. Clay moulds of silver and gold currencies of various countries, principally belonging to the period extending from the middle of the 5th Century B.C., and among others, of the staters of Cyzique, are frequently found at Athens.

The learned Sicilian Numismatist M. Antonio Salinas during his stay in Greece, collected a large number of these monuments, either as originals or moulds, or drawings. The purpose of this special class of objects that are of course connected with numismatics, is very obscure. But it can be conjectured that such pseudo-currencies of baked clay moulded from existing types (of money) had a fiduciary circulation of quite a private character, however, similar to that of the credit notes whose emission is authorized in certain countries by particular institutions."

In other words the clay facsimiles functioned in much the same manner as did bank notes over the last three hundred years in the Anglo-Saxon world; they were money, privately created and emitted.

François Lenormant, however lived at a time when relatively little was realized by numismatists of the functions of "Ledger Credit Page Entry Money," or often enough of money itself as being so many numbers injected into a circulation amongst the people, either as pure abstraction and functioning as by transfer of such ledger credit page entry, or as tangible record on clay, paper, copper, silver, or gold, and functioning as by transfer from hand to hand of those defined commodities, intrinsically valueless or otherwise, on which its numbers were so imprinted. The value of such numbers in goods and services for sale being the most amount of such numbers as the people offered in competitive buying or the least as they accepted in competitive selling.

PER ME DEI REGNANT!

The city states of the rulers of Troy, Orchomenos, Tyryns, Bog-Haz-Koi, Mycenae, Cnossos, and cities and states without number and of which not even the name or memory, now remains, too often, little expectant of calamity from without, from whatever cause, finally went down into smoking ruin before the deluge of wild men, who, with their reeking swords brought all those god-ordered ages of ancient time to a bloody close; men such as the wearer of the golden mask whose grave was opened by Heinrich Schlieman in his excavations at Mycenae, and who he believed to be Agamemnon sleeping his everlasting sleep.

Buried sword in one hand, with the other this giant amongst men still clutched in death as in life, those disks of gold which so obviously were storehouse of wealth and power.

Thus it is clear that by permitting gold to be equated with wealth, or that which had been money, and forgetting thus the true nature of money as a thing apart, his law alone, merely a device of transferable numbers to assist and give order to the exchanges amongst his people, this god-king from whom descended the legend of that company on Olympus, was already surrendering his might, and the freedoms of his peoples, to those inscrutable shadows that lurked in the dimness of the distant Babylonian counting houses.

To these rulers, power was already in the merchant's and master miner's precious metal pieces. With such precious metals as they stripped from the bodies of living and dead in those cities they had so gleefully sacked and put to sword, when peace carne again, they were able to purchase those items of luxury so much desired by their women, such as were manufactured in the cities of the Mesopotamian plain and

Egypt,[54] if not further afield. More important still, they were thus able to obtain the finest of arms that skilled craftsmanship could fashion, such as the suit of bronze armour found at Medea in Greece (illustrated on Page 135 of *Dawn of the Gods*, by Jacquetta Hawkes); the very best of the master armourer's trade.

Thus they readied themselves for the next slaughter. It may very well have been as in today, when the new aggressors, designated Communist as according to the meaning of that word, may very well be preparing for the destruction of those easy-going people of the Anglo-Saxon world from whose skill and technique derive those finest of arms through which their world could indeed be threatened with total obliteration.

That in their position as ruler all gold flowed through their hands, whether in those forms given to it by goldsmith's art or in those shapes most convenient from the point of view of its use in international exchange, there is no doubt. The latter case was clearly shown by the rings and disks and the tiny double headed axes, as found at Troy, all of gold, and the four hundred round pieces of gold and the one hundred and fifty golden disks that were found in the Royal tombs of Mycenae (dating from c. 1500 B.C.) by Heinrich Schlieman[55] all of which clearly

---

[54] Heinrich Schlieman: *Mycenae*, pp. 157; 241; 242. Blom; New York, 1967 (reprint)

[55] It is also interesting to note that amongst so much precious metal was also found a large number of oyster shells and unopened oysters; also weapons of obsidian. Although Heinrich Schlieman was convinced he had found the grave of Agamemnon who had lead the heroes to before the walls of Troy, the obsidian weapons and the oyster shells indicated that this grave belonged to a much earlier age again than that of Agamemnon; an age perhaps even previous to that in Which occurred those disturbances that brought down into ruin so much of the ancient world, of which Sumeria, Crete, Mycenae, Egypt and the Empire of the Hittites were but part.

represented some form of exchange or money. Spirals of gold wire also found in the grave of one member of the Royal Family of Mycenae are suggested by Seltsman (Greek Coins, p.5) to be adjusted to the small Aegean gold talent of 8.5 grammes which he classifies as the Aegean gold unit. Herein would be implication of the use of a gold unit in international exchanges even at that early time. The rings of gold wire of a few grammes weight which circulated in Egypt (Breasted, p. 307) in the reign of Tahutmes III (1501 B.C. - 1447 B.C.), would appear to afford some verification of this fact. Gold or silver money, whether ring money or other form of money, if of definite weight and fineness would always be desirable in international exchanges.

As an interesting and pertinent digression, it also appears that spiral or ring money may have come to occupy a place in the economic life of Egypt too, as early as the latter years of the so-called Old Kingdom. Its use and abuse, considering the Egyptian trade that existed across the known world during the reign of Pepi pharaoh who reigned 90 years during the 6th Dynasty,[56] may have been one of the factors by which the

---

At the time of Schlieman's diggings at Mycenae, practically nothing was known of the extensive use of shell money in ages long gone by, but as a result of the extensive studies of recent years, particularly those of Paul Einzig (*Primitive Money*; London 1949.), and of Mrs. Kingston-Higgins (*A Survey of Primitive Money*, London; 1949.), it is quite clear that the oyster shells found in the Mycenaean graves were reference days more ancient again than those of Agamemnon and the Heroes. They belonged to a day already nearly forgotten, when shells were money, and money, not only amongst simple societies, but also amongst some highly organized societies was shells. In the I Chiag, one of the earliest books of the Chinese, 100,000 dead shell fish are given as the equivalent of riches. The famous dictionary of the Emperor Kang Hsi (1662 A.D. - 1723 A.D.) based on the Shuo Wen of Hsu Shin who died about A.D. 120, says pei denotes sea creatures that live in shells. The character pei was included in most characters relating to wealth. It is included in many such characters in the latest Chinese dictionaries.

[56] Henry J. Breasted: p. 142.

International Money Power of the time, in whatever form it existed, brought about the total collapse of kingly rule in Egypt in the years subsequent to the death of this ruler.

The Hebrew records also appear to verify this use of metal rings or spirals being used in settlement of trade balances between foreigners; or of being storehouses of wealth. According to Madden, however,[57] there is no mention of gold money in ancient Hebrew records, though gold constituted part of the wealth of Abraham, undoubtedly refugee from Ur about the time of its destruction by the Gutim. The six hundred shekels of gold by weight paid by David for the threshing floor and oxen of Ornan[58] and the 6000 shekels of gold taken by Naaman on his journey to the King of Israel[59] do not imply money. Nor can the passage: "they lavish gold out of the bag and weigh silver in the balance,"[60] or "Wisdom cannot be gotten for gold neither shall silver be weighed for the price thereof,"[61] be brought forward in favour of gold money. Gold was generally employed for personal ornament[62] and for adornment of the temple.

It is probable, therefore, that a system of "jewel currency," or "ring money," was in use. The case of Rebekah to whom the servant of Abraham gave "a gold earing of half a shekel weight,[63] and two bracelets for her hands of ten (shekels) weight," proves that the ancient Hebrews made their jewels of

---

[57] F.W. Madden: *Coins of the Jews*, pp. 9-10.

[58] *Chron.* I. xxxi. 25.

[59] 2. *Kings.* V.5.

[60] *Isaiah.* xlvi.6.

[61] *Job.* xxviii. 15.

[62] *Genesis*, xxiv. 22.

[63] *Genesis.* xiv. 22.

a specific weight so as to know the value of these ornaments in employing them in lieu of money. That the Egyptians kept their bullion in jewels and rings is not merely indicated by the scene on the monuments as mentioned by Lenormant and Masparo, in which they are represented as weighing rings of gold, silver and copper, but also by the findings of archaeology such as the copper rings found at Tel Amarna stamped with the cartouche of Kuen-Aten, Hyksos ruler.[64] These rings would appear to have been retained in the treasury at Tel Amarna, and therefore still were current two hundred years after the expulsion of the so called Hyksos. According to Breasted, gold and copper rings of a fixed weigh circulated in large scale business in the time of the "Old Kingdom," and (significantly enough to the student of "banking," or private money creation and regulation, as it might better be known) "stone weights were already marked with their equivalence in such rings."[65] The circulation as money of these "promises to pay" recorded on stone, pointedly suggests the likelihood of the activities of a secret fraternity whose hereditary trade was private money creation. It may very

---

[64] Alexander del Mar: *A History of Monetary Systems in Various States*, p. 38.

[65] James H. Breasted: *A History of Egypt*, pp. 97-98. Of the latter years of the Old Kingdom remarks made by the scholarly writer of the articles on Egypt in the Encyclopaedia Britannica (9th Edn.): "The sixth Dynasty was probably a family of a different part of Egypt. It has left many records which indicate less centralization at Memphis than those of earlier Sovereigns; and mark the beginning of wars for predatory purposes and extension of territory. This change is accompanied by a less careful style of sculpture and less pains in the excavation of tombs as though the Egyptians were gaining a larger horizon, or, it may be, exchanging religion for ambition."

However, speculation more to the point might very well be as to whether or not the Egyptians of this period were making an exchange of the deep harmony in living as had obtained under the true and natural order under which they had lived so long, for that disorder in life which necessarily derived from the ferment known as "Progress"; one of the essential factors by which private (and hence irresponsible) money creative power maintains its total hegemony, once its control is established amongst a people.

well have been the debilitating force that, with the death of Pepi II in 2476 B.C., brought about ending in turmoil and anarchy to the even flow of the undeterminable age over which the God-Kings reigning in awesome splendour, so long had spread their mantle of man-consideration and true benevolence.

Further evidence that the Egyptians kept their bullion in jewels or rings is indicated by the passage from Exodus[66] in which it is related that the Israelites, previous to their departure from Egypt, borrowed "jewels of silver and jewels of gold and spoiled the Egyptians."

In consequence it would appear that the money used by the children of Jacob when they went to purchase corn in Egypt was ring money, the use of which was permitted by the Pharaoh Egypt of the time; rightly or wrongly. Their money is described "bundles of money," as verified by the authorized translation Deuteronomy. "Then shalt thou turn it into money and bind up the money in thine hand and shall go unto the place where the Lord thy God shall choose"[67] The excavations of Heinrich Schlieman indicate that such ring money was also used by the Mycenaeans at perhaps rather later date.

Thus the Greek city state, owing its existence to an uncertain long period during which there took place those events that led up to the final days of Cnossos and Mycenae, was the result of the union of the forces of order in life and death that motivated the priest-king, were he at Cnossos, or at Thebes, or Tel Amarna, or serving the Moon god at Ur, leader amongst the Sumerian cities, and those forces that drove on the builders of the battlements first of all unearthed by Heinrich Schlieman at

---

[66] *Exodus*. xii, 35. *Exodus* iii, 22. (King James Version).

[67] *Deuteronomy*. xiv, 24-26. (King James Version)

Troy and Mycenae. Whether priest-king or peasant-king, their wealth was already assessed in terms of the weight of their store of precious metals which would be so eagerly accepted in exchange for the products of the master armourers employed by the bankers who already controlled trade and money creation in those cities of the Ancient Orient; from which cities, therefore, the glory of total guidance by the god-will had already departed.

He who was literally the Son of God on Earth as he meditated in his island fastness of Crete, was beholden to none other than the people below who he served from his place as the apex of the pyramid of life itself, and to the will of the one above who appointed him to serve. The peasant king at Mycenae or Troy or wherever it might be, for all his seeming rock-like strength, and a certain god-likeness in character of the kingship he bore, as was indicated by the title *Wanax*, necessarily existed as instrument of those who manipulated gold or silver supplies internationally, and at the same time the slave market; men of a class who, in that control of prices which they so clearly exercised, were able to control prosperity in all those seemingly powerful states that had accepted the international valuation of silver as the factor determining internal or national values; such as was the case with most of the mainland cities. They may have been, as it seems they are today, a close knit conspiratorial group threaded through the priest and scholar class of these cities and lards; thought not of themselves of such origin.

The answer may be found to lie in the existence in very ancient Sumeria of a privileged class, who, having access to the "credit" of the temple, thus were able to control the masters of the great donkey caravans who carried such "credit," or will of the god of the city, from one place of business to the other; incising record on their tablets, of loan of such credit made to enable purchase, or interest overdue, or repayment of such loan as had been made the previous trip. These persons, who may be considered themselves to derive from the hereditary caravaneers and who must have functioned as bullion broker and banker, would have been fully clear on the subject of silver and its function in settlement of foreign trade balances and its use as a standard on which to base money accounting. In the latter days of the city states of Sumeria, it is reasonably clear that during certain periods of decay, a languid and corrupted priesthood might delegate[68] to these persons, not only matters of trade, but also those decisions relative to foreign states so essential to the continuance of the might and right of the god of the city.

The special international character of the outlook of these people, sprung as they undoubtedly were from the donkey caravaneers, born to be at home amongst all peoples, yet to always bear in mind the peculiar business of the caravan merchants, their trade and profit, may not have made for decisions as from a true and dedicated god-servant. Thus it may very well be that we must look to the professional caravaneers, from whom descended the *Habiru*,[69] for widespread dissemination of the knowledge of the possibilities offered to merchants by development of the practices relating to private money creation deriving from a clear understanding of the meaning of accounting to a silver standard, and later the potentialities towards development of monopoly of trade inherent in the actual use of silver as the material on which the numbers of the abstract unit were stamped. The full extent of

---

[68] Such a period may very well have been the several centuries preceding the collapse of the caravan trade in Mesopotamia, in the 18th century B.C.

[69] In the words of Professor F.W. Albright writing of the findings of his studies relative to the caravan trade and the organization of the donkey caravans of the twentieth and nineteenth centuries B.C.: "It became particularly obvious that the previously enigmatic occupational background of Abraham becomes intelligible only when we identify the terms *Ibri* 'Hebrew,' (previously '*Abiru*) with '*Apiru*, later '*Abiru*, literally 'person from across or beyond.'" (*The Amarna Letters from Palestine; Cambridge Ancient History*; Vol. II, p. 17.)

the possibilities towards the accumulation of wealth through exploitation of varying ratios between silver and gold in different parts of the world, and the possibilities of a private and secret expansion of the total monetary circulation which was open to those who were held in such esteem in the cities that persons were glad to deposit their valuables with them for safe-keeping, may also have been known to them.

As such accounting to a silver standard had long been known in the lands of Sumer and Akkad, and the mainland generally, control of values had long since been in the hands of the silver bullion brokers, whoever they were, and the money lenders, and bankers and their satellite merchants, without reference as in former days, to priesthood and temple scribe. Through bullion they controlled money, and through money creation, on that bullion as base, they controlled manufactures. According to T.B.L. Webster in his book *From Mycenae to Homer*: "Undoubtedly Ugarit and Alalakh were more concerned with manufactures than Knossos and Pylos, and silver by weight was already for them performing the function of money, whereas as far as can be seen in the Mycenaean centres, no such standard existed"[70]. However the fact that the Achaeans derived their system of measurements from Mesopotamia[71] would certainly suggest that the most important measurement of all, the monetary unit would equally originate from such source. This opinion is further strengthened by the collaboration obviously existing in the Mycenaean settlement at Ugarit[72] with that money power which based itself on silver by weight, such as clearly controlled the manufacturies of Ugarit and Alalakh.

Further according to the same scholar:

---

[70] T.B.L. Webster: *From Mycenae to Homer*, p. 22; London; 1964.

[71] Jacquetta Hawkes: *Dawn of the Gods*, p. 226. New York; 1969.

[72] *Ibid.*

"The Alalakh tablets also record copper distributed to smiths, but note in addition it is to be used for making baskets or arrowheads; and the King of Assyria sent copper to Mari to be made into nails by the local craftsmen. A report from Pylos that the woodcutters in two places are delivering 150 axles and 150 spars for the chariot factory may be compared with the Ugaritic texts on the delivery of wood for the making of arms, and a note of wood delivered to the carpenters for the construction of wagons in Alalakh. We may add here also from Pylos a list of wooden objects made, a list of vessels received by men (perhaps Mayors) in various places and a note of pieces of ivory; to set beside this rather slender evidence of Mycenaean manufacture, Alalakh provides a record of sixty four business houses and their produce; they include smiths, leather workers, joiners, and cartwrights."[73]

Thus it seems that where the conception of money as to a silver standard existed as at Ugarit and Alalakh, so also existed organized industry, including outstandingly the private manufacture of arms under methods that appear to be those of semi-mass production. It is not without significance that this early era of privately issued money (such as was silver money), and consequent private industry, particularly that which was devoted to arms manufacture, was in certain areas so coincidental with the massive movements of warlike peoples, and the collapse of ancient empires that had lived long under the pattern of life known as that of the Ancient Orient. Conquering peoples needed the best of arms. It seems that the best of arms were obtainable from private industry; and private industry in its turn needed silver or gold or labour which was slaves, in payment. Both were obtainable as the result of war. Therefore parallel, though not entirely the same as in today, the more war, the more the industry, and the more the need for the products of the money creators' ledgers. Hence became the

---

[73] T.B.L. Webster: *From Mycenae Homer*, p. 22.

more absolute the control of that which most of all designs industry and its accompanying slavery in one form or another, namely, private money creative power.

Thus regardless of what strength still resided in the heart of the temple states of the Ancient Orient, if values were dictated by the international valuation of silver bullion, then, above all, the internationally dealing silver bullion brokers would be in a position to see to it that manufacture and distribution of arms was under their control, the factor most important of all in international power allocation.

They were in a position to have manufactured in some scale, controlling labour as they undoubtedly did through control of the slave trade, the finest weapons known in that day for those rulers who collaborated with them and served best their purposes. Clearly by the same token, with such total money control, they were in a position to withhold the best of weapons, or the materials for such weapons, from those who served them the least. In a world that had come to believe in money as an absolute, such was the position long ago, exactly as in today. Thus the state that rejected international money power, as did Sparta and Rome in ancient times, and Russia in modern times, had to be prepared to establish total military self-sufficiency.

The Cretan civilization that communicated its ancient language through the pictograph script known as Linear "A," which recognizably came to communicate Greek through that development of this script known as Linear "B," about 1500 B.C.,[74] would certainly seem to have been conquered by Greek speaking peoples some reasonable period previously; which would suggest about 1700-1600 B.C.

---

[74] John Chadwick: *The Decipherment of Linear "B"*; Cambridge; 1958.

At the same time, according to Breasted,[75] in 1675 B.C., the so-called Hyksos, a Semitic conqueror, entered the Delta regions of Egypt, establishing total military supremacy through the use of horse and chariot, previously unknown in Egypt.

The evidences of the Ugarit and Alalakh tablets, although of a substantially later date (about three hundred and fifty years) indicating semi-mass production in these areas of chariot parts, arrow heads, and arms of various kinds,[76] cannot but suggest that it was from this region, so close to the copper of Cyprus, and the wood of Anatolia and Lebanon, that money power armed those restless peoples that may have inundated Crete in earlier times, and Egypt somewhat later.

The chariots by means of which Egypt had been subdued, can only have been paid for out of the booty of conquest, the plunder of tomb and temple, and the sale of the enslaved peoples. The fact of the persistence of the thrust of Tahutmes III[77] into these regions substantially less than one hundred years after the eviction of the Hyksos by Ahmose I (1500 B.C.-1557 B.C.) from their last Egyptian stronghold at Avaris[78] on the Eastern marches of the Delta, would indicate no idle pointless advance, but definite design towards destroying the heart of the enemy, the elimination of his financial and industrial centres. Whether they were still in the regions of Ugarit and Alalakh, or now sheltered elsewhere behind the Kingdom of Kadesh, perhaps in Mittani, would not be known.

However, that both sides had equal access to the international arms industry would certainly be indicated by the spoil in

---

[75] Henry J. Breasted: *A History of Egypt*, p. 214.

[76] T.B.L. Webster: *From Mycenae to Homer*, p. 18.

[77] Henry J. Breasted: *A History Egypt*, pp. 284-321.

[78] Henry J Breasted: *A History of Egypt*, p. 217.

manufactures of war of the battle of Megiddo (1479 B.C.) as won by Tahutmes III against the King of Kadesh and his allies, amounting to nine hundred and twenty-four chariots and two hundred suits of armour.[79] By corollary, it may reasonably be assumed that opposed to these chariots as seized at Megiddo, would have been at least another thousand chariots. Alexander of Macedonia venturing far from home in later times, was a reckless adventurer, considering that at the battle of Issus (October, 333 B.C.) the whole Macedonian army amounted to little more in numbers than the Greek mercenary centre of Darius which was but a small part of the Persian's enormous, if undisciplined host.[80] Tahutmes, who ruled Egypt from 1501-1447 B.C. was the god-king of a great and ancient state to which occupation by the detested Hyksos had so recently taught a severe lesson in that which was modern warfare in those times. He was descendant of a line of kings 2000 years old or more, and it is very doubtful if he would have moved abroad without careful organization and planning. To build his thousand or so chariots was needed the wood of Lebanon and Syria, and those districts surrounding the Gulf of Antioch.[81] Also was the craftsmanship of its cities of Ugarit and Alalakh needed, or at least, of that so strategic district, whatever its name at that time; also equal financial and industrial organization to that which clearly was available to the kingdom of Kadesh, suggested by Breasted to be the last flicker of political and military power of the Hyksos.[82]

---

[79] *Ibid.* p. 292.

[80] According to J.B. Bury (*History of Greece*, p. 744; Random House edn.), Alexander's total army numbered no more than 30,000 foot and 5000 horse. The Greek hoplite centre of Darius, against which was thrown the full weight of the relatively puny Macedonian phalanx, itself numbered 30,000 men.

[81] *Encyclopaedia Britannica*; 9th Edn.; Vol. XXII; p. 823.

[82] Henry J. Breasted: *A History of Egypt*, pp. 293, 305.

Thus it would appear that money creative power had definitely reestablished some form of agency in Egypt, where, under the conditions of the empire, its best interests lay. The agreement between Tahutmes and the Phoenician cities, particularly Tyre,[83] demonstrates concessions made to traders in order to obtain the sea-power which he so much needed for the success of his campaign against Kadesh. The fact of gold and silver rings of a few grains weight circulating in Egypt as against day-to-day purchases,[84] indicates the nature of the concessions by Tahutmes to that money creative force which undoubtedly drove the world-wide trade of the Phoenician cities. The gifts in silver bullion from the Kheta (or Hittites),[85] natural enemies of the kings of Mittani, indicate that they knew that which would be most welcome to the Pharaoh, and would most of all weaken his leanings towards friendship with Mittani, or other peoples likely to have been their enemies.

The temples of Egypt clearly retained immense wealth and holdings in land,[86] and still conducted their own trading expeditions.[87] However, from the reckoning of Breasted that one person in fifty, and one seventh of the land was owned by them,[88] it is clear that by the times of Rameses III (1198-1167 B.C.) and to whose reign this estimate is applicable, the true force behind kingly rule which is the will of the god, so that king and temple needed to own nothing, as being all in all, they owned all and were all, had long ago been gathered up by those promoting the conception of private ownership. Such

---

[83] Henry J. Breasted: *A History of Egypt*. p. 298. New York; 1956.

[84] Ibid. p. 307.

[85] Ibid. p. 304.

[86] Ibid. p. 491.

[87] Ibid. p. 485.

[88] Ibid. p. 491.

conception of private ownership would naturally derive from that right these persons had already arrogated to themselves to create and manipulate the monetary unit, tangible or abstract, and thereby stimulate the growth of a private enterprise for good or ill. To such an extent had this change in the substructure of life proceeded, that, by the time of Solomon, first Hebrew king in Jerusalem[89] (955 B.C. approx.), the chronicler was able to write: "And a chariot came up and went out of Egypt for six hundred shekels of silver";[90] therein being indication that the international money power of the day deemed it safe to locate its most important industry, which was that of armaments, in the land of Egypt; at least after the barbaric but definitely more "pliable" Libyan dynasty had become established.

Ancient ways and ancient morale gave way to foreign influences and the period of self-criticism and therefore self-immolation that always seems to follow the advent of the penetration of international money creative force. Such money creative force and its key arms manufacturies so much needed by the war powers of that day, would always continue to maintain itself, come what may. Possibly its heartland was some area such as Switzerland today, that by tacit consent of all powers, remained neutral in all this strife, and whose neutrality would always be respected by the armed force of each of the struggling states.

Kadesh, and its allies, Arvad and Symyra, were the military force towards the destruction of which Tahutmes III directed his efforts.[91] The manufacturing cities of Alalakh and Ugarit on

---

[89] Ibid. p. 529.

[90] Kings. 10, 29.

[91] Six hundred years later these cities of Arvad and Symyra seemed also to have attracted the special attention of Assyria. In this case they were friend and ally set up in opposition to the other Arameo-Phoenician cities.

the lower Orontes river and bordering on the Gulf of Antioch, respectively, because of the widespread extent of their trading operations during the 13th Century B.C. until the time of their destruction at the end of that century by sea rovers, either ally or enemy of the confederacy known as the "Peoples of the Sea," might very well be suspected of being headquarters of a money market at that time, even if the deep source of their money power existed in the Babylonian cities.

In being a centre for international trade and arms manufacture during the 13th century B.C., this area may very well be considered to have been a similar centre during the 15th Century B.C.: the more especially in consideration of the agreement which seemed to have existed between the Arameo-Phoenician cities (excluding Arvad and Symyra) and Tahutmes; at least those who guided his policies.

While therefore the neutrality of such areas was respected, money power in control of the movements of bullion internationally, safe behind this shield of neutrality as designers of the international money market, would be able to continue to manipulate war industries; always remaining in a position to allocate the latest of weapons to those states which offered them the best advantage in respect to their particular affair. The rulers of that great Egypt after Tahutmes III and his conquests, although probably completely unaware of the extent of the power of this same international force, deriving as it did from the bazaars of the ancient cities of lower Mesopotamia, obviously needed its good graces when it carne to obtaining those materials and weapons so necessary for what in that time was modern warfare.

As a result, although the Egyptian empire in the earliest years might very well be described as a common market existing independent of Babylonian money power, and deriving its strength from the will to be of a dedicated and instructed Ruler, the sequence of events shows that through those concessions it obtained for its best services in war, it was not long before international money power re-penetrated the substructure of Egyptian life and established its usual behind-the-scenes influence, if not control, as in the earlier time that denoted the collapse of the "Old Kingdom." It may safely be considered to have reassumed the position of hidden power it had held a thousand years before during the closing years of the 6th Dynasty, a period in which the stone weights indicating equivalence in metal money[92] circulated in much the same way as the clay facsimiles of contemporary coinages circulated in the Eastern Mediterranean area during the days of the Athenian empire, or as circulated the paper notes of today that formerly indicated claim on precious metal. Further indication of the activities of private money creative force in this same period exists in the evidence of an extensive world-wide trade on land and sea revealed by those items of Egyptian manufacture discovered at Dorak in Anatolia by James Mellaart,[93] and the stone vases and ivory seals that were found in Crete;[94] all of which dated from this time, and bore little evidence to suggest that they were in the nature of gifts between rulers.

Through "liberalism," and so-called "progressive teachings," its most ancient instruments, wittingly or otherwise, towards the continuance of its secret hegemony, reinstituted international money creative force seems to have brought the host land of Egypt to where it was at the time of Akhenaton (1375 to 1358 B.C.), and the Tel Amarna letters which tell of self-destruction and decay, the rejection of old values and beliefs, and the indifference of the a Egyptian rulers to their trust, and to the crumbling of Empire. The degeneracy and complacence of the

---

[92] Henry J. Breasted: *A History of Egypt*, pp. 97-98.

[93] Stuart Piggott: *Dawn of Civilization*, p. 168. (New York; 1961) See also p. 28 in T.B.L. Webster (Mycenae to Homer).

[94] Colin Renfrew: *The Emergence of Civilization*, p. 448.

age was revealed by the fruitless outcry out of Asia from the vassals of the Pharaoh; being particularly exemplified by the despairing pleas of king Abdikhiba of the most ancient city of Jerusalem for assistance against the pressure of the armed assaults of the *Habiru*.[95]

In the meantime the military might of those grim warriors of the shaft graves of Mycenae continued to grow, and they clearly could be relied on to supply the master moneyers of that ancient world with gold and silver and slaves. Therein these robber rulers, best known from the Homeric sagas, were but the instruments by which the mysterious worshippers of the anti-god, the controllers of the extensive money creative force deriving from the Mesopotamian cities, unseen, but all-seeing, slowly undermined the walls of the temple states of the ancient world, of Crete, of Mycenae, of Troy, of Bog-Haz Koi and of Egypt too, so finally and so completely, that little memory or record existed, except in the case of Egypt; even during that period which is known as antiquity; that is the period of the flourishing of Greece and Rome.

What, therefore, did the international money creative fraternity of that day need from those states that clearly forbad their trade

---

[95] One of the most eloquent of his letters to the Pharaoh (Winkler's Translation of the *Tel Amarna Letters*. p. 181.) is as follows: "The King's whole land which has begun hostilities with me, will be lost. Behold the territory of Shiri (Seir) as far as Ginti-Kirmil (Carmel), its princes are wholly lost, and hostility prevails against me. as long as ships were upon the sea, the strong arm of the King occupied Narahin and Kash, but now the Khabiri (Habiru) are occupying the King's cities. There remains not one prince to my lord the King, everyone is ruined. Let the King take care of his land, and. let him send troops. For if no troops come this year, let the King send his officer to fetch me and my brothers, that we may die with our lord the King." While the Pharaoh and his court, drenched with foreign influences, meditated at Tel Amarna upon the illusion of One World and its alien gods, the One World that had been the reality created by the sword of his more vigorous forebears, was crumbling to dust.

or settlement as corruptors of all true order and peace in life, and that thus rejected their blandishments; or from any other state for that matter? What other than the plunder out of sack and ruin by those wild men they brought in from distant lands to North and to South. and to whom they offered the sweet-smelling women, the sunlit gardens, the gold and the silver; which of course would soon be theirs in any case.

Of all those cities and states without number, and many without name, why they disappeared, or when, both as actual sites, or names intertwined with historical memory is not known; nor the story of the ending; for as at Pylos,[96] and Cnossos,[97] and Ugarit[98] too, in so many cases the flames were the final gesture of fate which made durable to the end of time, the clay libraries and archives thus sharply defining the end of their compilation and leaving no record further.

The last thrust of the relatively wild men of the North and West against Egypt, and that Egypt survived to still continue to write its name upon the page of history for yet a thousand years, even if with a hand growing ever more weary, if successful, would have revealed the same picture. It is clear that the organization of all those Western and Northern peoples in

---

[96] Jacquetta Hawkes: *Dawn of the Gods*, p. 209. (New York; 1968).

[97] T.B.B. Webster: *From Mycenae to Homer*, p. 23.

[98] W.F. Albright: *Syria, the Philistines and Phoenicia*; p. 31; Cambridge, 1966. Of the case of the identification of the date of destruction of Ugarit through finding the last tablets placed in the oven, Professor Albright writes: "Publication of the documents from the Tablet Oven excavated in 1954, provides a solid basis for dating the fall of Ugarit which must have occurred within a very short time after the tablets were placed in the oven. Two letters are particularly important: RS 18.38 and RS 18.40. The second letter, written by an Ugaritic official to the king of Ugarit, says that he is in Lawasanda (Lawasantiya), watching the approaches from the East together with the king of Siannu. The latter 'has fled and. was killed.'"

confederation against Egypt during the reign of the Pharaoh Merneptah (1236 B.C.-1236 B.C.) was not of haphazard design. Tehennu, Sherden (or Sardinians) Shekelesh (or Sikeli, the early natives of Sicily), Achaeans, Lycians, Teresh (or Etruscans), Danae (obviously deriving from the Goths of the Northern shores of Europe and very likely the forefathers of those in the Israelitish confederacy who described themselves as "Dan"),[99] all these nations known as "The Peoples of the Sea," could not have been brought together as a fairly disciplined group without some more internationally wise advisors in the close circle surrounding King Meryey of the Libyans than his own Libyan advisors. Egypt still contained in temple and burial house a great part of the gold washed from the rivers of Africa over a thousand years or more, despite the plunder in gold the so-called Hyksos had carried with them into the desert some three hundred and fifty years before. Whether Egypt fell, or the confederate host fell, either way was profit to the international bullion traders whose agents would have equally followed Egyptian or confederate.

After this total victory, largely won by the skill and discipline that existed in the Egyptian archery, of copper, still a most valuable metal of war, 9000 swords alone were surrendered to Merneptah. A further one hundred and twenty thousand pieces of other copper military equipment were also surrendered; of weapons and vessels in silver and gold, over three thousand pieces were taken from the camp of the rulers and chiefs; this latter spoil including many swords of gold and silver.

---

[99] Clearly the Danae were the Argives or Danaän of Homer's *Iliad*. The arrows of Apollo Shootafar that appear (Book I) to have driven the Danaän back to their ships with great slaughter, could very well have been those of the dreaded archers of Egypt under Pharaoh Merneptah; thus bearing no real relation to the events at Troy except as was convenient to the poet as he endeavoured to thread together fragments of a heroic tale out of the long ago.

The Kings are overthrown, saying 'salam!'
Not one holds up his head among the nine Nations of the Bow.
Wasted is Tehennu,
The Hittite Land is pacified,
Plundered is Canaan with every evil,
Carried off is Askalon,
Seized upon is Gezer,
Yenoam is made as a thing not existing.
Israel is desolated, her seed is not
Palestine has become a defenceless widow for Egypt.
All Lands are united, they are pacified;
Every one that is turbulent is bound by King Merneptah.[100]

It is interesting to note that although the hosts that fell at the battle of Perire, numbering at least nine thousand, were almost all from the West, according to the poem recorded above, Merneptah almost immediately turned his attention to the peoples of the East. Judging by this record of the stele, he paid some special attention to an Israel never previously referred to in Egyptian history. Such Israel would undoubtedly be a confederacy established during the 13th Century B.C. by Canaanitic tribes, elements such as the fragments of the "Hyksos" or Shepherd Kings, whatever their correct designation, and that had disappeared into the desert some 350 years before pursued by the chariots of Ahmose I,[101] elements deriving from the "Peoples of the Sea" perhaps, and the Habiru, also known as *'Apiru'* or *'Khabiri'*.

But who was who, or why, or what, little concerned that brain centre in Babylon or Ur, or wherever it was. Whoever they professed to be, or to belong to, meant nothing. Out of death

---

[100] Henry J. Breasted: *A History of Egypt*, p. 469.

[101] Sir William Mathew Flinders-Petrie; *A History of Egypt*, p. 256. London; 1897.

and destruction was their harvest, whether those they said were their own, were theirs or not. The only reality was control of precious metal. Out of death and destruction came the releasing in that day of the all important hoards of stored bullion, and the renewal of the slave herds to be consumed in mining ventures in distant places, garnering the increase of such precious metals.[102]

Further, as kingly rule weakened, with the increasing circulation of fraudulent receipts for precious metals and other valuables supposedly on deposit, this highly secretive interstratum of merchant classes controlled by these monopolists of money through monopoly of control of precious metal bullion, postulated by Professor A.L. Oppenheim to be Aramaic speaking during the first Millennium B.C.,[103] would be able of finance much larger manufacturing systems than had been

---

[102] Diodorus Siculus (A. del Mar: *History of the Precious Metals*, p. 40) gives striking picture of the horrors of marginal profit gold mining as carried out with slave labour in ancient times in the Bisharee district of Nubia (B.C. 50).

"There are thus infinite numbers thrown into these mines, all bound in fetters kept at work night and day, and so strictly surrounded that there is, no possibility of their effecting an escape. They are guarded by mercenary soldiers of various barbarous nations, whose language is foreign to them and to each other, so that there are no means of forming conspiracies or of corrupting those who are set to watch them. They are kept to incessant work by the rod of the overseer, who often lashes them severely. Not the least care is taken of the bodies of these poor creatures; they have not a rag to cover their nakedness; and whoever sees them must compassionate their melancholy and deplorable condition, for though they may be sick, maimed or lame, no rest nor any intermission of labour is allowed them. Neither the weakness of old age, nor the infirmities of females excuse any from the work, to which all are driven by blows and cudgels; until borne down by the intolerable weight of their misery, many fall dead in the midst of their insufferable labours. Deprived of all hope, these miserable creatures expect each day to be worse than the last, and long for death to end their sufferings."

[103] Leo A. Oppenheim: *Letters from Mesopotamia*; p. 57, Chicago 1967.

possible from the highly discriminatory temple loans of earlier days. Ugarit and Alalakh previously mentioned, were but early instances. While the purpose of the temple was to cause the people to live godly lives as according to the customs of the day and to preserve them from straying out of the ways of righteousness as it were, the secret and private money creative power, being more concerned with the opposite, the needs of the anti-god, the destruction of the people's lives, whether of king, priest, nobleman, or merchant, or he who laboured in the field, loaned without such discrimination. Out of the resulting confusion amongst rulers could come nothing but advantage to themselves and their purposes; out of the break up of family and home and tradition, all that the dedicated servant of the god has in life, would come an exhausted and confused people, more ready to accept slavery.[104] Corruption of the priesthood, as in today, was the chief aim of money conspiracy, and by causing such priesthood to lose sight of its high purpose and itself as the voice of god on earth, success in all its other purposes, naturally followed.

"Documents of the third level originate in autonomous economic bodies ranging from collective agricultural organizations centred in families, to what often constitutes *de facto* private enterprise inside and outside cities. The distribution

---

[104] Criticising the prescription by Plato of community of wives, etc. for the ruling classes of his Republic, Aristotle wrote: "It would be far more useful applied to the agricultural class. For where wives and children are held in common (and, as according to Plato, all love was to be indiscriminate as between male, female, relation, or otherwise), there is less affection, *and a lack of strong affection among the ruled is conducive to obedience and not to revolution.*" (*The Politics*. Book II. Ch. 4.). Aristotle, as tutor and advisor to Alexander "The Great," also as husband of the niece of Hermias, banker-tyrant of Assos and Atarneus, had clearly seen efforts towards practical application of these mischievous "philosophies" of political conduct.

of the evidence in volume and importance varies with time and region."[105]

Private enterprise depended on privately issued money and of such was silver. Thus towards the establishment of manufactures, they, the international bullion controllers needed the connivance of those corrupted temple officials who had lost sight of the meaning of that god-given power of money creation which had been theirs, and without which the god himself, the real ruler of the city, could not be truly maintained. By the time these temple officials were brought to enter into such connivance, they would be past realizing or caring, for that matter, about the destructive effects to their powers and purposes which lay in so permitting private issuance of money into circulation amongst the people by way of precious metals, or receipts for such precious metals or valuables, supposedly on deposit for safekeeping with prominent merchant houses; thus they would be easily manipulated.

With the extension of the growth of exchanges to a silver standard such as would derive from the circulation of false receipts issued against silver or valuables reputedly on deposit for safe keeping, no special outlay in precious metals was needed other than possibly bribes to court and temple officials. These men, the controllers of bullion movements internationally, and of almost equal consequence, the slave trade, now that their knowledge of the frauds relating to the use of precious metal money, and consequently their knowledge of that which is now known as "capital" was becoming perfected, were bringing into being extensive private industries, the most important of which, as pointed out previously, were the industries relating to war. Towards the promotion of any particular industry as required by the bankers, no doubt

---

[105] Leo A. Oppenheim: *Letters from Mesopotamia*, p. 30.

ambitious slaves or freedmen as eager for money as their counterparts today, could be always found.

It was clearly understood that those receipts representing the weight of silver or the valuables assessed as according to a silver standard, that the bankers were supposed to have on deposit for safe keeping, which circulated by custom, or by law which is custom, as money as to represent a definite amount of exchange units, while accepted as money, were money. The fact that the people accepted them as such, made them so. Their cost to the money manipulators, bullion brokers, or whatever their designation, being but that of the clay in the tablet and the scribe's entry thereon.

After the final triumph of the international money creative fraternity which may be identified in Mesopotamia with that period of conquest, reconquest, and conquest again that began with that invasion of Sumeria by the Gutim in 2270 B.C., and ended with the collapse of the Empire of Ur of Ibi-Sin before the Elamite rebels with their Amorite allies in 2030 B.C., and their taking away to Susa as captive, both the cult statue of the Lord Nannar, the Moon God together with the King Ibi-Sin himself, earthly viceroy of that God, those agents of International Money Power, quickly concluded the work of destruction[106] through liberalism and permissiveness, no doubt, so that by 1900 B.C., the Sumerian had totally lost his national and racial identity and will to be. What continued from then on

---

[106] The relative poverty of the tombs of the 3rd Dynasty at Ur and the pathetic substitutes for the precious metals with which the dead had been adorned in earlier days, reveal the same withering up process that seems to attack any state exposed over any length of time to the exactions of a private money creative power maintaining itself by control of precious metals and the merry-go-round of trade for trade's sake.

was, without a doubt, a mixed breed with no special allegiance to anything other than "money."[107]

Such agents are shown by the general evidence of history to be a class of dubious origins and antecedents. Imbued with racial self-hatred, these rascals, who are raised up in a time of national exhaustion, against the former natural system of rule, by a triumphant money power, too often are particularly distinguished by a readiness to please those who it seems to them are the masters; even to the downgrading and debauchment of their own kind. The apathy of a controlled public opinion to the deluge of perverted sex drenching the Anglo-Saxon countries today, which could not take place without the connivance of the so-called rulers, if only through their failure to take any serious steps towards controlling its source, is, herein, instance enough.

However, until the violent disruptions of caravaneering about 1800 B.C.,[108] the manufactures of Mesopotamia continued to flow Northwards as against precious metals, principally silver and raw materials; and no doubt that trading area or common market formerly controlled by the rulers of the IIIrd Dynasty at Ur, continued to exist; though no longer with the Lord Nannar[109] as signing authority.

The growing manufacturies of Mesopotamia, Syria, Egypt in the time of the Empire, Ur in the reign of Ibi-Sin, and of all the

---

[107] Thus the way was paved for the Semitic city of Babylon to institute itself as the leader of Mesopotamia. However, although politically displacing and absorbing the original race of Sumer, it functioned as but the prophet of Sumer, a mirror of the past giving renewed vigour to a culture that had been evolved long ago. (*A History of Babylon*, pp. 2-3, L.W. King.).

[108] Albright: *The Amarna Letters from Palestine*. Cambridge Ancient History; Vol. II; pp. 17-18.

[109] The Moon God of Ur.

well-populated world which is now known as the Near East, were instigated as a result of those secret money creative processes known only to that class of persons who have already been detailed as best as is possible out of the fragmentary evidence available, to be controlling external trade out of the Mesopotamian plain. Such manufacturies, trading to the ends of the known world, would have drained south the silver of Greece, of Thrace, of Illyria, and Carpathia; indeed from wherever it could be obtained, it would have flowed as against settlement of trade balances, to Mesopotamia.

Consequently, by the time of the Assyrian assumption of control over Aram, and Arabia, and Egypt during the first half of the first Millennium B.C., money, as being a creation of the god of the city toward the well-being and good life of his people, had become a conception of which sight had been almost completely lost. It had come to be the silver injected into circulation by private persons, who by then, in reality, if not so far as went general appearances, through manipulation of that inverted pyramid of ledger credit page entry money erected on the silver they claimed to hold in reserve, as apex, had now completely usurped the essential power of the temple: the creation and allocation of the unit of exchange. Thus the total design of the city which derived from the power of rejection or preferment formerly exercised through the money creative powers of the god through king and priesthood, fell into their hands, and where in earlier days a devoted priesthood exercised its prerogative of preferment through money creation, towards the people living a god-ordered and pious life, each man in harmony with his neighbours,[110] those new

---

[110] There are evidences of a piety and reverence in those ancient days, and of longing by mankind for guidance from an unknown God, little different to that piety to which the rise of Christianity gave revival, and which still exists in homes that withstand the uproar of the age, and stand aside from the destructive forces that seek to guide it. According to E.G.H. Kraeling in *Aram and Israel* (p. 26):

international forces that now exercised the reality of such rule from the counting houses, contemptuous of all kingly and godly power as undoubtedly they were, but still needing such power as front behind which they might shelter in order to better pursue their nefarious purposes, spread hate and suspicion, each man of his brother.

Secretly promoting the concept of "Permanent Revolution" as being most suited towards the maintenance of their control, no sooner did stable and natural god-ordered government come again, then, feverishly digging at its roots, they tore it down. Out of break-up of family and home, out of lust and drunkenness, out of the people living in disorder, and love giving way to hate, they throve. Where they saw signs of nobility and natural aristocracy in living and thought, returning, financial preferment was automatically withdrawn. He who was consumed with animal desires and ignobility of purpose, was their man and eagerly their slave, and willing betrayer of his brethren into what was planned for them by his master.

Even though certain priesthood continued to maintain vigorous temple organizations long after the international control came about such as was exercised by the great Babylonian financial houses, it may safely be assumed that such

---

In the scriptures of Sumeria we have: *Si dilini* — "*Sin* (or Si) hath set me free." *Si idri* — "*Sin* is my help (in a time of need)." *Si aqabi* — "*Sin* hath endowed (or bestowed upon me)." *Sin* or *Si* being the name of the God.

In the adoration of Nashu (or *Nusku* of the Assyrians) we have: *Nashu-dimri* — "*Nashu* is my protection." *Nashu gabri* — "*Nashu* is my hero." *Nashu sagab* — "*Nashu* is exalted." *Nashu Qatari* — "*Nashu* is my rock (of salvation)." *Nashu aili* — "*Nashu* is my strength." In the adoration of *Adad* we have: *Adad hutni* — "*Adad* is my protection."

In the adoration of *Ai* (The Lunar Deity of the Arabians) we have: *Ia abba* "*Ai* is my Father." "*Ia Manis*" *Ai* is my Right Hand. "*Alla sharu*" God is King! (and Lord of all!)

temple organizations continued to exist only on account of their deference to these new controllers of international exchanges. In a similar manner did the Egyptian priesthood defer to the power of Joseph as Vizier to the Pharaoh; as a result of which, while all other lands in Egypt were expropriated and returned to State ownership and administration, its lands, such as appertained to the temples, were not touched in any way.[111] Thus was a corrupted and short-sighted priesthood brought to acquiesce in the enthronement of its enemies, and the enemies of the god it represented. For Joseph clearly was agent of an external Money Power, and while the Pharaoh leaned on him, he and that force behind him were clearly the rulers. *de facto* if not *de jure*, they were in the place of the Pharaoh.

---

[111] *Genesis*. Chapter 57, Verse 22. According to Michael Grant: (*Jews in the Roman World*, p. 7), there are scholars who consider this Pharaoh to have been Akhenaton.

DAVID ASTLE

THE LEFT HAND OF DAWN

Both according to François Lenormant[112] and the Cambridge Ancient History,[113] cheques were in use in Babylonia from the earliest times. Such use of cheques has also been verified as having existed at Ur during the 3rd and 4th Millenniums B.C. by Sir Charles

L. Woolley, and no doubt, by other archaeologists at other sites.

As the only clear meaning that can be given to the law No. 7 of Hammurabai, indicates that also were known in the 3rd Millennium or earlier, the principles of private money creation through the creation of receipts as against valuables on deposit with persons of "Repute," the existence of all the abuses against the men of the city, deriving from the exercise of the principles of inflation and deflation of the total number of such receipts indicating given numbers of the unit of exchange, may be deemed to have existed. These inflations or deflations of the volume of the mass of abstract money, which indeed such false receipts may be called, and such as are particularly associated with the custom of making payments by cheque drawn on "deposits" created by such receipts as issued by such persons "of repute," and which could be manipulated as suited themselves and their friends etc., were directed towards creation of total monopoly of wealth and industry.

---

[112] François Lenormant: *La Monnaie dans l'Antiquité*; Book l; pp. 113-122.

[113] *Cambridge Ancient History*. Vol. I; p. 392.

Further, as according to Paul Einzig, "a credit system developed in Greece as in other parts of the ancient world long before the adoption of coinage,"[114] it may reasonably be supposed that well before the flood of refugees that must have poured out of Aram in the earlier days of the first millennium B.C. as a result of the Assyrian onslaught, Babylonian money power had already established branch agencies on the coast of Greece, and in the Mycenaean centres generally, from which they loaned their clay "promises to pay," expressed in terms of silver no doubt, as against collateral. Such loans could be used to purchase those luxury goods and arms which were brought from the Syrian or Mesopotamian cities; but although the original loan had been but an entry in the ledger of the agent, probably, in the final analysis costing little more than the labour of slave scribe, the repayment demanded would be silver or slaves, or other equally desirable goods.

Clear evidence of the existence of this Babylonian force in the Mycenaean cities was yielded by verification of the fact of the existence of the mythological Cadmus of Grecian Thebes, reputedly Phoenician (Phoenician being simply a word used by the Greeks to describe those people that came to trade from the ports of Syria and Canaan), having probably been reality. This historical fact was revealed by the discovery in modern day Thebes in the area that in ancient times must have been the national storehouses, of cylinders containing seals of a high dignitary of the court of King Burraburias who reigned in the city of Babylon in the first half of the 14th Century B.C.; which unmistakably suggested Cadmus, and his real part in the affairs of Thebes and those cities with which it was connected.[115]

---

[114] Paul Einzig: *Primitive Money*, p. 225.

[115] Jacquetta Hawkes: *Dawn of the Gods*, p. 205, (New York, 1968). Also Britannica 1898, Vol. XI. p. 92. Also the deductions of Professor Sayce in *Mycenae*, p. 265. p. 365.

Further evidence of the activities of the Babylonians is indicated by the discovery of their seals in the Cyclades.

These trading stations established in Mycenae long before Homer, would have functioned very much as did the European trading stations on the West Coast of Africa during the eighteenth century A.D.[116] They were points from which agents of international money power could instigate internal warfare amongst the tribes, so that they would always have ready market for the products of their arms and other industries; the most desirable payment for these products being precious metals and slaves; as much in ancient times as in modern times.

As previously pointed out, the warrior princes of Mycenaean Greece had undoubtedly maintained steady supplies of these commodities as the result of their depredations over many years. But once they had thrown all their resources and military power into the gamble across the sea which was the campaign of the King of Lydia and the "Peoples of the Sea" against Pharaoh

Merneptah of Egypt, and which ended in total disaster for them at the battle of Perire, the years of strength, and plenty, and being feared by their enemies were over.

It may reasonably be assumed that their total destruction while in confederation with the tribes and kingdoms of the Western Mediterranean at Perire on the Western marches of the Egyptian Delta in 1234 B.C., by the discipline of the massed archers of Pharaoh Merneptah, would have marked the Apogee of the parabola of their rise and fall.[117] In that battle it was

---

[116] Captain Theodore Canot: *The Adventures of an African Slaver*, (New York; 1928). Also *Cambridge Economic History*, Vol II; p. 16.

[117] W.F. Albright; p. 32.

proven that they had over-reached themselves, and, as history records, their descent from that Apogee was swift. Despite the excellence of their weapons and the skill at diplomatic manoeuvre of those forces supporting them, such as lay hid within the Babylonian money power, although so much of that world of ancient time had fallen before their fine copper weapons and their chariots, as a result of that unhappy battle, all such equipment was gone; and more than thinking of further conquests abroad, thought had to be for defence of hearth and home.

If then the latest estimate of the date of the battle of Perire, given as 1234 B.C. by W.F. Albright,[118] is correct, that the destruction of Egypt itself was planned over the period of years or so following the sack of Troy (1250 B.C. according to the modern dating and that of Herodotus), is reasonable supposition. The organizing, arming, and training of such widely diverse peoples as formed the army of King Meryey of Lybia, would have taken many years of careful planning.

---

[118] The details of the mining, treatment and smelting of unoxidized ores as took place about this time in the Austrian Alps, are evidence of a long and tedious process (*Cambridge Economic History*, Vol II, pp. 19-20.).

According to Professor W.F. Albright in *The Amarna Letters from Palestine*, (p. 12.): "when we glance through the Amarna letters, we cannot but be impressed with the smallness of the garrisons which were considered adequate by the local princes when clamouring for aid; the prince of Megiddo wants a hundred men, but three other chieftains including the princes of Gezer and Jerusalem, are satisfied with fifty each. Even the prince of wealthy Byblos who constantly asks for assistance, is generally satisfied with two hundred to six hundred infantry and twenty to thirty chariots. Brigawaza of the Damascus region also wants two hundred men."

Correlating these informations, it is clear, that although populations were much less in that day (the latter half of the second millennium B.C.), the limiting factor to military force was the availability of arms, not as is today with its unlimited supplies of metal, the availability of men (hence "conscription").

Considering that the plunder that acceded to Pharaoh Merneptah, after the battle, of at least ten thousand swords, mostly copper and bronze, the rest gold and silver, and the 120,000 pieces of other military equipment in copper and bronze, under the methods of production of that day represented years of work, perhaps Merneptah did not on this occasion melt them into bullion, or sell them to the agents of international money power who undoubtedly were amongst those camp followers appearing to support his army. He may have made the obvious move, as is suggested by the fall of Pylos about 1200 B.C.[119] of using this plunder in weapons to arm the tribes of Epirus, and perhaps farther North, who clearly would be the natural enemies Achaeans. These tribes, although recorded by some as being shepherds, were just as likely to have been slaves revolting from the mining industries established by the Babylonian money power through the instrumentality of the Achaeans and Mycenaeans; which mining industries produced the gold that was such a commonplace in the homes of the nobility of Mycenaea and the silver that was so much needed for the maintenance of that financial system based on silver by weight which was the foundation of what may have become, by this time, a total world hegemony of private money creative power.

Following is a digression on the mining industries that existed in Greece and to the North about the time of Cadmus who, as previously pointed out, was one of the principal Babylonian agents to the Mycenaean world. His approximate date may very well be known from the dating of the seal found at Grecian Thebes;[120] which reveals that Cadmus probably lived during the reign of King Burnaburiash (sometimes known as Burraburiash) of Babylon, who was contemporary of King

---

[119] Jacquetta Hawkes: *Dawn of the Gods*, p. 24.

[120] Ibid. p. 205.

Tutankhamen of Egypt (1358-1353 B.C.). The same Burnaburiash is best known by his letter to King Tutankhamen as was found in the Tel Amarna archives, in which, pleading for gold in no uncertain terms, he achieves an immortal fame.[121]

Nearly one hundred years before the more extensive knowledge of these times, such as exists today, Alexander Del Mar, relying on his own observations as a mining engineer, and on the records of the ancients, wrote as follows respecting the mines from which the agents of the world-wide Babylonian financial hegemony, such as Cadmus of Thebes drew their steady flow of gold and silver.

After description of the thoroughness of Roman mining in Spain in the Asturias, and detailed mention of Laureion near Athens, he continues: "Thassus, an island off the Thracian coast (written Thasso by the Greeks and Thassus by Livy) was originally colonized by the Phoenicians. Thassus itself is probably a corruption of Iassus for Pausanias informs us that Thassus was the son of Agenor, the brother of Europa, and the leader of the Phoenicians (and therefore, brother of Cadmus

---

[121] Letter 9 of the *Tel Amarna Tablets*; Vol I; p. 29. (Samuel A.B. Mercer; Toronto, 1939.). The translation reads as follows: *To Niphururia, king of Eg*[ypt], say. *Thus saith Burraburias, king of Karadunias, thy brother. I am well. With thee, thy house, thy wives, thy land, thy chief men, thy horses, thy chariots, may it be very well. Since my father and thy fathers with one another established friendly relations, they sent to one another rich presents, and they refused not one another any good request. Now my brother has sent [only] two minas of gold as a present. But now, if gold is plentiful, send me as much as thy fathers. But if it is scarce, send half what thy father did. Why didst thou send only two minas of gold? Now, since my work on the House of God is great, and vigorously have I undertaken its accomplishment, send much gold.*

There is little doubt that it was about this time that gold was beginning to augment silver in Babylonia as reserve in the ratio of 13:1 approximately. Hence it might reasonably be assumed that the worthy Burnaburiash could very well have been egged on by force other than that of sheer godliness.

the founder of Thebes)[122] which are details that belong to the myth of Iassus. Herodotus says that he himself visited the island of Thassus, where he saw a temple to the Thasian Hercules 'erected by the Phoenicians, who built Thassus while they were engaged in the search for Europa, an event which happened five generations before Hercules, the son of Amphytryon, was known in Greece." The "Thasian Hercules" was Iassus.

We know but little more of the early history of Thasus beyond the fact that its mines were celebrated for their yield of gold and silver; that the most productive ones were in the S.E. district between Aenyra and Coenyra; and that the Thasians, in addition to the mines of the island, owned and worked those of Scapte Hyle (or Scaptesyla) on the Thracian main. These last in the time of Darius yielded an average annual product worth or equal to 80 talents. The mines on the island did not produce so much at this period, although at an earlier one they had annually yielded between two or three hundred talents.

About 60 miles S.S.E. of Cape Sunium is the island of Siphnos, which in the time of Polycrates B.C. 580-22 and perhaps long before, was famous for its rich mines of gold and silver. 'Their soil produced both gold and silver in such abundance that from a tenth part of their revenues they had a treasury at Delphos equal n value to (all) the riches which that temple possessed.' In the Roman period, time of Strabo, Siphnos was noted for its poverty: for says Pausanias, speaking of the interval, 'Afterwards their gold mines were destroyed by an inundation of the sea.'

Mount Pangaeus is in Thrace on the River Nestus, about two hundred miles W.N.W. from Constantinople. Pliny says that the gold mines in this range were opened by Cadmus: indeed it

---

[122] Bracketed comment by present author. *Britannica*, 9th edition, Vol. VIII.

is probable that all the mines in ancient Greece were opened by the Phoenicians or the Venetians, before they were worked by the Greeks. Phillip of Macedon about B.C. 358, being informed that in ancient times (that would be previous to the so-called Dark Ages of Greece)[123] these mines had been productive, caused them to be reopened, with the result that he obtained from them annually more than a thousand talents. It is from the gold of Pangaeus that he struck his "Phillips," whose type during the following century was so extensively copied by the Gauls.

The island of Samos, once called Cypar-Issa, is on the west coast of Asia Minor near the mouth of the Caystrus and ruined Ephesus. It was colonized originally by the Bacchidae, who were presumably Phoenicians or Venetians and who, on being driven out of Samos by the Ionians, settled afterwards in Samothrace. We know little of the early history of Samos. The Samian mines were of gold and silver, the ores of which were reduced on the river Imbrasus. The extant gold, silver, and electrum coins of Samos are numerous. Some of those commonly attributed to Sardis, were ascribed by Sestini to Samos. Herodotus reports that Polycrates bought off the Lacedaemonians, who tried to deprive him of the island, with a subsidy of lead coins thinly cased with gold, and thus cheaply got rid of his unwelcome visitors. The mines of Samos were still worked in the time of Theophrastus, about 240 B.C., for he wrote concerning them: 'Those who work in these mines cannot stand upright, but are obliged to lie down either on their sides, or their backs: for vein they extract runs length-wise and is only two feet deep though considerably more in breadth and is enclosed on every side with hard rock. From this vein the ore is obtained.'

---

[123] Bracketed comment by present author.

Mines of gold or silver or both were worked by the so-called Pelasgians in many parts of Greece, chiefly in the mountains of Albania, Dalmatia, Croatia, Bosnia, Servia, Thrace and Bulgaria. The remains of a smelting furnace composed of colossal hewn stones (once again the cyclopaean stone works of Mycenae?),[124] together with heaps of refuse silver ores, can still be seen in Albania, almost in sight from the houses of Corfu (Corcyra). Similar structures and remains are said to exist in Dalmatia. In Bosnia at Slatnitza, on the road to Scopia, six miles from Traunick, the Romans worked gold mines on an extensive scale and they were probably worked by the Greeks before the Romans. There are reported to be gold mines in several mountains near Zvornick and Varech. The rivers Bosna, Verbatch, Drina, and Latchva are auriferous. Many silver mines have been worked in the neighbourhood of Rama or Prezos, Foinitca and other villages, called Sreberno, Srebernik, or Srebernitza. Cinnabar is obtained near the convent of Chressevo, and this deposit was probably worked for mercury in very ancient times. About B.C. 470, Alexander, son of Amyntas, possessed a mine near lake Prasis and Mt. Dysia in Macedonia, which yielded him a talent per diem.

In Servia there were silver mines near Nova-Berda, and (Roman) gold mines near Saphina. Ancient mines of both gold and silver, chiefly the latter exist in other parts of Servia, but little is known of their early history. There are some twenty thousand acres of alluvions within fifty miles of Belgrade which might yet richly reward the hydraulic process. There is plenty of water with good heads and good grades for the gravel. Bulgaria also abounds in mines of the precious metals, but like most of those within the territory comprised within Ancient Greece, they have fallen to ruins and their history is forgotten.

---

[124] Ibid.

.In many parts of Greece or European Turkey, where ancient mines were worked, a superstition is said to prevent the peasantry from visiting them. Malte-Brun especially mentions this of the old Roman mines near Traunick, and we ourselves have noticed the same superstition in the vicinity of the Roman gold mines in the Carpathian foothills. This superstition is probably due to the traditions of that cruel and relentless slavery to which their forefathers were subjected by the Greek and Roman Lords who once owned these mines. Valdivia, writing to the Emperor Charles V, declared that every castellano of gold from Peru cost a measure of human blood and tears. What was the cost of gold to the ancient Romans or the still more ancient Greeks, it would be hard to say: but a human life for every ounce would probably be well within the mark.[125]

For further information on mining in very ancient times in S.E. Europe, the activities of the Beaker people etc., the Cambridge Economic History should be consulted, though no special significance, such as obviously exists, will be pointed out therein relating this search for silver and gold to the private money creative system already well established in Babylonia at that time.

So to return to the main thread of this tale. It is clear that a relatively extensive, and hardened, and brutalized population existed in the localities of the mining industries of Epirus and farther North at the time of the flourishing of Crete, and Mycenae and of Cadmus of Thebes; formerly considered mythological, but clearly powerful agent of the Babylonian money power towards its search for the precious metals. This population, largely slave, given weapons and organizations, as the vanguard of the so-called militant shepherds, could be a serious threat to the civilizations of the South, so concerned

---

[125] Alexander del Mar: *History of the Precious Metals*, pp. 47-50.

with peace and the pleasures deriving from trade etc., which is born out by the records of history, scant as they are.

It is to be noted that Ugarit, wherein the Achaean had trade centre after 1300 B.C., great port, and location of manufacturies, fell well previous to 1190 B.C., when Rameses III of Egypt appears to have finally checked the Southward advance of its destroyer;[126] which suggests likelihood of them as having been those Northern people, not connected with the "Peoples of the Sea," with whom Egypt undoubtedly established alliance at the time of the battle of Perire. Such allies may very well have been those we know of as the Dorians, who, as is revealed by the tablets of Pylos, clearly were sea raiders in their earlier days in the Mediterranean area. Further verification of these conclusions, though not of the Dorian alliance, exists in the deductions of Professor Albright (*Syria, the Philistines, and Phoenicia*; p. 31.), deriving from the information on the documents found in the Tablet Oven at Ugarit, that the sack of Ugarit, having obviously occurred shortly after the tablets were placed in the oven, dates from about 1234 B.C., which would be about the time of the victory of Merneptah of Egypt over the "Peoples of the Sea" at Perire.

The destruction Ugarit may very well have been an act of political revenge of a reawakened Egypt, working through the allies it would be raising up. For it is clear that the raiders who struck down this important city were well advised in that they chose the time for their attack as being when the ships of Ugarit had been ordered elsewhere, perhaps to Lydia, by the Hittites who appear to have been the overlords of the kings of Ugarit.[127] These raiders obviously were also well armed. In that day, much more so than today, the question was not so much

---

[126] Breasted, pp. 480-481.

[127] Cyrus H Gordon: *Ugaritic Literature*, p. ix, p. 120. (Text 118) Rome, 1949.

as whether men were available, as whether effective arms were available for them to bear.

Ugarit was undoubtedly centre from which arms and supplies were shipped to the Libyans and the "Peoples of the Sea." In such, therefore, it would have been agency of that greater force seeking to design the end of Egypt as it bad been known; and waiting for its plunder of sliver and gold.

The main Achaean states, suffering serious shortage of arms as a result of the battle of Perire, which appears to be verified by the dearth of military equipment recorded by the Linear "B" tablets unearthed at Pylos, obviously written shortly before the full force of the attack came from the North, were wide open to the enemy. On the reasonable assumption that Pharaoh Merneptah would have arranged for armed uprising of the numerous mine slaves to the North of Mycenaean Greece, together with organized attack from those nations of mid Europe, perhaps from as far afield as Denmark, trading partner of Mycenae,[128] it would have been reasonable for him to have supplied them with officers particularly instructed in siege work, and the arms with which, as a result of Perire, his arsenals would have been so well equipped.

One thing is clear, the Dorians known to be destroyers of Pylos, an action which paved the way for their conquest of the Peloponnese, were well organized, with a strong *esprit de corps* which remained with them until the last days of Sparta, and were well armed as armaments went in those days. Having ships, as the tablets of Pylos reveal,[129] they thus could maintain adequate supplies down the coast of the Adriatic. Above all they must have had previous experience in siege work such as

---

[128] *Cambridge Economic History*, Vol. II, p. 16.

[129] Jacquetta Hawkes: *Dawn of the Gods*, p. 209.

could have been gained in the wars against the Canaanitic cities, for the tremendous walls of both Mycenae and Tyryns could not have been taken but by well organised armies with a strong and experienced engineering corps. It may safely be considered that a considerable part of the excellent arms with which the Dorians must have been supplied, was the plunder of Perire. The only uncertainty is whether these arms were obtained, as seems to be the usual thing in such circumstances, from the international money power direct, or from a scheming and resurgent Egypt where the god-king shone once again on the throne of the two lands, giving universal illumination as guide of his people's destiny. After Perire, terrible battle that it must have been for the times, he certainly would have been in a position to "Divide and Rule."

After all these events, largely indicating frustration of the schemes of international money creative power, particularly in its failure to bring about total collapse of that most ancient world which was Egypt, so far as Greece was concerned, there came a period known today as the "Dark Ages"; dark, because too little is known thereof. Such was the magnitude of the disaster that swept over the Achaeans, weaponless as they very well may have been, that for a time those trading stations established by the Babylonians, and that had flourished for so long, through the crumbling of so much of what had been in ancient days, may have been reduced or even closed.[130]

As however the turbulence died away, money power as centred in Mesopotamia. now with the plunder of half a dozen civilizations in its strong rooms, and a steady inflow of the precious metals deriving from the rapid expansion of the mining industry at that time, due to the improvement of the methods of exploration and smelting brought about by the use of tools of hardened iron, together with the availability of

---

[130] *Cambridge Economic History*; Vol. II: p. 19.

ample slave supplies as derived from all these wars, began to look around for new fields in which its power to create "Capital" could be used to best advantage. Thus once again the money creators of Mesopotamia turned their eyes towards the idyllic shores of Greece, and its forested mountains and hills; Greece which was clearly the gateway to Europe, and, through its command of the routes to the Hellespont and the Black Sea, to further Asia.

Analysing the sources, either Dorian or Ionian from which derived the impulses which gave driving force to the growth of the Greek industrial revolution, the *Encyclopaedia Britannica* (1898) says:

"The Ionian was that which most actively influenced the early development of Greece. But the Ionians themselves derived the most impulses of their progress from a foreign source. Those Canaanites or 'lowlanders' of Syria, whom we call by the Greek name of Phoenicians, inhabited the long narrow strip of territory between Lebanon and the sea. Phoenicia, called 'Keft' by the Egyptians, had at a remote period contributed Semitic settlers to the Delta or 'Isle of Caphtor'; and it would appear from the evidence of the Egyptian monuments that the Kefa, or Phoenicians, were a great commercial people as early as the 16th Century B.C. Cyprus, visible from the heights of Lebanon, was the first stage of the Phoenician advance into the Western waters; and to the last there was a Semitic element side by side with the Indo-Europeans. From Cyprus the Phoenician navigators proceeded to the Southern coasts of Asia Minor, where the Phoenician colonists gradually blended with the natives, until the entire seaboard had become in a great measure subject to Phoenician influences. Thus the Solymni, settled in Lycia, were akin to the Canaanites and the Carians, originally kinsmen of the Greeks, were strongly affected by Phoenician contact. It was at Miletus especially that the Ionian Greeks came into commercial intercourse with the Phoenicians. Unlike the dwellers on the southern seaboard of Asia Minor, they showed no tendency to merge their nationality in that of Syrian strangers. But they learned from them much that concerned the art of navigation, as for instance, the use of the round built merchant vessels called, and also a system of weights and measures, as well as the rudiments of some useful arts. The Phoenicians had first of all been drawn to the coasts of Greece in quest of the purple fish which was found in abundance off the coasts of the Peloponnesus and of Boeotia; other attractions were furnished by the plentiful timber for shipbuilding which the Greek forests supplied, *and by veins of silver, iron, and copper ore.*

Two periods of Phoenician influence on early Greece may be distinguished: first, a period during which they were brought into intercourse with the Greeks merely by traffic in occasional voyages; secondly a period of Phoenician trading settlements in the islands or on the coasts of the Greek seas, when their influence became more penetrating and thorough. It was probably early in this second period, perhaps about the 9th century B.C. (probably the time of the first major Assyrian attack on the Arameans in 933 B.C.), that the Phoenician alphabet became diffused through Greece. This alphabet was itself derived from the alphabet of the Egyptian Hieroglyphics, which was brought into Phoenicia by the Phoenician settlers in the Delta. It was imported into Greece, *probably by the Arameo-Phoenicians of the Gulf of Antioch*, not by the Phoenicians of Tyre and Sidon, and seems to have superseded, in Asia Minor and the islands, a syllabary of some seventy characters, which continued to be used in Cyprus down to a late time. The direct Phoenician (I.E. Babylonian), influence on Greece lasted to about 600 B.C. (significantly about the time of the *Seisachtheia* at Athens, and the Laws of Lycurgus in Laconia). Commerce and navigation were the provinces that concerned the higher culture, the Phoenicians seem to have been little more than carriers from East to West of Egyptian, Assyrian, or Babylonian ideas."[131]

Although the existence of the cities of Ugarit and Alalakh in the region of the Gulf of Antioch was unknown when the above was written, neither therefore had knowledge of those days received the impetus of the information recorded in their tablet hoards, nor were Linear "A" and "B" known, much less deciphered, revealing so much of Mycenae and its time, and that which had been before, the opinions expressed by this 19th Century writer more or less agree with those recently expressed by Sir Charles Leonard Woolley,[132] despite the belief of Sir Leonard some 26 years previously, that the script of the (Aramaic) tablets of Ras Shamra, site of ancient Ugarit, derived from the cuneiform of Sumeria and Akkadia.[133]

.And so to continue with the main thread of our narrative, it being thus quite clear that by 933 B.C., agencies for Babylonian imperialism were once again well established, in Greece, certainly in Ionia, and almost certainly farther afield on the Greek mainland, considering those favourable conditions existing in Greece at that time, the international money power of that day, in reality as blind a force to its own needs and purposes as it is today, on the advice of such Aramaean refugees no doubt, decided to reduce exports to Greece, and to finance the growth of native Greek manufactures. Such financing, whether through forgery of the existing currency of Greece, the iron or copper spits, out of the bloody scrap garnered from the fields of battle in Aram, or Arabia, or Israel,

---

[131] Britannica. 1898: p. 90: Vol. XI.

[132] Sir Charles Leonard Woolley: *Prehistory and the Beginnings of Civilization*, pp. 651-658, London, 1937.

[133] Sir Charles Leonard Woolley: *Abraham*, p. 23, 24. Also see p. 80 present work.

or Egypt; or by other methods known to them, as previously described, would present no problem.

Thus renewing more permanently the base from which their trade into Northern Europe might be conducted, winter or summer, they were guaranteed a more steady flow of Carpathian, Illyrian, Thracian, or Attican silver. A base was also established from which the similar trade into the Pontic regions and South Russia could be better maintained; in addition could be reckoned on a growing industrial population to assist in the absorption of both Egyptian and South Russian surpluses of grain.

The petty but vigorous city states of Greece as existed and would come to exist, would form a good ground for experiment with money systems, and with new systems of government and, what is now-a-days called social systems. In the fevered imagination of the money changers scheming in their shaded courtyards of Babylonia, such experiments might even show the way towards that for which their souls yearned above all, and which still they had not been able to bring about: the total disintegration of the last great kingdoms of earth, which, it seems, no sooner had they been brought to the point of collapse, than somehow they came to rise again. "Kingship again being sent down from on High."[134] The way might be shown to them by which they too, their God, themselves and theirs, might become Lords of the Earth; and indeed, whereby out of their midst might be set up that God-King who would preside over the governance of the Universe; its total and absolute ruler.

---

[134] This quotation which comes from Sir Charles L. Woolley's translation of the Sumerian King Lists, (*Excavations* at Ur, p. 249.), reads in full: "The Flood came. After the Flood came, Kingship again was sent down from on High."

.And much of these strange yearnings came to be realized. The possibilities inherent in circulating pieces of precious metal of equal weight and fineness, and with the seal of state stamped thereon, as money, after the first major experiment therein in the Lydia of Croesus, were fully exploited in Greece. No doubt these ancient Greeks, the same as our people in this day, fondly imagined that the state imprinted marks on their so-called coinage, denoted the absolute integrity of their money; and while they continued in this belief, they were the more easily manipulated.

Thus the power of rejection or appointment fell out of the withering hand of a decadent, if not dying priesthood, into that hand that moved over the disks of precious metal in the shadows of the counting house; and rather than noble and selfless men in positions of power, came low and venal men wielding but the appearance of power. Such men being raised up from the blind mob, exercised no more control or rule than that which the forces behind money creation and issuance permitted to them; nor did they exercise guidance further than that limit dictated by the inferiority of their quality.

The Greek of those days, as the Englishman during the 17th Century A.D., was highly intelligent, industrious, and frugal, and he clearly served under his ancient and natural aristocracy proudly and gladly in war or in peace. His land was then covered with forests from which was available an ample supply of charcoal such as would last kilns and furnaces for a long time to come; from Thrace, not so far distant, came suitable timbers for shipbuilding. Hence the spark that gave light to the life of the Greek city state must have been smouldering well before the introduction of coined money from Lydia and its attendant possibilities of controlled credit manipulations much greater than had ever been before.

Consequently, at the time of its emergence into the light of history as we know it, Greece was to the known world in the same way as was England during the 16th and 17th Centuries, when, due to the stealthy stimulation of a "Credit," or abstract money economy, money greed injected into the nobility caused them to forget their trust. The major manifestation of the forgetfulness of such trust was their seizure of the common lands for the purposes of sheep pasture, the growing wool trade now yielding good return in the expanding money economy; thus depriving the villagers of their rightful livelihood on the land, and leaving them with no option but emigration into the cities. In the cities these villagers served as labour in mine or factory, there being totally at the mercy of rascals from foreign parts, or those who bad been raised up from their own ranks as most eager for food, and who were least critical of the hand that offered it to them.

So far as Greece was concerned, on to a scene idyllic in the loveliness of its tree clad hills and mountains and shores, came men from that Aramaic speaking money power out of Syria and Aram, plausible men who wept and moaned to the pitying Greek the slaughter of their people by the Assyrian. Refugees from the Hittite city of Carchemish, from Aramean Damascus, Kummuh, and Sama'l, and other cities. Cities which had crumbled to dust before the ferocity of the Assyrians under Shalmanezer and Ashurnazirpal; but whether Syrian or Babylonian, these men spoke and wrote Aramaic in one form or another, as the evidence of the Greek alphabet reveals,[135] and which would be further suggested by the nature of the tablets that were found (about 1935) on the site of Ugarit (now known as Ras Shamra), on the North Syrian Coast.[136]

---

[135] Frederick William Madden, M.R.A.S.: *Coins of the Jews*, P. 29; London; 1881.

[136] According to Sir Charles L. Woolley in his book *Abraham* (pp. 23-24.): "At Ras Shamra on the North Syrian coast, there have recently been unearthed documents of a very surprising kind; there are clay tablets bearing

These men brought with them the knowledge of precious metal commodity exchange, and amongst other deceptions easily perpetrated on a simple and trusting people, knowledge of the possibilities of creation of money and wealth through the rackets of storage of valuables as for safe custody; or the creation of credit as it is now euphemistically known, and its power as a driving force towards the establishment of industry amongst a healthy, trusting, and warlike people; and its power towards the creation of monopoly of ownership and control of such industry.

What must have been cottage industry in Greece, soon became industry under organization and under methods of semi-mass production, long since known in Sumeria, and Akkadia, and Assyria etc. Such industry could only be organized on the basis of money wages in the case of freemen, and therefore only with labour, slave or free, trained to the concept of *money*, and the *making of money*, as the *be-all and end-all* in life.

Athens made pottery and ships; Corinth made pottery and ships; Megara made textiles. Athens, with ample surpluses of olive oil sufficient to maintain a substantial export trade in that commodity, and with the production of silver from the Laureion mines but a few miles from the city, became centre of

---

inscriptions in cuneiform, but the signs represent not syllables as in Babylonian, but letters of the alphabet, and the language is a form of Aramaic closely related to Hebrew: they date from the 14th Century before Christ. Consequently we see that by the time of the Exodus people living in Syria and speaking a tongue akin to the Israelite were so accustomed to the idea of writing that they had modified the old established script of Sumer and Babylon to suit the peculiarities of their own language." However, in his latest book: *Prehistory and the Beginnings of Civilization*, (pp. 651-658), Sir Leonard Woolley states that the various scripts of Ancient Syria deciphered or otherwise, and including Phoenician which he definitely claims to be parent script of ancient Greek, all derived from the Egyptian picture writing or Hieroglyphics (via the Hieratic of 2000 B.C.) in agreement with Madden who wrote one hundred years ago. (See chart on p. 75 of the present work.)

an entre-pôt trade with those other Greek city states that relied on copper or iron fiduciary money systems to drive their industry and exchanges; money systems if of state design and control, that international banking had little use for.

But without the economic organization deriving from participation in the orbit of the international money market controlled by the international silver bullion brokers and their agents, the bankers of the Piraeus who controlled above all the flow of silver from Laureion and Thrace, and Samos, and mines further afield, it is doubtful if that dynamic force engendered from the union of Dorian and pre-Dorian Greece could ever have become that which it did become: the point to which a great part of the power and learning gravitated from those fast dying worlds of the most Ancient Orient; thence being thrust forth again amongst men to constitute that which may prove to have been one of the last stages of man's endeavour upon this earth.

It was the beginning of an apparent reassemblance, a false renewal of learning and life which was to reveal momentarily, in fading glory, the fusion of that world of the companions of Zeus, golden-headed giants descended to earth from their home amongst the gods, and the world of Crete where dark children of the sun basked in the light and comfort of him who to them was god on earth as he walked in his gardens at Cnossos.

Both god, priesthood and people lived in this distant sunlit world in the mystic harmony of ancient systems of life. They lived with little knowledge of warfare or weapons of war. Their cities were without wall or visible defence so long had they been without fear. In a mild warm climate, they needed little clothing, and their women who wore no more than a heavy flounced skirt, proudly and fearlessly displayed the loveliness of their breasts.

BLOOD, SORROW, AND SILVER

The growth during the early years of the first Millennium B.C. of the use of hardened iron tools in the mining industry[137] and the development of a highly efficient system by the Phoenicians, for smelting calamine and other silver bearing ores, as shown by the almost complete absence of silver in the slags or scoria left by their mining operations at Laureion,[138] released a heavy flow of silver on to the bullion markets of the Near East; with the consequence that silver, further than being a standard for money accounting between merchants and also the temples "in relation to staples, other metals, and customary services."[139] became an actual means of payment." and as currency of all levels of transaction."[140] This practice, with all the possibilities inherent therein towards the virtually unlimited private creation of money in opposition to that money which had originated as entry in the temple ledger, spread westward with all its attendant evils during the first half of the first millennium B.C., as already pointed out in respect to Greece.

While certain temple organizations still survived as previously mentioned and were strongly maintained, the instances quoted being those of the temples of Sippur and Uruk (Oppenheim; p.46), the flood of privately issued and controlled money which in reality was this new silver in circulation, together with the pyramid of ledger credit page entry money raised thereon, had

---

[137] Alexander del Mar: *History of the Precious Metals*, p. 45.

[138] Miner's and Smelter's Magazine, Vol. VI, pp 286-322. (A. del Mar: *History of the Precious Metals*, p. 46.)

[139] Leo A. Oppenheim: *Letters from Mesopotamia*, p. 46: Chicago: 1967.

[140] Ibid.

almost completely effaced even the memory of that law in relation to exchanges, that was the word and order of the god of the city himself, and that had been the issue of kings and priesthood of former times. These kings may have been aware that the source of all their powers was the power inherent m the creation and emission of the units of exchange, which was the power to discriminate, the power to reject or prefer from amongst their subjects; and of course they may not have been so aware.

Of the evidence revealing the steps by which this god-power was undermined, the first and most important was the establishment of internal values in the exchanges within any state to the same standard as the value of silver in the international exchanges, which did not happen overnight as it were, and may have slowly taken place over several thousand years; for at least 1500 years before what was supposed to be the invention of coined money in Lydia, silver ingots already circulated in Babylonia bearing the stamp of the issuing and guaranteeing authority, whether temple, state, or merchant. Before this time "Silver was used in many instances as a standard of value even though it was not actually employed in payments."[141]

It is not until the Assyrian, Neo-Babylonian, and Persian eras that clear evidence can be traced of the total degeneration of kingly power and of kings and so-called emperors as quite often being little more than gloriously be-medalled front men for private money creative power striving to create world-wide hegemony. They still continued to be needed principally as a point towards which the eyes of the people might be diverted in order that the people might not realize that all was not well

---

[141] Paul Einzig: *Primitive Money*, p. 206. Also as according to the records of the city of Kish as pertain to the Azag-Bau Dynasty (3268-2897 B.C.). See page 1 of this work.

in that direction towards which their loyalties naturally leaned, nor glimpse the destructive forces that were gnawing at the roots of the Tree of Life itself. Even as far back as 2500 B.C. Sargon of Akkad proceeded into Anatolia to chastise the city of Ganes on account of the commercial community of Mesopotamia;[142] probably to enforce payment of interest on loans, or repayment of principal. One of the reasons of the success of Cyrus, though but a petty Persian prince formerly to 550 B.C. when he deposed his sovereign, Astyages the Mede, is clear from the circumstances of his victory over Croesus of Lydia in 546 B.C.

Croesus had offended international money powers by seizure of their treasure held by their agent Sadyattes[143] and by the total assumption of monetary issue by the state. Example had to be made of him to deter other princes from similar action, and the eager and ambitious Cyrus was obviously the one chosen for this purpose. According to the article on Babylonia in the Encyclopaedia Britannica, 9th Edition, by Professor Sayce, Croesus had rashly joined battle with Cyrus without waiting for the arrival of his Babylonian allies under Nabu-Nahud[144] the father of Belshazzar of the Book of Daniel. It is more than likely, however, that a truer reading of these events would be that international money power, patron of the rise of Cyrus both through organization of his supplies of mercenary soldiers, and of the best of weapons, had been the principal influence in these events as in other enterprises of Cyrus, such as the siege of Babylon 14 years later. Thanks to its influence, while the progress of Nabu-Nahud towards junction with the forces of Croesus would have been sabotaged, Croesus himself

---

[142] Sir Charles Woolley: *Abraham*, p. 122.

[143] Ernest Babelon: *Les Origines de la Monnaie*, p. 106; Paris; 1897.

[144] Herodotus: *The Histories*, Book I.

would have been misinformed of the intentions and strength of both Cyrus and Nabu-Nahud.[145]

Cyrus won the day, and Croesus was totally humbled. Having thus proven his "suitability," and his readiness to promote the policies of his financial backers, the relatively easy conquest of Babylon was arranged for Cyrus some fourteen years later.[146] Cyrus from then on was designated "The Great," and assumed the title of "Great King" of the vast Persian domains over which he now ruled.

As the most valuable by-product of their being and existence, kings and "conquerors" were also needed towards the maintenance of the steady inflow of slaves, sufficient to take care of the fearful death rate in the mines, and no doubt, to permit of the opening of new mines due to the rapid expansion of the mining industry on account of the growth of the use of hardened iron tools and improved methods of exploration.

This growth of bullion supplies, also meaning growth of the money economy, meant growth of industry. Such growth of industry meant further demand for labour, which labour then was principally slave, as money economy had not arrived at the totality of its modern development. Therefore not only was an increasing and continuous flow of slaves needed for the mines, but also for the industry to which the products of the mines gave rise.

There were two ways alone by which new supplies of precious metals became available to rejuvenate a monetary circulation withering, and even disappearing from wear and tear,

---

[145] The Nabonidus of modern books of reference who reigned in conjunction with Belshazzar.

[146] Actually through his general, Gobryas, 558 B.C.

exportation or hoarding, with the economic collapse that such condition could bring about: one was through mining using slave labour as mining with free labour was rarely profitable,[147] and the other was through sack and plunder. For the first method "Conquerors" were needed for free men did not willingly become mine slaves; for the second method "Conquerors" were obviously needed again, for to cause a people to reveal and surrender their hidden hoards of precious metals, would only be possible as a result of the nights of terror immediately following on the "Conquest," and the abuse and rapine infected by a lust crazed soldiery such as followed such conquerors and achieved such "Conquests." For instance, according to the *Iliad*, (Book IX), promise of the gold and bronze plunder (of Troy) was the principal lure used by Agamemnon (besides the return of Briseis), to bring Achilles back into the fight.

For further instance, may be accepted the main information in respect to Shalmanezer the Assyrian and his campaigns in 858 B.C., leaving no doubt of the purposes of the hidden forces who guided him, and wherein lay their chief interest. The conquest of Damascus, in 803 B.C., yielded 20 talents of gold and 2300 talents of silver, not to speak of 300 talents copper and 5000 talents of iron. The sack of Carchemish by Sargon, 717 B.C., yielded 11 talents of gold and 2100 talents of silver.

The following table reveals what was extracted from several lesser cities and their rulers.

---

[147] Alexander del Mar: *History of Monetary Systems*, pp. 413, 425, 410, 441, 442.

Ruler & City	Gold Indemnity
Hattinean	3 Talents
Sangar of Carchemish	3 Talents
Harii of Sam'al	10 Talents
Arame son of Bitaqusi	6 Talents
Katazil of Kummuh	20 minas of silver

Silver Indemnity	Annual Tribute
100 Talents	10 Talents of Silver
70 Talents 1 m. gold, 1 t. silver	
16 minas of gold	

Tyre, Sidon, and Jehu of Israel, though clearly sitting on the fence as it were to secure the best advantage as might be offered out of these events, without openly committing themselves as ally of Assyria, hastened to pay tribute when after the battle near Wadi Zerzer in 842 B.C. in which Hazael, usurper King of Damascus was finally put to flight with the slaughter of some 6000 Arameans,[148] and likely the enslavement of many more, Shalmanezer, victorious but totally exhausted, came down to the coast unable to continue with the investment of Damascus[149]. It would be an interesting speculation as to what was really in the mind of Shalmanezer in turning towards the coast. What money power had armed Hazael to the point that he could be such a real threat to the Assyrian? Had Shalmanezer planned bloody revenge? Then realizing that in the destruction he planned, he might further destroy his own source of arms, and those slave traders who organized the sale

---

[148] Emil G.H. Kraeling: *Aram and Israel*, p. 80; Columbia. 1918.

[149] Ibid.

of his captives, had he hesitated, finally deciding to settle for tribute?

The States of Arvad, Symyra, and Ushana in the fact that they paid no tribute to Nineveh,[150] while being much closer than the Aramean States, revealed themselves as ally; the absence of any savage thrust by Assyria at that time against Israel, or Tyre, or Sidon, in the first phase of Assyrian conquest, would suggest such states, if not actually as ally, as harbouring forces in one form or another which would be controlled by agents of that highly secret international bullion broking fraternity, which indubitably existed, and which was connected to the extensive organization of camp followers and slave traders that must have been yet another host behind the Assyrian host, and therefore, profitably, enemy of the Aramean.

Money power, international in scope, being that it sought at this time, to institute precious metals as the governing factor of exchanges over the rest of the known world, was deeply lodged in the heart of the Assyrian, a people to whom it had early imparted the secret Hittite skills and processes in iron working, and who, in their home land, had the necessary materials for such industry. Assyria for the time was their sword arm. Whether the Assyrians were aware of its significance or not, they must have been closely connected with that fraternity whose business was mining of the precious metals, trade in certain staple commodities and manufactures, and slaves, and who must have conducted their operations in all the cities of Babylonia, Aram, whether enemy or not, and especially, Phoenicia. Considering that Phoenician mining operations extended as far North as Britain where was mined the tin so necessary in bronze manufacture, it may be assumed that Phoenicia, above all, dealt in Assyrian war captives. In places as distant as Cornwall where they would have been in a relatively

---

[150] Emil G.H. Krealing: *Aram and Israel*, p. 80, Columbia, 1918.

weak position so far from home, they would have relied on imported slaves, rather than on local conquest. There is no missing the connection between the floods of slaves as released on to world markets by the Assyrian conquests, and the rapid expansions of that which is now known as "Credit," the same silver and gold mining that was taking place all over the known world at that time.

Of some interest is the story of the easing of the pressure on Damascus by the departure of Shalmanezer in 839 B.C. during the first phase of Assyrian conquest, to more pressing business in the North. "Hazael, King of Damascus was able to turn again to Israel."

Once Assyria, abandoning the Israelites whose alliance they must have been accepting at that time, either to assure themselves of a source of supply of mercenary soldiers or of slave-master camp followers, turned a deaf ear to the pleas of Jehu, the Israelite king, the Philistines, the Idumeans, the Amorites, and even their ancient ally, the Tyrians, viciously turned on them[151]. Could it be to seize a share of the plunder gathered off the battlefields of Shalmanezer?

The renewed stream of precious metal money that must have followed the sack of all those cities of Aram at this time, flowing through the coffers of the international money power located in the cities of Nineveh or Babylon or Ur, would have been accompanied by vast expansions of that which is now known as "Credit," the same being emitted in all the major cities of the Near East. Also[152] Bills of Exchange, Letters of Credit, but above all the ubiquitous receipts for valuables reputedly on deposit for safe custody, came into being: clay

---

[151] Emil G.H. Kraeling, Ph.D.: *Aram and Israel*, pp. 83-84 Columbia: 1918.

[152] Paul Einzig: *Primitive Money*, p. 225; Oxford, 1949.

"Promises to Pay": all forming expansion in one form or another of the working money supply. By manipulation of such abstract monetary units in relation to what might have been described as the visible symbols of the monetary unit such as was gold or silver money, powerful business houses combining the operations of banker, goldsmith, silversmith etc., with branches in all major cities, were certainly able to manipulate the destinies of so-called empires, just as they have so done in this day. That Babylon itself should have been able to rise again, and lead a frightened world against Assyria to form the so-called Neo-Babylonian empire, is proof, however, that international money power at that time was not monopoly of the Hebrew who now whatever his origins, as ally of the Israelite who had come out of Egypt, appears clearly in history, a distinct entity; even if the part he plays as native of Palestine was relatively insignificant.

It seems the fall of the Assyrian in finality in the defeat of Ashur-Uballit by Nabopolassar in 605 B.C, was also the fall of the Hebrew. No sooner had Nabopolassar destroyed the last remnant of Assyrian military power, than, at Carchemish, his son Nebuchadnezzar destroyed that of a resurgent Egypt under Pharaoh Necho, recently victor over Josiah of Judah on that ominous place of battle Meggiddo,[153] better known as

---

[153] According to II *Kings*, 17, 6, 'In the ninth year of Hoshea, the king of Assyria took Samaria, and carried Israel away into Assyria, and placed them in Halah and in Habor by the river of Gozan, and in the cities of the Medes,' and according to the records of Sargon of Assyria: 'Samaria I looked at, I captured; 27,280 men (or families) who dwelt in it I carried away.'

As a completely new population was brought to the now empty land (II *Kings*, 17, 24), it is curious that 120 years later a so-called Jewish prince should go out of his way to seek battle with Pharaoh Necho, vigorous king of a resurgent Egypt, who according to the Biblical record (II *Chronicles*, 36, 21) 'sent ambassadors to him, saying, what have I to do with thee, thou king of Judah? I come not against thee this day, but against the house wherewith I have war: for God commanded me to make haste (to Carchemish): forbear thee from meddling with God, who is with me, that he destroy thee not.'

Armageddon, (II *Chronicles*; 25, 20-27.), and where eight hundred years previously Tahutmes III had put the confederate armies of Syria to flight.

In this battle of Carchemish in which Pharaoh Necho had suffered complete defeat, was destroyed the last protector of Israel, and as a consequence, in 586 B.C. Israel itself was totally destroyed. Its leaders, overtaken by the same fate as its Aramean blood relatives, if not co-religionists, were carried off to servitude at Babylon; where in the case of some, they were used to keep the wheels of industry and finance turning in that great city, while in the case of others, they seem to have been permitted settlement in the region of the river Chebar, a large irrigation canal near Babylon, where they were allowed to establish homes, to farm, and to maintain themselves as a racial and religious group, clearly living a national and exclusive life, as was shown by the very fact that an intensely nationalistic prophet such as Ezekiel could exist in the settlement at Chebar, preaching amongst his own people without restriction.[154]

During this time the city was yet again sold to the new imperial power risen out of old Elam and the Persian Highlands, and in 536 B.C., the Persian forces under Cyrus, "The Great," quietly entered the city by night march down the drying river bed after they had completed diversion of the river. According to the book of Daniel, the proud Belshazzar, King in Babylon, was slain that night.[155]

It is interesting to note that shortly after the entry of the Persian forces into the city, the "Children of Israel" were permitted to return to that which they considered their

---

[154] *Ezekiel*, Chapter I, V.1,3. Chapter 3, V.15, 23. Chapter 10, V.15, 22. Chapter 11, V.4, (Prophesy) 25, (Expounding Prophesy to Chebarites).

[155] *Daniel*, Chapter 5, V. 30.

homeland, and every assistance was given them towards renewal of their national life and the rebuilding of their temple, which, of course, was its heart. In the very first year of his reign at Babylon 536 B.C., Cyrus issued a decree permitting the rebuilding of the temple at Jerusalem, and the gold and silver vessels carried away by Nebuchadnezzar supposed to be 5400 in number, were returned to Sheshbazaar, the Prince of Judah who was leader of the migration.[156] Although the proclamation of Cyrus had been addressed to all servants of God throughout the Empire, the 42,000 or so who responded to the call and went with Sheshbazaar, were but a small part of the Hebrew population of the total dominions of Cyrus. The special concessions made by Cyrus to the Hebrew almost on entry into the city of Babylon, would certainly suggest that he had received their substantial assistance, perhaps through financing towards the purchase of the finest of military accoutrements such as would only be obtainable through the good graces of the Babylonian commercial and banking houses, or through that information with which the Hebrew may have kept him constantly supplied such as the state of military preparedness within the city, etc.

It may reasonably be assumed that the Babylonian money power was completely international in outlook, whatever its outward profession, and totally unsympathetic towards the ancient faith of the Ziggurat and the worship of Marduk,[157] and towards the intended effects of the restoration of the Ziggurat of Ur, at that time, by Nebuchadnezzar. If in earlier Assyrian times such money power certainly was not the Hebrew, though possibly linked thereto through members of the latter Israelitish Confederacy such as the *Habiru* or even those who derived

---

[156] William Smith: *History of the Bible*, p. 476 London, Ont. 1885.

[157] Marduk was the national God of Babylon, just as Nannar was National God of Ur, and second only to Énlil.

from the Hyksos, the fact of the existence of powerful Hebrew influence in international finance in Neo-Babylonian times, seems a reasonable supposition.

The Hebrew, being aggressive and intelligent, may have risen to especially privileged position in the Babylonian money industry, if that is what it can be called, and may have come to learn at that time those secret practices of the money changers craft, which he was certainly forbidden in his native land, according to the Laws Moses. In Babylonia the law No. 7 of Hammurabai has long since become a dead letter.

That ungodly and cruel order of Ezra compelling the Israelites divorce their foreign wives after their return to what was considered their ancestral homeland,[158] might very well have been related to the needs of total religious, racial, and commercial security, as indeed might the ordinance existing today amongst English Quakers forbidding them to marry outside their own sect,[159] whose leaders, any brief study will show, were deeply involved in the growth and control of modern banking,[160] which had lead, and still leads mankind along a road that offers little peace or rest, and finally, exhaustion and calamity; a road of non-return.

One thing becomes clear out of this turmoil of rising and falling "Empires" of the first millennium B.C., particularly that calamitous succession of Assyrian, Neo-Babylonian, and Persian "Empires," from 933-605 B.C., 625-538 B.C., and 538-

---

[158] *Ezra*, King James Version; Ch. 10.

[159] "Membership in the Society is now either by 'convincement' of the Spiritual Truths to which Friends witness, or, in England, by birth if both parents are Friends:" James Hastings in Vol. 12 of the *Encyclopedia of Religion and Ethics* (New York 1914.).

[160] Sir Ernest Cassel: *Lloyd's Bank in the History of Banking*, p. 20 et seq. Oxford, 1933.

332 B.C., respectively, and that is: in a world where treasure had become totally equated in the peoples minds with "Wealth," as expressing relatively large sums of the monetary unit, no sooner had one power gathered all such treasure in a given area into its store houses and safe deposits, by conquest, plunder, and sack, than such treasure, temporarily creating boom, moved on again, as likely as not to form the base of those "credits" granted by international money power towards the purchase of arms and the best of mercenary soldiers by that next power destined to arise and be the new "conqueror."

Dealing in money, and bullion which was the foundation of the money system, had become a highly specialized and closed trade now able to operate quite apart from the temples; even if in many cases the temples still continued to permit themselves, and that which they stood for, to be used as front, and so had offered sanctity to those most sinister and destructive operations of the money, bullion, and slave brokers; in themselves and their attitude towards mankind, the antithesis of God, the Anti-God.

The money masters had only one purpose besides maintenance of secrecy: which was growth of themselves and those through whom they worked. Those through whom they worked were too often the criminal castes of the civilizations; criminal because the nature of so much of their activities, such as fencing, counterfeiting of coinages, clipping and sweating of coins, was criminal; as it had to be. Towards this purpose, consciously or not, they sought the total destruction of that natural order of life of god, king, priesthood, and temple and the devoted, and its eradication from the Book of Life itself. For piety and love and man living with hope and will for the future, guided by his trained shepherds had to be substituted an order of the *exploitation* of mankind. The rulers in such an order would be its previous rejects, its outcasts. God, king, temple and the devoted were to become a thing forgotten, and man, into whom was to be injected raging animal passions, was to be left wandering without guide, except such thrusting hither and thither by such as could only be called living sores of man-hatred and which were embedded in mankind itself, could be called guidance.

The unfortunate masses of the Ancient Orient, who had so trusted their rulers, had no idea or understanding of the new reality, and that the ruler they saw, far from being the Son of God on Earth, was in reality a puppet manipulated by that conspiratorial force exerted by those controllers of precious metal bullion particularly, that lurked in the Aramaic speaking middle class mentioned by Professor Oppenheim.[161] These powerful classes could have had no more than a secret contempt for the gods, kings, priesthood, of the peoples amongst whom they lived, able as they were by this manipulation, to bring about the decay or growth of power, without reference to such "State" power structure, of those whose undoing or otherwise, they planned.

They themselves, through triumph of their system of private money issuance, had now in reality come to sit in the place of the gods. From this time on it seems, there was not even that periodic interference of the king against the money-lender, which gave the people respite from time to time, as in the old Babylonian period,[162] and the Kingdom of Israel of record.[163]

Cruel private monopolization of wealth and capital grew, and where the people had been sheep in the flock, and the king their loving and devoted guide, now that kings concerned themselves with those false policies prepared for them in the interest of the private money creators, the people became lost

---

[161] Leo A. Oppenheim: *Letters from Mesopotamia*, p. 51; Chicago; 1967.

[162] Ibid., p. 46.

[163] *Leviticus*, Chapter 5, King James version.

and disheartened, driven hither and thither as they were by the crazed wolf masquerading in the place of the shepherd's diligent sheep dog.

In this time, as today, the people were almost entirely at the mercy of the private persons controlling their money, who then controlled the inflow of precious metals, silver and gold, the foundation of the people's money. The policies of these controllers from their standpoint as internationalists, were necessarily directed towards the stimulation of war *against* the well-being of mankind. Frequently wars were above all the prime essential, firstly towards the destruction of the natural system of rule[164] previously defined, which had been the protection of the people; secondly towards the reinjection into the system of hoarded coin and bullion, and consequent reinflation of the money supply; thirdly, but not the least important, the gathering of a new crop of slaves to replace those stocks of silver and gold, so necessary to the foundation of their money power, and the maintenance of their international hegemony in consequence.

---

[164] The nobility have always been the first to disappear in major warfare. As leaders of their men in battle, their young men are the first to die. During the recent first 'Great' war, it may safely be said that the best part of the young men of the natural aristocracy of Europe had perished by 1917.

BABYLON, BANKING, AND BULLION

Without a doubt, the ramifications of Babylonian banking as operated from Nineveh during the eighth and seventh centuries B.C., extended in more or less degree over that total area from Tartessus to India,[165] and from the gold washings of that great bend in the Nile in Nubia known as the Bisharee, to the mines of Cornwall; and of all such area it was the focus of land and sea routes. In absolute degree during the first millennium, it extended as far afield as there is evidence of Aramaic as language of official and merchant classes; that is to say from Peshawar to Greece.[166] In Greece the evidence however is not so much from Aramaic as language, as from the fact that the Greek alphabet derives from Aramaic,[167] and therefore may be assumed to be the design of refugee Arameans of the period after 933 B.C., when Assyrian policy after forty years of unremitting pressure from the Arameans, became the extirpation of the Aramean, achievable from much strengthened military resources.

---

[165] F.W. Madden: *Coins of the Jews*, pp. 4-5; London; 1881.

[166] Charles Seltsman: *Greek Coins*; London; 1933.

[167] F.W. Madden: *Coins of the Jews*, page 29. According to Herodotus "the Phoenician letters were adopted but with some variation in the shape of a few," but according to Professor Sayce of much more convincing opinion, "since the names of the letters of the Greek alphabet nearly all end in 'a,' it would appear that it must have been brought into Greece, not by the Phoenicians of Tyre and Sidon, but by the Arameans of the gulf of Antioch since the emphatic Aleph is a characteristic of Aramaic, not Phoenician. Even the names of the letters in the Hebrew alphabet disclose their Aramaic origin." Which conclusions were further verified by the Ras Shamra tablets discovered some fifty years later, mentioned on page 80 of this work. (See chart on pp. 75-76.)

Accolytes of the bankers of Babylonia, whether from Nineveh, Carchemish, or the Babylonian cities themselves, who sought their own fields abroad, or prominent but unsuspecting natives of the area chosen for penetration, were selected as "suitable" to open the trade in a given area; "suitability," as in today, being advanced training in money worship, basic lack of integrity, and preferably some black mark in their secret past making them amenable to pressure and willing to grind down their own kind, or sell them to the slave trader without the gate, and without mercy and without compunction.

Those refugees skilled in money, from the cities of Aram in particular, though perhaps not qualifying in every specific trait detailed above, being dispossessed, and with therefore bitterness in their hearts, would have served best. They would have considered that alignment with the Babylonian banking houses would be alignment with enemy and destroyer of that which had destroyed them. Such silver money as they later minted and circulated from Aegina and Argos, appears, as is explained below, to have been of the same weight and fineness as the Babylonian shekel, being that it was eighty-five grains to the drachma. Thus it is evident that the financial organization these Arameans created in Greece previous to Solon was outright extension of the Babylonian; in a way it might have been the instrument of Babylonian imperialism, just as was the entry on the tablet of the traveling agent of the Temple of Ur, recording loans made to enable purchase, instrument, two thousand years before, of that imperialism of Ur[168]. Thus the coinage as used at Athens at this time, wherever minted, could be exported and circulated in Babylonia or other cities of this common money market; and while it could be profitably used in settlement of unfavourable Indian trade balances, it could also be returned to Athens without loss or remitting.

---

[168] Sir Charles L. Woolley: *Abraham*, pp. 124-125, p. 16.

In the so-called Solonian monetary reforms, according to Groseclose,[169] the Mina consisting of 73 drachmas was made legal tender to the value of 100 drachmas, though according to some scholars, there is no evidence of Athenian mintage at this time.[170] Assuming Groseclose and his authorities to be correct, it follows that the real meaning of these currency reforms was the establishment of Athenian home mintage inaugurating a new coinage of a less weight, made legal tender for debts incurred in terms of the previous heavy weight coinage minted at Aegina or Argos. However of this matter Seltsman in his *Greek Coins* writes,."That was the change brought about by the Solonian currency reform, the purpose of which was not to relieve debtors by lowering the value of the standard coin, but rather to free Athenian trade from a weight system such as bound the merchants to a local Peloponnesian standard which did not extend beyond the Aegean sea.

Instead the Athenians now had a currency based on the old and famous bronze Age "Euboic talent and mina, and his standard coin was of the same weight of those of the Corinthians, Samians, and later of Cyrenaeans. But he retained the Pheidonian system of dividing his stater into two drachmas and his drachma into six obols. At Athens, too, the rival systems of currency met and merged for she began to coin on the Dorian system, whence she derived her obols, drachmas, and didrachmas, but under Solon's reforms she went over to the Ionian system and adjusted her money to the Ionic Euboic talent."[171]

---

[169] Elgin Groseclose: *Money, the Human Conflict*; p. 16. University of Oklahoma; 1934.

[170] W.P. Wallace: *The Early Coinages of Athens and Euboia*, p. 23, Numismatic Chronicle, 1962, and reply by Colin M. Kraay on p. 417.

[171] Charles Seltsman: *Greek Coins*, London, 1933.

The very fact of the stress on weight shows that such reforms were designed for, and perhaps only really understood by, a group that was only concerned with silver by weight; in other words, large scale movements of bullion; and who would be none other than our old friends the international bankers or bullion brokers; possibly even in some opposition to a situation in the Peloponnese and Aegina, such as may have been occasioned by the institution of the Laws of Lycurgus at Sparta,[172] when consequently, they and their agents had virtually been ejected from those areas controlled by Sparta or influenced by her policies.

Solon was more likely the front man they put up to put into effect a programme they had designed as a result of the conclusion reached amongst themselves that the notion of Greece as source of the slaves so desperately needed in a world which consumed so much labour, would have to be forgotten if their agents were to be able to continue operating in Greece, and if they themselves were to be able to maintain that confidence and respect of the Greek people so essential to their particular affair.

From henceforward it is clear, the issue was to be loans to industrial workers on the security of their wages. No longer would the banks or money lenders lend to the peasantry being that now they were forbidden to bind their persons as collateral security, and sell them into slavery across the seas, in the event of non-payment; or to alienate their lands. To get such loans, which the poor and trusting of the countryside were always craving for one special occasion or another it was necessary to go to Athens and work for a wage in some industry. It may safely be said that the main industry was mining at Laureion, and possibly in Thrace, where "Free Men" for a trifling wage

---

[172] Plutarch: The Lives, "*Lucurgus*."

could join the gangs of slaves clawing their way into the hard rock, until further sources of cheap slave supply were found.

Although some modern numismatic scholars[173] disagree with the findings of the scholars of even thirty years ago, and with some reason, and certainly may be more accurate in their dates, in the case of Alexander Del Mar, who had both practical experience of mining and practical experience in the field of government finance, and who had made considerable study of the workings of money and finance in antiquity, his opinion is not to be so lightly brushed aside. In his *History of Monetary Systems in Various States* on this subject he writes:[174]

"According to Boeckh, p. 28, one hundred of the new drachmas of Solon who was Archon of Athens B.C. 594, were equivalent to 72 or 73 more ancient drachmas. If this were quite reliable, then to Solon belongs the merit or demerit of altering the ratio from 13:1 to 10:1; because, as we have some of the drachmas of Solon and know their contents, the proportion given would make the more ancient drachmas contain about 85 grains fine silver, the weight of the shekel. As twenty of these were commonly exchanged for a gold coin, which, whether a dharana of India, a medimni of Media, a daric of Persia, or a stater of the Levant, contained about 130 grains of fine metal, the Athenian ratio, previous to the lowering of the drachma, must have obeyed the ratio of Assyria, Media, and Persia, which was 13:1. But according to Quiepo, who is a more reliable authority on the weights of coins than Boeckh, although we have drachmas older than Solon, they do not contain more than 65 grains of fine silver; so that the change of ratio from 13:1 to 10:1, assumed to have occurred at Athens,

---

[173] W.P. Wallace: *The Early Coinages of Athens and Euboia*, p. 23, Numismatic Chronicle; and the reply by Colin M. Kraay, p. 417.

[174] A. Del Mar: *History of Monetary Systems in Various States*, p. 47; reprint, New York; 1969.

must have taken place before Solon was Archon. However, it is certain from the coins that the ratio under the administration of Solon was 10:1 and that it continued for nearly three centuries; for it is impliedly mentioned by Menander about B.C. 322, as being still in vogue at a recent period. During this interval, the ratio in the Orient was 6¼ or 6½, and in Persia 13:1 or double the Indian ratio."

In other words, if these weights of drachma and of shekel as at that time are correct, just as the Roman denarius was later issued to practically the same weight as the post Solonian drachma which was in use in Sicily and Magna Graecia,[175] so was the early Greek drachma, whether Aeginetic or of Argos, I.E. Pheidonian, minted to the same standard as the shekel, the unit of exchange in Babylonia, Assyria, and Phoenicia, clearly creating extension of the Common Money Market of that area and its financial dependencies. Thus the Greek coin could be exported, circulated at par with the shekel, and even returned to Greece without loss through remitting or smelting to bullion; and also more important still, could realize that sure profit that the international bullion traders had guaranteed themselves in

---

[175] "Mais lorsque, par la guerre de Tarente, l'Italie eut été soumise, ... alors se fit sentir, en premier lieu, la nécessité de plus en plus vive d'un système général de bonnes monnaies; ... On fit choix, dans ce but, d'un pied monétaire, qui déjà avait été généralement accepté, et on frappa le Denier, de valeur de la Drachme Attique, qui était en usage non seulement dans les monarchies de l'Orient mais encore en Sicile. Assurément le Drachme de l'Attique pesait 4 gr. 37, tandis que le plus ancien Denier, quelque peu plus lourd, était taillé sur un poids moyen de 4 gr. 55 puisqu'il valait quatre Scrupules, c'est-a-dire 1/72 de livre ou 1/6 d'once. Mais cette différence fut supprimée, a la suite d'une réduction qui eut lieu vraisemblablement pendant la première guerre punique, et porta le denier à 1/84 de livre ou 1/7 de l'once c'est-à-dire 3 gr. 90; de sorte que les derniers de ce poids devaient en général être accepté sur le même pied que les Drachmes qui étaient en circulation et n'avaient pas tout à fait le poids légal.": Théodore Mommsen & Joachim Marquardt: *Manuel des Antiquités Romaines*, p. 14, Tome X, "*De l'Organisation Financière Chez les Romaines.*"

the Indian trade, by prevailing on rulers to maintain the ratio of silver as to gold at 13:1 as opposed to 6½:1 in India.[176] In other words the real significance of the monetary reforms of Solon was the separation of Athens from the financial hegemony of Babylonia and its nearer agencies in Lydia, Aegina, Argos etc.; which, as previously pointed out, may very well have been rendered ineffective by the Laws of Lycurgus,[177] considered now, a point of great significance, to have been enacted in the early sixth century.[178] From now on it was going to be forbidden to Athenian merchants to settle unfavourable trade balances with slaves, and almost profitless to settle such balances with silver, either as coin or bullion. Henceforth the bankers would have to serve Athenian interests and would have to derive their profits from local business, I.E., there would be much more money circulating in Athens, and therefore a healthier industry; which history records as being exactly what transpired.

According to Grote, the banking system assumed after Solon a more beneficial character. The old noxious contracts "mere snare for the liberty of a poor free man and his children," disappeared and loans of money "took their place founded on property and prospective earnings of the debtor which were in the main useful to both parties, and therefore maintained their place in the moral sentiment of the people."[179]

---

[176] Alexander del Mar: *History of Monetary Systems in Various States*, p. 29, pp. 35-53.

[177] Formerly, as according to Mythology, considered to have been enacted in the 9th Century B.C.

[178] Humphrey Michell: *Sparta*, p. 27.

[179] G. Grote: *History of Greece*, Ch. 9; (Elgin Groseclose: Money, the Human Conflict, p. 18.)

Thus to such an extent did Athens abjure the international bankers who must be loosely described as centering in Babylonia, that, insignificant as she relatively was, through the *seisachtheia* ('shaking-off-of-burdens'), she in reality severed from Babylonian Imperialism and its financial hegemony world wide, and established herself as minor competitive force, as was shown by the Persian efforts at encirclement; towards which their seizure of control of the Thracian mines in the year 512 B.C. constituted the first clear step. Even if the reforms of Solon were not so absolute as those of Lycurgus in Sparta, and still left silver as the material of the basic monetary unit, and therefore still left Athens at the mercy of those forces whose secret activities contributed towards the functioning of what is known as Gresham's Law, "Bad money drives out the good," the Persian move of 512 B.C., by no means took the strength out of Athens and her allies. While securing ship timbers for the fleets they were planning, and also further silver supplies, Persia, wherein nested international money power at that time, thought that she would be cutting off from Athens these commodities so essential to the promotion of war industry. Somehow Athens still continued to maintain itself free of this Babylonian Imperialism which now sheltered behind Persia, and despite the enormous resources of Persia, was able to defeat the "Great King," both on land at Marathon, 490 B.C.; Platea and Mycale, 479 B.C.; and at sea at Salamis in the famous naval battle of 480 B.C. It may safely be assumed that the huge issues of the owl drachmas during the decade that followed the discovery of the 3rd level or contact at Laureion[180] and its fantastically rich ore, substantially contributed to this success. Those designing international money power were just that: international! If the other fellow too, looked to be on to a good thing, and could offer what its controllers needed most of all, which was precious metals, then a way could always be found

---

[180] W.P Wallace: *The Early Coinages of Athens and Euboia*, p. 35, The Numismatic Chronicle, 1962.

to do business! Out of war could only come good to them and theirs. Whether the "Great King" remained great, or Athens took his place, was not of that much importance. They would see to it that none who might be a real threat to them, would achieve a similar power to theirs; that is, from an international standpoint.

So to sum up the situation so far as pre-Solonian Athens was concerned, a simple unlettered people offered all the luxuries of another world as against the new money whose function is so little understood by lettered people even in this day, without going back 2500 years, had become swamped in debt. The law in respect to this debt had been upheld by a corrupted nobility in favour of the bankers. No doubt it had been represented to them by these same bankers that this pressure of debt on the growing population would keep the masses docile and tied to the land as was indicated by the prevalence of the mortgage tablets on the farms of Attica.[181] This condition, favouring the corrupted nobility of Greece and the international money power, ignored the needs of the new-rich manufacturers of Athens, who were neither able to obtain sufficient supply of local free labour, nor to obtain slaves.

Where credit institutions had long since existed as in the Grecian ports,[182] in a land of relatively simple folk, where the ways of money were no more understood than they are today, by loans of ledger credit page entry money against collateral, demanding in repayment silver coinage, Money Power obviously had made a very good thing of it in Greece. By the bankers of a given area using the same standard of weight in its precious metal coinage, calling loans in unison, the money

---

[181] Elgin Groseclose: *Money, the Human Conflict*, p. 16; University of Oklahoma, 1934.

[182] Paul Einzig: *Primitive Money*, p. 225; London, 1949.

supply could be shrunk to almost nothing; on which, their agents abroad could send ships, and buy crops and men and women and children for a song.

The Laws of the Archon Solon, by making no provision for employment for the freed debt slaves, nor providing for redistribution of the land, gave the Athenian manufacturer that labour, which he most of all needed. The Solonian ordinance offering Athenian citizenship to any free man from the countryside who came to Athens and took up a trade, further improved the labour market.

The monetary reforms of Solon reducing the export of coin or bullion, gave the Athenian manufacturers the money they also needed, for they remained the only market for the "funds" of the bankers, native or Peloponnesian; the latter having had no option but to find new lands to "conquer," as it were, after their virtual ejection by the laws enacted under the patronage of Lycurgus of Sparta.[183]

Finally, it might be said that the laws of the Archon Solon were the manifestation of the growth of the Athenian principle and the rejection, compulsory or otherwise, by all classes, of the Babylonian Money Power; including that growing class, who for the time being, seeing which way the wind lay, might now be called National Money Power.

---

[183] According to Gertrude Coogan, the first act of Solon after having had the Dictatorship urged on him by a powerful sector of the Athenian population, was abrogation of the privilege of silver mining, and, as a consequence, the privilege of money issuance by the nobility. I am, however, of the opinion that Miss Coogan missed the point here. What actually happened, it is true, would have been abrogation of the privilege of money issue by the nobility, but not as directly exercised by such nobility, but as through it being farmed out by them to the Arameo-Phoenician traders, i.e., the Babylonian Money Power.

PHRYGIA, FINANCE, AND FRONT MAN

The Assyrian conquests must have released a very flood of bullion on to the markets of the Middle East. Steeply rising prices that would have followed must have made it more profitable for bankers and money lenders and manufacturers from this most ancient area to look further afield for lands where money as denoted by treasure was not so plentiful, and therefore wherein such treasure might serve them best. The gold, silver, and electrum bullion with which, after 671 B.C. and the Assyrian thrust into Egypt during the second phase of Assyrian conquest, their store houses and strong rooms were overflowing, could be put to better use than lying inactive in these same store houses or strong rooms, at Nineveh, Babylon, Lagash, or Ur or wherever they were situated.

The privately issued electrum staters of Lydia of the seventh and sixth century B.C. denoted a highly significant possibility. Lydia was the source of something Assyria badly needed. The first thing such military organization such as existed in Assyria would need, would be financial organization, and secondly, stemming from its financial organization, organization above all towards the purpose of the purchase of the best of arms. Phrygia was famous throughout the ancient world for its arms.[184] Lydia bordered on and indeed may very well have been part of Phrygia in earlier times. Hence the secret of the electrum staters. Assyria needed Phrygian arms and at the same

---

[184] "But I perhaps, owing to the number of advocates may be classed in the common body; the battle of Cannae has made you a sufficiently respectable accuser. We have seen many men slain, not at Trasimene but at Servilius. Who was not wounded there with Phrygian steel?" Cicero: Orationes, *"Pro S. Roscius"* (Vol. I, p. 65; C.D. Yonge; London, 1883.).

time had to accept such financial terns as the suppliers of such arms decreed, and it may safely be assured that such terms stipulated payment was to be made in gold, silver, or electrum.

The extraordinary treasure of such as Sadyattes, latter dispossessed and executed by Croesus, cannot be explained any other way. It had to derive from the plunder gathered up by Assyria from all its conquests, as much as from the river washings of Lydia. The evidence of the gold artifacts, of the ancient civilizations of Anatolia of thousands of years previous to this time, such as Hacilar, Catal Huyuk, Dorak,[185] would indicate that the Anatolian rivers had been well washed for gold many ages before[186]. Although according to the *Guide to the principal coins of the Greeks* published by the British Museum, pages 12-13, electrum for the Lydian coinages came from the Pactolus river, the question still stands: "what happened to the enormous gold, silver, and electrum plunder, of Assyria; that had been taken from Aram, Israel, Arabia, and above all from Egypt?"

The great temple cities such as Karnak must have literally gleamed with gold and silver monuments and finishing. According to Diodorus in 57 B.C.: "So that there was no city under the sun so adorned with so many and stately monuments of gold, silver, and ivory, and multitudes of colossi and obelisks, each cut out of an entire stone.

.The decorations of these buildings were as magnificent as their design. The walls and pylons were covered with paintings and sculpture, the gates and pillars were overlaid with gold and the

---

[185] Kenneth Pearson: *The Dorak Affair*, London, 1967.

[186] Strabo, XIII, iv, 5. (Del Mar: *History of the Precious Metals*, p. 51.)

floors with silver, which, to the Egyptians was a metal hardly less precious than gold itself."[187]

The electrum obelisks of Hatsepsut[188] as removed by Ashurbanipal from before the Temple of Amon at Karnak in 661 B.C., contained, according to Breasted 2500 talents of electrum,[189] and according to other writers as much as 2900 talent; not to speak of other more massive plunder stripped from temple and tomb. The electrum from the obelisks alone, assuming the correctness of the percentages of gold, silver, and copper given on the cylinder reported by Desroches-Noblecourt to be in the Louvre, as being 75%, 22%, 3%, respectively,[190] would value at $186,648,000 (166,650 lbs. at approximately $70.00 to the fine ounce), having a buying power infinitely greater than in today. Skilfully used as the basis of a pyramid of ledger credit page entry money, it would be sufficient to maintain the finances of great enterprise, if not of kingdoms. Lydia, peasant kingdom that had emerged from the ruins of Phrygia after the Cimmerian invasion,[191] could very well have functioned in its institution in a similar manner to Switzerland during the last few hundred years; somewhat in the nature of a bullion broker's or international banker's refuge.[192] Which might account, perhaps, for the ferocity of the destruction by Cyrus of the hapless Croesus, who was said to have been flayed alive; as example no doubt to other kings, and

---

[187] Christopher Dawson: *Age of the Gods*, p. 295.

[188] James H. Breasted: *History of Egypt*, p. 281.

[189] *Ibid.* p. 559.

[190] Christiane Desroches-Noblecourt: *Tutankhamen*, p. 33. New York, 1963.

[191] *Encyclopaedia of World History*, p. 37, Boston, 1948.

[192] The fact that after the destruction of Croesus by Cyrus, 547 B.C., Sardis remained the principal mint for the whole Persian Empire, and for which it turned out Sigloi as to the Babylonian standard, gives further strength to the idea.

to remind them that while their power was national, there was another power which was international; above and beyond the power of petty kings.

Similarly, the other metals, copper, bronze, and iron, no longer deemed precious, and which therefore were often left on the battlefield, would fall into the hands of members of those semi-criminal castes such as Sadyattes, previously mentioned, who would control the camp followers that stripped the dead and thus garnered this scrap metal. These metals offered considerable profit by way of manufacturing counterfeits of the currencies of those states wherein base metal currencies were used.

Many Northern states and cities to which considerable industry was being transferred, used copper or iron fiduciary currencies in earlier times. Such was the iron currency of Clazomenae mentioned by Aristotle[193] and the iron spits of Pre-Pheidon Argos, examples of which were dedicated to the Goddess in the Temple of Hera at Argos at the commencement of silver coinage by Pheidon, and were actually exhumed from the place of their dedication by the archaeologists who explored that site.[194] Herein would have been fertile field for profit for those that dealt in money in Greece or elsewhere, for that matter.

Though the Greek himself obviously must have been the foundation of Greek industry, the Aramean or the Phoenician, bringing the ways of money and banking and who brought an alphabet and writing to Greece, became the cornerstone of that industry. He also brought agencies from the great banking houses of Babylonia such as that firm mentioned by Professor

---

[193] Frederick William Madden, M.R.A.S.: *Coins of the Jews*, p.29; London; 1881.

[194] Charles Seltsman: *Greek Coins*, pp. 34-35.

Sayce in *Babylonian Literature*, which flourished from the reign of Nabopolassar, the father of Nebuchadnezzar, to the reign of Darius Hystaspes; approximately one hundred years; and of which evidence remains in the clay cheques and deeds found by some Arabs in a great earthen jar.[195] Since the time of Professor Sayce, which is nearly a hundred years ago, much more evidence of the existence of powerful banking and merchant institutions has come to light; outstandingly those of the Egibi Sons, and the Murassu, who, according to Professor Humphrey Michell in his work, *The Economics of Ancient Greece* (p. 334), carried on very large and complicated business; even by modern standards.

Just as Babylonian business and banking houses maintained extensive branches in the Sumerian cities, such as at Lagash where their records were found to exceed the records of the king,[196] so it may safely be assumed that they maintained branches within any state within the limits of the communications of the day, and where profit was to be made.

The sturdy intelligent people of Greece were a fertile field for the renewal of industry and trade after the disturbance that must have followed the rise in prices deriving from the augmentation of precious metal reserves resulting from the flow of Assyrian plunder on to the bullion markets, and later, with Babylonia once again supreme following the victories of Nabopolassar in 605 B.C., from the similar flow of Babylonian plunder. At the same time Greece was a place of refuge from the war clouds drifting over all that Near East world, and the stench of slaughter that followed the warring hosts.

---

[195] Frederick William Madden, M.R.A.S.: *Coins of the Jews*, p. 6. (footnote).

[196] *Cambridge Ancient History*, p. 392, Vol. 1.

It would not be long before the skill of the Aramean at letters, money, counterfeit or otherwise, and in organization of industry, stirred the peasant kingdoms of Greece. Industries rose under the guidance of these refugees similar to those of their homelands, to be later followed by a money economy as to the silver standards of Babylonia, and by the systematic spreading of money madness amongst the landed aristocracy of Greece, thus separating them from their peoples for whom they had been the hereditary guides. For their peoples and their labours had now become but cyphers; desirable wealth assessed as according to the figures in the banker's book.

The people who drifted into the cities as slave or freeman, and found employment in the organized manufactures of these strangers who by now were calling themselves Greeks, and were by now bearing Greek names, not unnaturally gave their allegiance to that new hand that seemed to feed them. Eagerly, just as in today, they drank at the fountain of hatred of their former masters, who through their sanction of the activities of these "New Greeks," and connivance with them in respect to the new money system they set up, betrayed both their people and themselves.

Among the first steps towards the total monetization of the wealth and labour of the Greek peoples to a precious metal standard controllable by the great banking houses of Babylonia, was the permitting of the striking of a silver coinage on the island of Aegina by Pheidon,[197] "progressive" King of Argos in 680 B.C., similar to the private coinage that was issued in Lydia

---

[197] According to the table on p. 35, *"Greek Coins"* by C. Seltsman, the Aeginetan drachma was established without any doubt at its given standard, because in the time of Pheidon, the ratio of silver to iron was 400:1. He clearly had been advised to establish the new silver drachmas and obolos so that they would have the same purchasing power as the now discarded iron obolos and "Drax." according to their valuation in an International market where money was metal by *weight*.

prior to Croesus. "Progressive" King of Argos meant in this case a king ready to listen to the blandishments of money power, luring him into that trap which was the use of precious metal currency, over which he could have relatively little control; since silver as its base was to be obtained only at great expense by slave labour at localities too often far distant, and, relative to localities yielding iron or copper, few and far between. True, the silver used by the moneyers of Aegina probably came from Laureion, in sight across the sea. But even though the source of supply was so close at hand, a coinage of which so small a unit represented so much value, placed the economy, through the practices of banking, in the hands of the international bullion controllers.

That the bankers, known as *trapezitae*, conducted almost the same business as bankers today is clearly indicated by the article in Seffert's Classical Dictionary, even if, as the word *trapezitae* indicates, they but sat at a bench in the market place, instead of sitting in gilded halls surmounted by sixty story buildings, as indeed they do today. Within the limits of clay tablet and stylus, the same confidence game was operated, though probably there were few who understood it as being such; yesterday it was a conspiracy against the men of a city, or a relatively small state; today a conspiracy against the whole world. Those that have their hands on the throttle of this all embracing evil do not however bear the faintest resemblance to whole hearted demons in hell, or gods who in their mountain halls contemptuously plan the total eradication of man who may be their complete failure. They are but pudgy and sly little men as much overwhelmed by the monster they have raised, as are the foolish nations that permitted them so to do.

Of Ancient Greek banking Seffert says: "Bankers were called by the Greeks *trapezitae* because they sat at tables in the market places, the centre of all business transactions. They acted as money changers exchanging for a commission heavy money or gold into smaller coin, and the moneys of different systems with each other. In commercial cities they would do a considerable trade in this way, the different standards and the uncertainty of the stamping of the coins in Greece creating a great demand for their assistance. They also acted as money lenders both on a small and a large scale. *Finally they received money on deposit. People placed their money with them for safe custody, partly to facilitate the management of it. The depositors, according to their convenience, either drew out sums of money themselves, or commissioned their banker to make payment to a third person. In this line the business of the banks was considerable. If a citizen had a large sum of money circulating in business, he probably preferred to put it in a bank and to hand over to the banker the business of making his payments. Strangers too found that the banks offered them such facilities that they were glad to make considerable use of them.*[198] The bankers kept strict account of all monies in their charge. If a person were making a payment to another who was a depositor at the same bank, the banker would simply transfer the requisite sum from one account to another. The bankers were generally well known from the public character of their occupation, and they naturally gained great experience in business. Consequently their advice and assistance were often asked for in the ordinary affairs of life. They would be called in to attest the conclusion of contracts, and would take charge of sums of money, the title to which was disputed, and of important documents. Business of this kind was *generally in the hands of resident aliens.*"[199]

The above quotation from the great German scholar, Oskar Seffert, leaves those of us who understand the origins and meaning of today's banking, little doubt, as previously pointed out, that within the limits of clay tablet and stylus, every fraudulent practice known to banking would have been

---

[198] Obviously for discounting Bills of Exchange, raising money against Bills of Lading, Warehouse Receipts, and the realization into that which circulated as money of the promissory note issued as between friends or otherwise.

[199] Oskar Seffert: *Dictionary of Classical Antiquities*, p. 91.

practised. Also the commonly accepted idea that instruments used in foreign trade, such as Letters of Credit, Bills of Exchange, etc. were a discovery of the 12th Century A.D., is further clearly proved erroneous by the sentence: *"Strangers too found that the banks offered them such facilities that they were glad to make considerable use of them."*[200]

Therefore behind the monetary reforms of King Pheidon of Argos we must see not the wonder of what so many so-called scholars would call the arrival of the "Invention" of coinage in Greece, but the comings and goings of strange aliens with letters from mysterious "Important" men who dwelt in Tyre, or Sidon, or Sardis, or who dwelt in Babylonia itself; everything to be in the name of "progress," everything to be joy and light! The only thing our poor peasant king had to ask himself was. "Joy and light for whom. Us or these panders, pornographers, and luxury pedlars who now flock to our shores?"

Very soon, no doubt, the answer became apparent. Behind the Aramaic speaking banker came the slave trader, and it was not long before the poor people found that the king's law was no longer for them, and was but a measure behind which these glib and double talking "Bankers" operated. "We must protect the people's savings!" no doubt was their cry, yesterday, as in today.

Such silver coinage as was produced at Aegina or Argos would have been no more than a few seen symbols, the apex of an inverted pyramid of unseen or abstract symbols of which only the money master really understood the meaning and purpose, and only he knew how to manipulate. Through manipulation of these "Credits" in relation to the silver that people now thought was their money, King Pheidon himself could have been tricked into believing himself a slave because he could not

---

[200] Visiting Merchants and Ships' Captains.

repay his so-called "debt." However the banker needed the king as such, for a while yet no doubt.

In the meantime peasantry and lesser nobility were drawn into this trap of irredeemable debt, and, as the king's law had to be upheld, they and their families would be sold into that cruel slave system that was growing up all over the Mediterranean world and through which, money economy, now grown into a very monster, could find docile labour for the dreary grind of the new methods of semi-mass production in manufacture, such as it had brought into being, and against which the reforms of Solon as described in the previous chapter, were directed.

History should not be misled by the Greek names of those significant figures and families concerned with money and money power at that time, whether in Lydia or in Greece. Oskar Seffert states quite clearly that the bankers or *trapezitae* were resident aliens.[201] Controlling the undercurrents of city life as undoubtedly they would have so done, in those days it would have been no more difficult than it is in these days to secure the services of a front man to promote their interests, and secure them citizenship if necessary. Just as aliens who seek trade and power amongst whatever people they maybe, so often change their names to suit the circumstances while retaining allegiance to that group into which they were born, so it was in that day, nearly three thousand years ago. In the early days of the Greek cities, citizenship was easy to obtain and persons with pretence at power, influence and money, in a society where worship of money had replaced worship of the gods, in truth, would have no great difficulty in that direction.

Out of the weakening of what was left of the true power of kingly rule at Athens, such as descended from Mycenaean

---

[201] Oskar Seffert: *Dictionary of Classical Antiquities*, p. 91.

Greece, and consequent growth of "Aristocratic" democracy, doubtless deriving from concession to international money power for its assistance against the Dorian previous to 1100 B.C., and before whom it appears the city of Athens never fell, came the replacement of the title *Wanax* indicating god-king reigning in earthly splendour, for that of *Archon-Basileus* of lesser degree.[202] Out of the further weakening of such aristocracy of the Greeks as later existed, whether Achaean, Ionian, or Dorian, and the soul destruction sown amongst them as consequence of their betrayal into slavery and abuse of their followers who had so trusted them and looked to them for guidance, derived those conditions out of which the so-called tyrant rose to power. Out of the involvement of the natural leaders of the people[203] with things ignoble and inimical to their own kind, such as trade and "Money-making," and with strange luxuries and vices, rose those men, often traitors to their own class, who fronted for the conspiratorial money power of the age. Such men steered the restless aspirations of the wage slaves of the cities; those dispossessed masses so easily stirred to active resentment against their former leaders deriving from the ancient nobility; and who, of course, had no more understanding than themselves of that force by which they were both being manipulated.

---

[202] Jacquetta Hawkes: *Dawn of the Gods*, p. 262; New York; 1968.

[203] Referring to the Hellenic terminology in connection with banking transactions and professions etc. Professor Heichelheim of vast scholarship recorded "That the banking transactions of the individual bankers, money lenders, and debtors influenced the whole economic life and even, to a certain degree, the intellectual development in Attica, the territories of the Delian League and in many other polis territories of our period, since the fifth, if not occasionally sixth centuries B.C. will be obvious from the above list which has a surprising number of specializations." Fritz Heichelheim: *An Ancient Economic History*, Vol. II, pp. 196-197; Leyden; 1958-1970.

TYRANT AND TRAPEZITAE

Of the tyrants of Greece and Asia Minor in ancient times, the learned Professor Heichelheim wrote:[204]

"These tyrants were for the most part members of the nobility themselves who had made the grade using the new political and economic possibilities of their time to overthrow their own equals and to subdue their whole home state temporarily. The tyrants were often compelled to introduce the coin economy pattern into the area over which they ruled, or at least to promote its development officially, in order to gain the upper hand over their enemies. To stabilize the position of the peasantry on the land, and to expand and rebuild state economy, a central distribution of money and goods in kind partly directed towards mercenaries, bodyguards and various political friends, and partly indirectly to the masses of poor people in the form of wages paid for extensive building operations and improvements, is characteristic of tyrant economy."

The above remarks of Professor Heichelheim indicate there were "new political and economic possibilities" in that period 650-500 B.C. when the tyrannies most of all flourished. The question then becomes, what were these "new political and economic possibilities?" The answer is arrived at readily; they derived from the activities of the agents of the international silver bullion brokers, who, from ports such as Argos, Athens, and Aegina where King Pheidon struck the first Greek silver coinage c.680 BC., promoted the luxury traders who sold their

---

[204] Fritz Heichelheim: *An Ancient Economic History*, Vol. 1, p. 290; Leyden. 1958. 1970.

wares from wigs to harlots as against the new silver coinage or promise thereof. The opportunities clearly were for those who assisted in the monetization of the city, and all its activities and possessions, and its population, man, woman, and child, and their possessions too, and thereby assisted in the firm establishment of the rule of bankers, trade, and traders, as against the gods ruling over mankind living in his natural order.

"The aristocracies refused political equality to the landless traders and manufacturers, the peasants were oppressed by the rich and encouraged to get into debt and then were reduced to slavery and exile; slaves began to compete with free labour. Ambitious individuals capitalized this discontent to overthrow the constituted government and establish themselves as tyrants in all the Greek cities with the notable exception of Sparta."[205]

The situation is very clear. The kings and aristocracies as descended from ancient days, as a derivative of their folly in permitting the unrestricted activities of the new bankers, who were now well established in all the major cities of Greece outside of Sparta, saw a class of manufacturers and entrepreneurs come into being, largely foreigners and men of lowly origin. These men, more often than not with the means of nobility but the outlook of slaves, were clearly a serious threat to kings and nobility and the order they represented.

In the same manner during the sixteenth and seventeenth centuries A.D., the worthy tradesmen of London, while still deferring to the natural nobility of the land, more and more realized, that they too were lords of the land through control of labour by the wage rates and needed little encouragement from that true source of their power, the bullion brokers, towards

---

[205] Houghton Mifflin (Publishers): *Encyclopedia of World History*, p. 48; Boston; 1940.

hatred of a government[206] which still gave them little say, for all the wealth that they were possessed of according to the new standards. This government still continued, at least until Charles I, to consider one of its main duties was to prevent the oppression of the poor and the trusting,[207] regardless of the so-called "needs of trade."

The similar class that rose in Greece some two thousand years previously, more and more realized that they were the new reality, and that they were now in actuality the lords of the land through labour, which they owned outright as slaves, or controlled as through daily wages. If the land itself they still did not own and control, it mattered not; for there were those voices that told them that land too was but a trade and a tool in the new order. As their textiles (as at Megara), or pottery (as at Corinth), that every ship leaving harbour carried to the ends of the earth, so the land of the great lord was but the capital investment that grew the food that he the manufacturer purchased for himself and his slaves or the raw materials needed for his particular trade; and he himself, in the money creator's kingdom on earth, was as assessable in coin as was potter, weaver, or armourer. The land owning nobleman was a man controllable as themselves through the arts of taxation in terms of money, could they but institute a system of government in which the natural ruler had no more power to rule than themselves.

No doubt these worthy tradesmen of Megara, or Corinth, or Athens, led on by the attitude of their true masters, the *trapezitae*, the money creators, agents of those great and ancient banking houses of Babylon city, said to themselves of the

---

[206] A. Andreades: *History of the Bank of England*, p. 22; London; 1966.

[207] Sir William Ashley: *Economic Organizations of England*, p. 96-118. London; 1933.

natural lords of Hellas "Who are these men?" "For all their fine manners and clothing, we could buy them up a hundred times did they but know it!"

And so the stage was set for the arrival of the tyrant financed into existence by the bankers towards the total destruction of the old way of life, which still had within it the seeds of a strength sufficient to root out its enemies such as, in the case of Sparta, had been outstandingly proven by the renewal of the ancient life system through the financial and social reforms of Lycurgus. Classes of manufacturers and entrepreneurs, contemptuous of a nobility that seemed to have betrayed its trust, were easily stirred to envy and resentment, and the work of destruction by the tyrant received little or no opposition.

"In order to level the class of large landowners and nobles economically, Theagenes of Megara simply allowed their herds of cattle to be slaughtered without remuneration. A frequent political device of tyrants from Asia Minor to Sicily was to murder or banish nobles, confiscate their possessions, and redistribute their wealth amongst the poor."[208]

The poor, needless to say, soon returned to being poor again. "The poor ye shall always have with you." The poor merely being those who trust that their rulers are attending to serious matters as indicated by their position in the scale of life, such as governing. The word "poor" having existed, of course, long before the crafty banker, standing in the shade beside the ways of life, arranged it that measure of poverty and riches was in that number of (privately issued) units of exchange in which a man could be assessed according to success or failure in the conflict of life, as he the banker had established it.

---

[208] Fritz Heichelheim: *An Ancient Economic History*, Vol. I, p. 290.

The tyrant, therefore, was that force by which international money power as it derived from the control of silver bullion and the slave markets, destroyed all resistance to its total ownership of life and labour and human hope. The status of all, slave or free, in some degree, depended on their relations with the *trapezitae* who presided at their table in the *agora*; and should they be kings or rulers of states, no doubt their destinies would be much influenced by those shadowy figures furtively watching from the counting houses of far away Mesopotamia. According to the special nature of the times, the tyrant, in his capacity as ruler, would above all be guided instrument; but that the tyrant no more understood the true significance of his existence than do these so-called revolutionary "leaders" of today, is a certainty.

The so-called "revolutions" of today are clearly similar in their origins to those of the time of the tyrants; the main difference being more of a technicality. Until 1870 A.D. the arbitrary valuation of gold bullion as according to the decision of the bullion brokers, was common denominator of values internationally, with silver bullion in second place at the ratio as decided by the leading states; but still rarely varying a great deal from that ratio decided on nearly 2000 years ago by Julius Caesar and his financial advisors, of 12:1.[209] After the demonetization of silver in almost all the major states of the world, in the seventies of the last century,[210] the common denominator of values was gold alone, with silver just another commodity moving up and down on world markets according to supply and demand.

More than ample evidence exists of those persons designated international bankers in "Modern Times" as also the instigative

---

[209] A. Del Mar: *History of the Precious Metals*, p. 81; New York, 1968.

[210] A. Del Mar: *Money and Civilization*. Also John R. Elsom. pp. 49-50

factor in the principle so-called revolutions of the last three hundred years. According to Commander Guy Carr,[211] the so-called English revolution was totally the work of the international bullion brokers who seem at that time to have been lodged in Amsterdam, although the loan of silver bullion to Queen Elizabeth I[212] for the recoinage that took place shortly after her accession to the throne as negotiated by the famous "Sicile,"[213] later Lord Burghley, came from Antwerp.

Some of the Crypto-Jews of the Commonwealth,[214] of whom many would have been in England during the reign of Charles I, would also appear to have been a factor in such revolution as witting or unwitting agents of the Amsterdam bullion brokers.[215] The main designer of the events of those days seems to have been a Manasseh Ben Israel, "a remarkable character," who apparently took the initiative in the financing of Cromwell;[216] which enabled Cromwell to obtain the best of arms, the first requisite of the would-be conqueror throughout history.

The arrival of the Spanish and Portuguese Marranos[217] in Holland in 1593 A.D., with the consequent harnessing of the Dutch, a seafaring people, naturally aggressive, to their world wide trade activities, and the resultant so-called "prosperity," immediately produced its impact in Britain. The regrowth of

---

[211] Commander Guy Carr: *Pawns in the Game*, pp. 19, 20, 21.

[212] G. Ravenscroft Dennis: *The House of Cecil*, p. 61. London, 1914.

[213] Illustrated London News, Nov. 11th, 1911, p. 762.

[214] Lucien Wolf: *The Resettlement of the Jews in England*; London; 1888.

[215] A. Andreades: *History of the Bank of England*, p. 28.

[216] F.P.G. Guizot: *Histoire de la République d'angleterre*, pp. 154-155; Paris; 1854.

[217] Max Dimont: *Jews, God, and History*, p. 291. New York; 1962.

the commercial power of these "New Dutch," more especially as deriving from the bullion trade which they seemed to continue to control internationally, principally due to the connections they continued to maintain in Spain, directed towards them a great part of the flood of the precious metals which was being wrung out of the wretched natives of South America particularly; not to speak of that which came from Japan, China, and India, of which not so much seems to be known.[218] No sooner did these precious metals arrive in Spain or Portugal than almost immediately they moved on to other parts in settlement of trade debit balances created largely by the Spanish wars in Europe, particularly in Italy.[219]

This superfluity of the precious metals in Northern Europe certainly was one of the instigative factors, in the growth of "Banking," which had spread from Venice and Genoa, to

---

[218] According to the letters of Quang Chang Ling (1878); (*History of the Precious Metals*; p. 348; A. Del Mar): " It was in the year 1498 that the Portuguese made their way around the Cape (of Good Hope). In 1510, under Albuquerque, they treacherously seized the East Indian city of Goa, and leaving a garrison in it, sailed away to Malacca which they had seen and coveted in 1508. They plundered Malacca of a booty so enormous that the Quinto, or fifth, of the king of Portugal amounted to 200.000 gold cruzados, a sum equivalent to $5,000,000.00."

"We have our own theory concerning the sources of your present riches. We ascribe it in part, to your gains from the piratical conquest, enslavement and murderous extinction of the American races, but chiefly to the profitable trade with the Orient. From the opening of this trade to 1640, when the Portuguese were driven from Japan, and the British first acquired territory in Hindustan, three of your European nations alone took a thousand million dollars in gold and silver from Asia; two thirds as much as they wrung from all America during the same period. From Malacca alone they took 25.000.000; from Japan, up to the date mentioned, four hundred millions; from India and China still greater sums (in gold or silver coin, or bullion)."

[219] The Chapters in Del Mar's *History of Civilization* dealing with this period, will repay the reading.

Amsterdam, and from thence to London,[220] where, evinced by the activities of the goldsmiths, it had set itself up against kings, as the whole story of the downfall of Charles I would indicate.

The political picture of Northern Europe derived a great deal of its changing character from the rise in prices which came about both as a result of the relatively tremendous influx of new precious metals at that time, and as a result of the growth of "Banking," that is private abstract money creation, which affected prices equally with that precious metal that could be seen as it circulated as money. Kings, often in the hands of the venal advisors to whom the age gave rise, were no longer able to make both ends meet, and not understanding the true nature of the activities of the bankers or goldsmiths, they neither knew how to put a stop to such activities nor, if they permitted them, how to tax them.

The sullen resistance experienced by Charles I from the puritanical and self-righteous burghers of the City of London,[221] most of whom were by then deeply beholden to the goldsmiths for their finances, who, in their turn were no doubt beholden to the Amsterdam bullion brokers for the gold they sometimes needed in a hurry when rumour went round that their receipts which circulated as money, were largely false and had nothing behind them except lies, may be traced to these same bullion brokers of Amsterdam.

Their policy above all required the weakening of kingship in England, for the "Banking" monopoly they saw they might come to institute in England, could not flourish with a king on the throne such as Charles who truly regarded himself as the Lord's anointed. A king who was aware of the source of his

---

[220] Andreades: *History of the Bank of England*, pp. 14-32.

[221] Ibid, p. 19-20.

power, even if not widely instructed therein, that is to say, who was aware of the true meaning of monetary creation and emission relative to his kingship, was not much to their liking. The reinstitution of the office of a Royal Exchanger, abolished by Henry VIII in 1539 on the advice of a Sir Thomas Gresham,[222] was also not much to their liking, nor the seizure by Charles of the £130,000 deposited in the Tower supposedly by the London merchants, reputed to have come from Spain *en route* to Dunkirk, Spanish possession at that time. The reinstitution of the office of Royal Exchanger meant that one of the major sources of revenue of the goldsmiths, and therefore their masters, the bullion brokers was cut off: that which obtained from the exchange of coins, foreign or domestic; which meant, therefore, they were denied the opportunity to clip, or sweat, or retain for export those full-weight coins that came their way.[223]

"The unsafe condition of a Bank under a Monarchy."[224]

These words of Pepys indicate the trend of thought of certain circles at the time. Although Charles I could not be considered the most effective opposition to banking and its proponents, nevertheless, he was in the way; even if the cure to him — Cromwell— proved perhaps to be even more in the way! Cromwell's "Bills of Public Faith," of which very little record remains, a true currency being intrinsically valueless, state issued, and inconvertible, must have been cause for grave misgivings on the part of the goldsmiths, and all concerned, as to whether they had done right in supporting the enemies of the king! It was not long after the return to the throne of

---

[222] Ibid. p. 22.

[223] A. del Mar: *History of Monetary Crimes*, PP. 7-44.

[224] Pepys Diary, Aug 17th, 1666. *Diary and Correspondence*. 5 vols. London, 1848.

England of the Stuart Line in the person of the amenable Charles II, in 1660, that these "Bills of Public Faith," the real key to sovereignty, were repudiated;[225] showing that the son had even less understanding of the realities of money than had the father.[226]

To return to Cromwell and the principal factors that lead up to his success, and his assumption of the powers of tyranny: when it became clear that Cromwell was as "suitable" a man as could be found to fit the needs of the occasion, Manasseh Ben Israel supplied him with the gifted Fernandez Carvajal, for the reorganization of his army, which became known as the "Model Army". Trained revolutionaries then poured into the country, presiding over whom was the Portuguese Ambassador, a De Souza, who loaned them the diplomatic immunity of his house for their meetings. One such revolutionary was the man known today as Calvin, whose father had been fiscal agent to a prominent French Bishop.[227]

These revolutionary leaders, besides developing the technique of spreading religious differences, also exploited the use of truculent mobs, a practice known to this class of people from most ancient times, for the gaining of political ends. According

---

[225] Anderson, Adam, p. 485, *An Historical and Chronological Deduction of the Origin of Commerce*, Vol. II, London, 1787-1789.

[226] Charles II was totally in the hands of the bankers and goldsmiths as is revealed by the following extract from D. MacPherson's *Annals of Commerce*, (p. 428). "Charles being in want of money, the bankers took 10% of him barefacedly, and by private contracts on many bills, orders, tallies and debts of that King, they got 20, sometimes 30% to the great dishonour of Government. This great gain induced the Goldsmiths to become more and more lenders to the King, to anticipate all the revenues, to take every grant of Parliament into pawn as soon as it was given; also to outvie each other in buying and taking to pawn bills, orders and tallies, so that in effect, all the revenue passed through their hands."

[227] Will Durant: *The Reformation*; p. 459.

to Commander Guy Carr, who is a relatively recent writer on this subject:[228] "The evidence which *absolutely* convicts Oliver Cromwell of participating in the revolutionary plot was obtained by Lord Alfred Douglas, who edited a weekly review known as Plain English published by the North British Publishing Company. In an article which appeared in the issue of Sept. 3rd 1921, he explained that he and his friend, Mr. L.D. Van Valckert of Amsterdam, Holland, had come into possession of a missing volume of records of the Synagogue of Muljeim. This volume had been lost during the Napoleonic Wars. The volume contained records of letters written to and answered by the directors of the Synagogue.

They are written in German. One entry dated June 16th, 1647 reads: From O.C. (i.e.) Oliver Cromwell to Ebenezer Pratt.

'In return for financial support will advocate admission to England; this however impossible while Charles living. Charles cannot be executed without trial, adequate grounds for which do not at present exist. Therefore advise that Charles be assassinated, but will have nothing to do with the arrangements for procuring an assassin, though willing to help in his escape.'

In reply to this dispatch the records show E. Pratt wrote a letter dated July 12th, 1647 addressed to Oliver Cromwell.

'Will grant financial aid as soon as Charles removed and. admitted.[229] Assassination too dangerous. Charles should be

---

[228] Commander Guy Carr: *Pawns in the Game*, p. 20.

[229] According to A. Andreades (*History of the Bank of England*. p. 30.), Frederick Harrison says in his biography of Oliver Cromwell: "Noble were the efforts of the Protector to impress his own spirit of toleration on the intolerance of his age. He effectively protected the Quakers; he admitted the Jews after an expulsion of three centuries, and he satisfied Mazarin that he had given to Catholics all the protection that he dared."

given an opportunity to escape. His recapture will then make trial and execution possible. The support will be liberal but useless to discuss terms until trial commences.'

On November 12th, that same year, Charles was given the opportunity to escape. He was, of course, recaptured. Hollis and Ludlow, authorities on this chapter of history, are both on record as considering the flight as the stratagem of Cromwell. After Charles had been recaptured, events moved apace. Cromwell had the British Parliament purged of most of the members he knew were loyal to the King. Notwithstanding this drastic action, when the house sat all night on December 6th, 1648, the majority agreed 'That the concessions offered by the king were satisfactory to a settlement.'

Any such settlement would have disqualified Cromwell from receiving the blood money promised him by the international money barons through their agent E. Pratt, so Cromwell struck again. He ordered Colonel Pryde to purge Parliament of those members who had voted in favour of a settlement with the King. What then happened is referred to in history books as 'Pryde's purge'.

When the purge was finished, fifty members remained. They are recorded as the 'Rump Parliament'. They usurped absolute power. On January 30th, 1649, he was publicly beheaded in front of the banqueting house at Whitehall, London. Oliver Cromwell received his blood money just as Judas had done."[230]

On the same somewhat obscure page of history, Professor Andreades pointed out in his *History of the Bank of England*,[231] that Cromwell's best known historians pay little attention to the

---

[230] Commander Guy Carr: *Pawns in the Game*, p. 19-21.

[231] A. Andreades: *History of the Bank of England*, p. 28.

subject of his relations with the Jews and their return to England. Carlyle and Morley devoting no more than a page to this highly controversial event.[232] The reader gains the impression that more was to be said on the subject. He asserts himself: "It is certain that as soon as Charles I was dead, the Jews attempted to return to England."[233]

The following statements by Benjamin Franklin in reference to the causes of the American Revolution are equally illuminating:

"About this time (the time of the Treaty of Paris, 1763), Benjamin Franklin made a visit to England. While there he was asked how he accounted for the prosperous conditions of the colonies. His reply was: 'That is simple. It is only because in the colonies we issue our own money. It is called "Colonial Scrip" and we issue it in the proper proportion to the demands of trade and industry.'" (See Senate Document No. 23, Page 98, by Robert L. Owen,[234] former Chairman, Committee on Banking and Currency, United States Senate.)

---

[232] *Ibid.*

[233] *Ibid.*

[234] Robert L. Owen was the senator who wrote and introduced the legislation setting up the Federal Reserve (Central Banking) system in 1913. His foreword to a book written by a Miss Gertrude Coogan shows that he lived to bitterly regret his part in writing and introducing this Bill. The remark made later by President Wilson, who had paved the way for the Bill — "I am a most unhappy man. Unwittingly I have ruined my country" — shows that Owen was not alone in his remorse. The Central Banking System known as the Federal Reserve System and towards the creation of which he had been the principal instrument, though apparently state department in the same way as the Bank of England, was in reality no more than the instrument through which the so-called International Bankers harnessed the burgeoning energies of the American peoples to themselves, their own world wide needs and purposes. From first to last, which perhaps has not yet come, it was a privately owned and controlled institution.

Robert L. Owen continues: "It was not very long until this information was brought to the Rothschild's Bank, and they saw that here was a nation ready to be exploited; here was a nation setting up an example that they could issue their own money instead of the money coming through the Banks. The Rothschild's Bank caused a bill to be introduced in the English Parliament., therefore, which provided that no colony of England could issue its own money. They had to use English money. Consequently the colonies were compelled to discard their 'scrip' and mortgage themselves to the Bank of England (the Amsterdam Bullion Brokers!) to get money. For the first time in the history of the United States our money began to be based on debt."

"Benjamin Franklin stated that in one year from that date the streets of the colonies were filled with the unemployed, because when England exchanged with them, she gave them only half as many units in payment in borrowed money from the Rothschild as they had in 'scrip'. In other words, their circulating medium was reduced 50%, and everyone became unemployed according to Benjamin Franklin's own statement."

Continuing the quote from Senate Document No. 23: "Mr. Franklin went further than that. He said that this was the original cause of the revolutionary war. In his own language: *'The colonies would gladly have borne the little tax on tea and other matters had it not been that England took away from the colonies their money which created unemployment and dissatisfaction'.*"[235]

The French Revolution, so called, left much less evidence of its origins than the so-called Russian Revolution 120 years later, though the instigating factor is clear enough. *The French Revolution* by Nesta Webster, *The Life of Napoleon* by Sir Walter

---

[235] John R. Elsom: *Lightning over the Treasury Building*, PP. 29-30; Forum Press; Boston.

Scott, almost unobtainable, and above all the chapters in *God and the Goldsmiths* by McNair Wilson, on Napoleon Bonaparte, give some light on this matter. A study of Louis XV and his relations to the Pâris Brothers, the state tax farmers, especially through Madame Du Pompadour, formerly Poisson, possibly illegitimate child of Pâris Duverney and god-daughter of Pâris Monmartel, yields impressions. The writings of Necker, front man for the international bankers of the time, and who Mirabeau described as "the Hero who arrived by famine" should be read, and also the writings of Turgot, finance Minister to Louis XVI, who fought against Necker and the evil fraternity behind him, and who nicely summed up the situation in his first memorandum to Louis XVI as follows:

"So long as finance shall be continually subject to the old expedients in order to provide for state services, your Majesty will always be dependent on financiers, and they ever will be the masters, and by the manoeuvres belonging to their trade they will frustrate the most important operations. Thus the government can never feel itself at ease, it can never be acknowledged as able to sustain itself, because the discontents and impatience of the people are always the means made use of by intriguing and ill-disposed men in order to excite disturbance."[236]

Clearly the Minister Turgot was a man of sincerity and integrity, a true God-servant, and the fact that it was only after prolonged scheming on the part of the international bankers, who mostly lived outside of France, that he was dismissed,[237] would suggest that his master also sought to do that which he was borne to do, that is, love, guide, and protect the people.

---

[236] R. McNair Wilson: *God and the Goldsmiths*, p. 48.

[237] His dismissal was effected through the agency of Marie-Antoinette. As she disliked Turgot personally, no doubt she was a ready instrument.

But neither master nor man understood the strength of the undercurrents which flowed, nor, it is to be feared, the true meaning of *l'etat c'est moi*, which in essence means "I am the fount of Life. I am that point through which the Almighty God injects your money amongst you that binds you together as one. I, and no other; not my steward, nor servant, faithful or unfaithful."

The men of intrigue he referred to, were such stewards, the international bankers. These men, standing behind thrones intercepted that God-Power from on high which was the force behind *l'etat c'est moi*, and, controlling the value of money of whatever kind, and therefore international price levels, with responsibility only to them and theirs, confused the nations with their sly schemes of fatuous purpose.

The instigating factor of the Russian Revolution so-called is common knowledge and is detailed in a hundred books. Perhaps one of the best sources of information relating to the financing of the same Russian "Revolution" is the book *Czarism and Revolution* written by Arsene De Goulévitch, a former officer of the Czar's army and founder of the Union for the Defence of Oppressed Peoples.

According to information deriving from the French Secret Service, one of the principal sources of finances for the International Revolutionary Movement prior to 1917, was Jacob Schiff of the International banking firm of Kuhn, Loeb, and Company, based in New York City. It was recorded that twelve million dollars had been donated to the revolutionaries by Schiff, in the years preceding the war of 1914-1918. This fact is apparently confirmed and amplified from sources other than the French Secret Service.[238]

---

[238] A. Goulévitch: *Czarism and Revolution*, p. 225.

The main funds for the so called "Revolution" and towards the steps which led up to it, do not appear to have come from that class of nouveau riche bred into being in Russia out of the activities over the previous 50 years, of the joint stock banks, and the men such as Sawa Morozov, and Tereschenko,[239] the socialistic sugar magnate. The extensive funds so necessary towards the effective disruption of a major state appear to have come from certain British and American circles, which it seems, had been lending their support to the Russian revolutionary "cause," for a long time. In his book, *My Life*, Trotsky speaks of a large loan granted in 1907 by a "Financier" belonging to the so-called "Liberal" Party in Britain. This particular "British" financier was apparently not alone in his monetary support of the "Revolution" in Russia.[240]

The conduct of Jacob Schiff, previously mentioned, towards Czarist Russia, once he was installed as head of the New York "International Banking" firm of Kuhn, Loeb, and Company, was that of an apparently unyielding enemy. References to his anti-czarist activities exist in the book by Cyrus Adler: *Jacob Schiff, his Life and Letters.*[241]

Further verification of the activities of Jacob Schiff is afforded by the New York "Journal American" of February 3rd, 1949; a time when pro-revolutionary activities were "The Thing" in New York City:[242] "today it is estimated by Jacob's grandson, John Schiff, that the old man sank about $20,000,000.00 for the

---

[239] *Ibid.* p. 223.

[240] *Ibid.*, p. 224.

[241] Cyrus Adler: *Jacob Schiff, His Life and Letters*, New York, 1928.

[242] Although it is really very difficult to see what exactly would have been left for this class of people, often multi-millionaires, to revolt against by 1949, which also includes the hegemony of the Anglo-Saxon in the United States.

triumph of Bolshevism in Russia."[243] According to Goulévitch (p. 231), various other persons well known in the world of international banking, whatever the expression "International Banking" might mean,[244] were also known to be associated with support of revolutionary activities. The ruin to the states of the world set on foot by these immensely rich, but otherwise trifling persons, whose solidarity, however, had enabled them to so profit from the unbelievable expansion of the use of Ledger Credit Page Entry Money in the Anglo-Saxon banking systems, could not better demonstrate the absurdity of allowing private, and therefore irresponsible, persons to exercise that power which should belong to the gods alone, the power inherent in the creation and issuance of the Unit of Exchange amongst the peoples.

In a speech made six weeks before the fall of the Kerensky Government, Lenin made one of his most significant recommendations and perhaps the one most suggestive of the possibility of his sincerity, even if in the rest he seems to have

---

[243] Also according to the author of Czarism and Revolution (p. 224), "in the Spring of 1917, Jacob Schiff openly boasted of having been instrumental in overthrowing the Czarist regime."

[244] According to Dr. Carroll Quigley (p. 52.) in the review by W. Cleon Skousen outstanding characteristics of the international bankers were:

"… they remained different from ordinary bankers in distinctive ways: (1) they were cosmopolitan and international; (2) they were close to governments and were particularly concerned with questions of government debts. (3) their interests were almost exclusively in bonds and very rarely in goods. (4) they were accordingly fanatical devotees of deflation. (5) they were almost equally devoted to secrecy and the secret use of financial influence in political life. These bankers came to be called 'international bankers' and, more particularly, were known as 'merchant' bankers in England, 'private bankers' in France, and 'investment bankers' in the United States. In all countries they carried on various kinds of banking and exchange activities, but everywhere they were sharply distinguishable from other, more obvious kinds of banks, such as savings banks or commercial banks."

been misguided. It was the one recommendation most indicative of his awareness of the deep-seated causes of the conditions that had given rise to himself and what he stood for. Additional to proposing nationalization of the great monopolies already existing in Russia, (primarily as the result of the admission of joint-stock banking into the country as concession to the victors of the Crimean war), above all he recommended the total nationalization of banking. In his own words he says: "all banks to be merged into one and the state control its operations, that is the nationalization of the banks."

"To talk about regularization of banks," continues Lenin, "means either to betray complete ignorance, or to fool the simple folk with high sounding words, to control the delivery of bread, or in general, the production and distribution of goods, without controlling banking practices, *is an absurdity* (Collected Works [1964], vol. 25, p. 329).[245]

Of course, six weeks later, when Lenin had physically seized power with the aid of his "armed bandits," it was a small matter to set up printing presses in the major cities in Russia that commenced to pour off paper roubles by the billion. Some fourteen or fifteen thousand workers were busily engaged in the government printing shops of Moscow, Leningrad, Penza, Perm, and Rostov-on-Don, turning out tons upon tons of

---

[245] Arthur Zapolsky Arnold, Ph.D.: *Banks, Credit, and Money in Soviet Russia*, p. 57; Columbia; 1937. Also see the article by Lenin in "Pravda," May 29th-30th, 1917: *The threatening catastrophe and boundless promises*. Of equal interest and strikingly similar in the language used is the comment of Lionel Rothschild on the subject of banking as quoted by Lord Beaconsfield (Benjamin D'israeli) in 1844: "Can anything be more absurd than that a nation should apply to an individual to maintain its credit, and with its credit, its existence as a state and its comfort as a people?"

paper money. The printing of notes was simplified to a point where counterfeiting became easy.[246]

At the same time safety deposit boxes were seized, all accounts frozen and the banks were closed, so that there was no addition to the circulation existing outside of banks at the start of this "operation," a great part of which circulation would have been gold; and no new money came on the scene other than the paper roubles of the Bolsheviki printing presses which immediately took the place of that Ledger Credit Page Money by manipulation of which the banks had previously controlled a great deal of trade.

For a year or two the Monarchist roubles were printed as if there was intention to keep the people half expecting that the Czar would be coming back, then for a short while a 'Kerenki' rouble was printed, presumably issue of the short lived Kerensky government, as if to prepare the people for total resignation, and then finally, the Bolsheviki rouble which let the people know that all was indeed lost. This continuing the money of a destroyed king seems to have been no new policy of international money power, especially in the case of those kings, its particular enemies. An illustration of which, occurring in ancient times, was the continued minting at the Sardis mint of the *sigloi* of Croesus long after he had been destroyed. The printing press money of the Russian Revolution entered the circulation against government expenditures and against gold coin which it became illegal to possess, no doubt being accompanied by an equal amount of counterfeit, also exchanged against gold.

These vigorous moves must have been cause for some misgivings amongst the bankers who continued to finance the

---

[246] Arthur Zapolsky Arnold: *Banks, Credit, and Money in Soviet Russia*, p. 96; Columbia; 1937.

"Revolution" so far as went Bolsheviki needs in foreign exchange. But no doubt so closely surrounded was Lenin by their agents,[247] they would have been justified in reasoning that they would come out on top again without too much trouble, especially with the new roubles being so easy to counterfeit. And during that period of the so-called "New Economic Policy," approximately 1920-24, they did so come out on top.

In the archives of the State Publishers of Moscow is recorded the following eulogy to the printing press as being as great a force in the so-called revolution as armies:

"Paper money of the Soviet Republic gave support to the young regime at the most critical period of its existence when there was no possibility of raising direct taxes to meet the outlays of the civil war. Hail to our printing press! It is true that its days are numbered but it has already completed three quarters of its work. In the archives of the proletarian revolution along with the cannon, rifles, and machine guns of our epoch that vanquished the enemies of the proletariat, the place of honour will be given to the printing press, the machine gun of the commissariat of finance that poured fire into the rear of the bourgeois system and that made use of the laws of currency and circulation of that regime for the purpose of destroying it, and of financing the revolution."[248]

Typically enough the "Tyrant" himself, Vladimir I. Lenin, saw little or no profit out of all this, for himself, the Russian people, or that ideal of world revolution in which it appears he sincerely believed. If he truly was the author of the above statements regarding banking, then, when he died not so long

---

[247] Fr. Dennis Fahey: *Mystical Body of Christ in the Modern World*, Dublin; 1964.

[248] (a) Arthur Zapolsky Arnold: *Banks, Credit, and Money in Soviet Russia*, pp. 96-97. (b) *Paper Money during the epoch of the Dictatorship of the Proletariat*, (Moscow State Publishers, 1920) p. 4.

after all these events, it was as a weary and disillusioned man. For that gold, still very much the base for total control of world finance, which was wrung from the Russian people during the period of terror between 1917 and 1922, seems to have almost all found its way back to the "Benefactors" of the original revolutionaries, Messrs. Kuhn, Loeb, and Company of New York (Jacob Schiff's firm), and it must have been clear to Lenin by the time he died in 1924 that he was but agent of a force that regarded him as merely another tool to be used towards the making of that which they designed.

"Mr. Bakhmetiev, the late Russian Imperial Ambassador to the United States, tells us that the Bolsheviks, after victory, transferred 600 million roubles in gold between the years 1918 and 1922, to Kuhn, Loeb, and Company (Schiff's firm)"[249] which makes pretty good return for the mere 20,000,000 dollars granted by the philanthropic Mr. Schiff and which would have been as credits against purchases at that!

At that time such amount of gold could be used to form the apex of an inverted pyramid of abstract money equal in amount to beyond thirty times the number of units such gold represented in U.S. currency according to its official price.

---

[249] A. Goulévitch: *Czarism and Revolution*, p. 225.

POTSHERDS AND OTHER FRAGMENTS

The glimpse at these cataclysmic events of relatively modern times, as in the previous chapter, will assist towards understanding of the implications of similar events in ancient times of which but the most fragmentary information exists. As was written three thousand years ago: *"Is there anything whereof it may be said; See this is new? It hath been already of old time which was before us."*[250]

So returning to that smaller world of ancient days, the theme of this book, it may safely be said that similar conspiracy and secret manoeuvre led up to all that fast changing sequence of social events that clearly followed a definite design, in Attica; particularly from the collapse of hereditary kingship in 683 B.C.; which date marks, it most reasonably may be assumed, the commencement of rule by Money Creative Power either international or home grown. A king created annually by vote has even less chance of ruling effectively than the so-called presidents of today, elective kings as they really are, though sorry enough spectacles some of them may be, and who have as much as five years to serve the purposes of whoever they front for.

Some writers dismiss the idea of a capitalism in antiquity, but accepting definition of capitalism as the condition of the unrestricted promotion of human activity through the instrument of the driving force of that power of creation, and loan against collateral, and at interest, of the unit of exchange, or of promises of the unit of exchange as denoted by Ledger Credit Page Entry, and which function as the same thing in

---

[250] Ecclesiastes. Chapter 1, Verse 10; King James Version.

exchanges between persons dealing with the same banker or interlocked system of banks, very little analysis of the circumstances that gave rise to the tyrants will show that a form of "capitalism" did exist, even if more local in character, and restricted to the individual city, or state, as a rule. The tyrant was front man towards the total monetization of the state, the land and its labour, and towards the transfer of that independent labour formerly firmly placed in the Natural Order of God-Life, to a condition of dependence on a wage of money, directed towards being able to keep on living as with the notion of being a free man.

Today we but repeat the mistakes of the past; however today it is not merely disaster to a small city or state and its way of life, but with the existing refinement of that which can only be described as the money swindle as it was conducted in ancient times by the *trapezitae* at their bench in the market place, made possible by mass paper manufacture and the printing press, and the enormous potentialities therein towards quickening the speed and drive of human life and endeavour, it almost certainly will prove to be, one way or another, total disaster, and to all mankind.

Those lines of Solon say enough:

But of themselves in their folly the men of the city are willing
Our great city to wreck, being won over by wealth.
False are the hearts of the people's leaders.[251]

A further couplet indicates the meaning of "our great city to wreck."
Great men ruin a city: for lack of understanding

---

[251] P.N. Ure, M.A.: *The Origins of Tyranny*; New York; 1922.

Under a despot's yoke lieth the people enslaved.[252]

These lines written after the seizure by Peisistratus of the Tyranny at Athens would indicate that the same Peisistratus had the assistance in his rise to power of those former great landowning families of Attica who had been drawn into the schemes of the foreign money masters to their undoing. These landowners had forgotten their duty towards their own people. Fascinated by strange luxuries and the stranger talk of the money men, the *trapezitae*, they had permitted themselves to be absorbed with visions of that new wealth measured by the numbers indicated by the precious metal symbols of these same *trapezitae*. They forgot that in the absolute analysis they themselves were but stewards of a higher power. Lacking understanding, above all, of the true nature of this money as being above all *their own law* towards the facilitation of the exchanges amongst themselves and their people, they had been lead astray from their duty. By conniving with the bankers and their protégées the new manufacturers, to drive their own people off the land into the cities, and into the industries rapidly speeding up from the new money economy, they forgot that in their capacity as rulers, the whole land was theirs in trust to their people, and that the people therefore were expectant of them to be their guides and shepherds.

These plausible aliens who set up the money economy via their so-called "banks," owned nothing but unmitigated gall, a vast contempt for mankind, and such as they could double-talk the naïve peasant rulers into giving them.

The folly of these rulers in equating possession with the master moneyers trifling pieces of gold and silver dated back to those grim Kings of the Homeric Sagas or before, who, being lain in their graves at Mycenae with all their riches, thus set off on

---

[252] *Ibid.*

their eternal journey with that small store of gold that the crafty Babylonian money-men had trained them to regard as wealth, as opposed to the real wealth of an organized state whose money was the benevolent law of the ruler in relation to surpluses, and directed towards the good and continuing life of the people and no more.

Those who had power and made men to marvel at their riches.[253]

This line indicates that Solon, like so many equally worthy people of this day, knew that money was an evil without understanding what it was about money that made it so. Not the *having* of the precious metal pieces of the banker recording the number of units represented, for such metal money lying inert beneath the floors[254] has no meaning so far as the quickening or slowing of the pulse of life is concerned. It has no more meaning than have abstract units of exchange media that have not yet been recorded in the ledger on account of no suitable (to the banker!) demand for them. and, of course, they are without limit. Nor even the spending of it as the holder, according to law, might choose. The evil is in the forgetfulness of the ruler that money is no more than a recording of his law of exchange, its magnitude being governed by the number of units indicated. It can never be treasure which is merely items carrying with them a high valuation in relation to such units, relative to their desirability and portability. The evil about money derives in consequence from lack of understanding of its true nature, and particularly from the confusing of money and treasure. It is the persistent failure of mankind to realize that money is but the result of agreement being arrived at amongst a sovereign people through their ruler, to provide

---

[253] P.N. Ure: *The Origins of Tyranny*, p. 8; New York; 1922.

[254] It was the custom in ancient times to bury hoarded wealth (tangible) beneath the floor of the house.

themselves with a system of numbers by which their exchanges might be facilitated, and so help them to live a better life. Treasure being but commodity by which the unit of value of whatever state may be, can best be stored; even though such state cease to exist; because of that ancient and international convention in respect to the valuation of such treasure such as has lasted from age to age; from the most ancient times, Palaeolithic or earlier, until today.

The evil lay and it may be said, lies, in the forgetfulness of the ruler to respect his duty to provide an adequate money supply for his people regulated by himself and free of obligation to external forces, in such manner as had existed in the Ancient Oriental civilizations in earlier times. It lay in the permitting to private and hence irresponsible persons the power to intervene in that which was the most sacred responsibility of the ruler through the priesthood, the creation and regulation of the medium of exchange: his people's money.

Therefore the hidden force behind the setting up of a tyranny was the far reaching power of a conspiratorial secret society, international in scope, controlling money emission in all countries which it penetrated through its continuing control of the sources of supply of that silver treasure by weight such as constituted the base of the exchange systems long ago established by itself.

The tyrant, therefore, was clearly the front man for the local banker more than actually being the banker himself. He it was who gave legality to the banker and the activities of that coterie of merchants, traders, and captains who flourished on the banker's financial organization, and, though this they did not understand, his connection with those international bullion brokers of the day. These worthy businessmen depended for tiding themselves over difficult periods on that which the banker loaned them as money: maybe an entry in a ledger transferable to the account of a fellow merchant, visiting captain, or trader in slaves, or other merchandise; they also depended on the banker to be safe custodian for such treasure as came their way. The tyrant was therefore, either naïve or corrupt, the instrument set up by the banker, firstly towards the legalization of his status, and secondly towards the removal of that class who might yet challenge his peculiar and secret power, the natural aristocracy of Hellas.

This natural aristocracy, in a growing system that clearly sought the alienation and subversion of its free dependents with the purpose of ultimately leading them into paid day labour or into slavery final and absolute, was uncertainly situated in states which now owed their existence to the bankers, and their coterie of entrepreneurs, and manufacturers, and merchants, as clearly did so many of the Greek states of the Greek industrial revolution.

The banker, lurking in the shade apart from men, knew that these proud noblemen, formerly lords of this lovely land which was Greece, had forgotten the meaning of their own existence, and its relation to the total ordering of their society, and he despised them as well he might, for permitting him to undermine the true order of life and cause these simple folk, their peasantry, to be driven off the land one way or another, to the wage slavery of the potteries at Corinth, or Athens, or wherever it might be or whatever it might be.

In the same way, the Lords of the Manors of England and Scotland had driven the peasantry off the common lands some 2400 years later; land now representing that magic of money of which previously they had seen little. The same peasantry drifting into the new manufacturing and mining towns, dazed and leaderless, then formed a plentiful labour supply for that similar putrescent wickedness which was the industrial revolution in England's green and pleasant land. If they were lucky they were able to emigrate.

In the lines of Theognis whose political aim was to prevent a recurrence of the Tyranny in Megara which was a centre for the manufacture of textiles:

Tradesmen reign supreme: the bad lord it over their betters.
This is the lesson that all must thoroughly master:
How that in the world wealth has the might and the power.
Many a bad man is rich and many a good man is needy.
Not without cause, Oh Wealth, do men honour thee above all things.
Must men reckon the only virtue the making of money?
Everyone honours those that are rich and despises the needy.[255]

The banker, trained from the money shops of Babylonia, knew that for him the only desirable political situation was where the lowly and vulgar[256] held the appearance of power and wealth and "money," for such would not question too intently the source from whence they derived that "money," nor the nature of that "money" such as had paved their way to so-called power, for fear its so necessary supply might be cut off. In the words of Aristophanes:

Often has it crossed my fancy that the cities apt to deal

---

[255] *The Origins of Tyranny*, p. 8, p.N. Ure, M.A., New York, 1922.

[256] Hence the situation at Athens so similar to the situation in the Anglo-Saxon world today. Athens at that stage of the Peloponnesian War was undoubtedly completely under the political control of the banks (or *trapezitae*). It was not long after the battle of Aegospotami, 405 B.C., in which Lysander of Sparta destroyed the whole Athenian fleet as it lay drawn up on the beach, that the war ended with the usual results of such "Great" wars in so called "democratic" states, and with Athens completely dependent on privately created money for its finances, that is, on the International Bankers, and with such types of persons suitable to them and their plans for the future, occupying key positions. The victor, Sparta, was equally dependent on their good will, as a result of those concessions undoubtedly made at the Treaty of Miletus, 412 B.C. in order to obtain money such as was desirable internationally, and with which could be purchased the ships so necessary to defeat Athens, and without which the war could not have been brought to definite conclusion.

With the very best and noblest of the Commonweal
Just as with our ancient coinage, and the fine new minted gold
These, sir, our sterling pieces, all of pure Athenian mould,
All of perfect die and metal, all the fairest of the fair,
All of workmanship unequalled, proved and valued everywhere,
These we use not. But the worthless pinchbeck coins of yesterday,
Vilest die and basest metal, now we always use instead.
Even so our sterling townsmen, nobly born and nobly bred,
Men of worth and rank and mettle, men of honourable fame,
Trained in every liberal science, choral dance and manly game,
These we treat with scorn and insult. But the strangers newliest come,
Worthless sons of worthless fathers, pinchbeck townsmen, coppery scum
(Whom in earlier days the city hardly would have stooped to use
Even for her scapegoat victims) these for every task we choose.[257]

Where, as in a city such as Megara, one banking house might control all credit or money creation, to question and seek to know how this was done would also mean search for knowledge of the banker's secrets and this, our tyrant instinctively knew, was dangerous for his continued success.
What are the gains that lead up to a tyranny? Is it not more probable that they are some form of payment received by the commons (those that are bad) from the would-be tyrant?

Not at all. Merely the word was passed by that banking institution to which the majority of tradesmen or manufacturers in that particular city were indebted, that the banker, giver of all, (and taker of all!), favoured this move. Ah! and indeed it would be good for all, and to please the common people there would be plenty of work! It may safely be considered that the first legislation passed by our new tyrant

---

[257] *The Frogs of Aristophanes*, lines 717 to 733, trans. by B.B. Rogers (with slight variations). (Page 138, *Greek Coins*, Charles Seltsman, M.A., London, 1933.)

would legalize the position of his backers, which previously, as likely as not, had been illegal!

The tyrant at this stage of history, was a necessity to Money Power, and while possibly having the appearance of being wealthy, he depended for his real finances on that backer whose interests he promoted. Those two officers of Alexander for example, who accepted the tyranny of Asiatic cities could in no way have understood the reality of finance, international or otherwise, except perhaps if they had been clerks in the paymaster corps of officer status. If they had so understood such finance, it is doubtful that they would have been promoted as they were.

The tyrant was one who the banker could rely on to put through his "Levelling" programme, or in the double talk of today, could be relied on to "Press ahead with Democratization," and to work against the class from which he was supposed to have come.[258] He was one who could be relied on to put through programmes of public works, maintain military expenditures etc.; for all such activities strengthened the banker's position as creator and regulator of the exchange unit, and therefore, from those exclusive courtyards wherein he schemed, designer of the life of the city. The banker could not maintain his hold over the city, except his product, ledger credit page entry money, however created, was in constant demand, and the local government deeply embroiled in his schemes. The tyrant had to be one completely in accord with that so-called "democratic" political attitude, which the banker always seemed to espouse. His ostensible purpose had to be to "Level"; such

---

[258] In exactly the same way as Lenin, Dictator (or Tyrant) of Russia 1917-1922 was supposed to be drawn from the Nobility, or as Mao-Tse-Tung, at a later date dictator in China, was supposed to have derived from a similar class in China.

levelling meaning of course, tearing down everything above themselves, (and above the banker too!)

Those fragments of verse as quoted here, reputed to be by Solon, leave little doubt of the sincerity of Solon, at least superficially. The fact remains that as a merchant, whether of necessity or otherwise, he must have been marked with some of the outlook of that class. His famous laws, amongst which was that law releasing the peasantry from the debt slavery into which their natural rulers had permitted them to be drawn, and that was eating into the very vitals of Attica, in view of the fact that he offered citizenship to any family moving to Athens with the intention of taking up some manual trade, might very well have been promoted by his backers. The city was clearly very short of suitable free labour. It very well might be that his backers were those money lenders and bankers that controlled the growing manufactures of Athens, and who saw that there was more profit and work for that which they loaned as money, in bringing the peasantry to Athens as free men (if a wage slave is really any more free than a slave owned outright!)[259] and in having thus a plentiful supply of labour, than in tying such peasantry to the soil by debt slavery, and in the case of distraint, their sale on to a surfeited market abroad. While there was still a healthy population of small holders as well as the great landlords, there was always possibility of recovery by the

---

[259] The following letter circularized amongst American Bankers by European Banking interests during the American civil war gives a most revealing light on this subject. There is no reason to suppose that the motives of the *trapezitae* of the Greek city states were in any way more altruistic: " Slavery is likely to be abolished by the war power and chattel slavery destroyed. This, I and my European friends are in favour of, for slavery is but the owning of labour and carries with it the care of the labourers, while the European plan, led by England, is that capital shall control labour by controlling wages." This letter, known as *the Hazard Circular*, is to be found on Pages 44-45 in *The Money Manipulators* by June Grem.

enslaved state, and themselves, the enslavers, as happened at Sparta in the time of Lycurgus, driven out of the land for hundreds of years. With a massive proletariat beholden to the men of the city for their freedom (as day labourers!), the former aristocracy even if they should ever awaken to their duty, would have no chance. Nor did they. All those "liberalizing" laws promulgated by Solon and his successors, steadily deprived the ancient families of Attica of their former power and prerogative. The shadow of power was put into the hands of ignoble persons, as indeed would have been so many of the "Demagogues," and other "Democratic" officials, who, too often would have been no more than blind creatures lifted up from the mob to the service of money power. By the devices existing as part of what is known as "democracy," such as *Ostrakism* through rumour put into circulation by the secret societies in the city, controlled, as in today, by the bankers without a doubt, "Leaders" no longer "suitable" could be removed.

"The tyrants themselves are repeatedly found making it part of their policy to keep their subjects employed on big industrial concerns. In more than one case we shall see their power collapsing *just when this policy becomes financially impossible.*"[260]

In other words if that tyrant proved unsatisfactory to his masters, money that source of strength in political life, was cut off just at the time it would be most needed, such as when he had become involved in heavy spending. Herein is further proof of the tyrant being not money power itself, but front man for money power.

"This part of the tyrant's policy is noticed by Aristotle who quotes the dedications (buildings and works of art) of the Cypselids at Corinth, the buildings of Olymphian Zeus at

---

[260] Ure: *The Origins of Tyranny*, p. 15.

Athens by the Peisistratids, and the works of Polycrates around Samos. To these names we add Theagenes of Megara, Phalaris of Agrigentum, Aristodemus of Cumae and the Tarquins of Rome, all of whom are associated with works of this kind."[261]

It is pointed out by Professor Ure that it can scarcely be an accident that the Tyranny of Athens ended almost immediately after the removal of one of its two roots; the mines of the country of the Thracians and Paionians.[262] Which is to say that if the source of bullion on which the money power of a so-called banker was founded, petered out, or was lost to enemy action, the tyrant he had promoted could be discarded as having no further purpose.

Such activities being ordered by a class of persons who had achieved despotic power in the same period of history, roughly the eighth, seventh, and sixth centuries B.C., the period which saw extensive development of mining in all of Europe including Lydia, Cyprus, Spain,[263] Carpathia, Epirus, Illyria, Thrace and Greece itself, without mentioning the flow of precious metal plunder deriving from the depredations of the Assyrian, can only have been the result of a policy deep laid, and far reaching in its consequences. This policy can only have been created in some central point from which flowed the springs of world power such as would have designed, wittingly, or unwittingly, so much of the ancient world.

The same period also coincided with the development of mining tools of hardened iron, highly efficient methods of reduction of silver bearing ores,[264] and the growth of an

---

[261] *Ibid.* p. 14.

[262] *Ibid.* p. 59.

[263] *Ibid.* p. 46.

[264] A. Del Mar: *A History of the Precious Metals*, pp. 47-51.

adequate supply of slave labour from various sources and due to the above mentioned depredations of the Assyrian etc.; all of which was so necessary towards profitable mining operations at that time. It may not unreasonably be supposed that this central point was still in the cities of lower Mesopotamia, such as Babylon, Ur, Lagash, Uruk etc. From this area the merchant houses would have continued to have spread their operations around the world[265] in the same way, as, it is recorded, had been done from Ur as much as fifteen hundred years before during the so-called IIIrd Dynasty;[266] or for that matter during the period of seeming glory and empire that so often follows the accession to power of private money creative force in any organized and potentially vigorous state. A most outstanding instance of the latter in modern times exists in the period of empire that came to Britain following the establishment of the Bank of England in 1694 A.D.[267]

The silver which the international bankers drew from Greece etc. at a ratio of 10:1 or more, would have been used in settlement of trade balances with India, Bactria, or China, at a ratio of 6:1 or less, as to gold. According to Alexander del Mar, this movement of silver to the Orient from Athens, was arranged by the Athenian Government;[268] but except this early

---

[265] *Cambridge Ancient History*, p. 392, Vol. I.

[266] Sir Charles Woolley: *Abraham*, p. 121-126.

[267] A. Andreades: *History of the Bank of England*. Also see *Tragedy and Hope*, by Dr. Quigley.

[268] A. del Mar: *The Halcyon Age of Greece*, p. 5. There also were to be found outlying places in the Orient where the ratio of gold to silver went as low as 1:1 during the 1st Millennium B.C., remaining so until a very late date, in certain instances. It is reported by Sir Henry J. Reid, who wrote during the 19th Century, in his book *Japan* (Chapter XVIII), that the ratio of silver to gold, governing the use of the precious metals in settlement of trade balances, was still 1:1 in Japan during the 17th Century A.D.; long after contact with Europeans. The advantage the European bullion brokers took of this situation with its resultant disturbance to the status quo, was one of

Athenian Government was fronting for the bankers, this could not have been so. International trade balances have always been settled from the world's banking capital or headquarters of the international bankers or bullion brokers, such as was London during the last three centuries until very recently. In the days of which we write, this world banking capital was still located in Babylon city, it may reasonably be assumed.

The money of the cities of lower Mesopotamia and the whole Near East for that matter, had been based for a long time on the international valuation of silver by weight, and therefore these cities had long ago sought to obtain control of all sources of supply of such silver. As far back as 2470 B.C., King Manishtusu of Akkad invaded Southern Persia with no purpose other than gaining control of its silver mines.[269] When the rapid expansion of mining, as mentioned above, brought on to the markets of the world a relative deluge of silver and gold, the latter taking no mean second place, those groups controlling International finance from Babylonia, and possibly from Nineveh, decided no doubt to seek for further worlds to conquer, as it were.

The thing was to find a use for their surfeit of bullion, particularly silver, and of which metal they were now in a position to arrange extensive supplies to any banker who would be able to use such advantageously towards the promotion of their general worldwide plans. The growing commercial and industrial vigour of the Greeks showed them an answer to this problem. Thus the significance of the advent of the tyrants as promoters of heavy public spending of moneys based

---

the main factors leading up to the almost total expulsion of Europeans from Japan during the period 1624 A.D. - 1853 A.D.

[269] Sir Charles Woolley: *Abraham*, p. 122.

originally, on the silver standards of Babylonia, cannot be dismissed.

The policy of the bankers, for whom the tyrants fronted, would be to spread the main practice, at least their most profitable one, of private money creation, one way or the other. Using silver as base, they knew full well the tremendous possibilities that existed towards the creation of an abstract money whose equally efficient units cost them no more than entry by the slave scribe on the clay tablet that sufficed as his ledger. Such policy spread, together with competition in manufacture, the need for that which the international bankers of that day, faceless as in this day, loaned against collateral as money. This money was based on the silver bullion they let it be known they were possessed of or held on deposit for their customers, be they individual, corporate body, or state.

It is reasonable to assume that there was little difference as between that first tangible money of private issuance in England as denoted by the goldsmiths receipts of the sixteenth and seventeenth centuries[270] and the money as issued by the banks of the Greek cities. Its efficacy in the exchanges, although it was in reality no more than a highly organized system of counterfeit, derived from the total secrecy maintained by those involved in its issue. Little clear information exists on this subject today as in ancient times and much of which, even if all the millions of tablets unearthed in Mesopotamia are ever translated and evaluated by scholars competent to do so, must remain as but faint outline.

One such faint outline of particular interest, though not deriving from the Mesopotamian tablets, is discernible in this information of Servius Tullius, slave king of early Rome:

---

[270] A. Andreades: *History of the Bank of England*, pp. 22-26.

"According to Charisius, Varro wrote: *Nummum argenteum flatum primum a Servio Tullio dicunt, is IIII scripulis major fuit quam nunc.*" "It is said that silver money was first made by Servius Tullius and was *IIII scripulis* heavier than now."[271]

As it was Servius Tullius who ordered the establishment of the census at Rome that gave the basis for both taxation and military service, both essential organizations as to a state being taken over by international money power, the truth of this statement by Varro need not be questioned.

It is interesting to note in passing that although Servius Tullius was a usurper undoubtedly of slave origin, Livy carefully draws him in rather more favourable light than the Tarquins, particularly Superbus, the last of the line. By the time of Livy (59 B.C.-17 A.D.) the most powerful sector of the Roman population, the equites or knights, was taken over by wealthy freedmen and enfranchised foreigners.[272] Livy, when writing in that day under the threat of *Lex Majestus*[273] would clearly have

---

[271] Theodore Mommsen & Joachim Marquardt: *Manuel des Antiquités Romaines*, p. 12, Tome IX; *De l'Organisation Financière chez les Romaines*, Paris, 1888.

[272] *Ibid.* p. 68.

[273] In its origins in 100 B.C., *Lex Majestus* (*lex appuleia de maiestate imminuta*) was an extension of the definition of treason as being internal revolt, to include any act impairing the "Majesty" of the Roman people. By the time of the early Empire, this law had been extended to cover almost any word or deed against the Emperor, and, it may reasonably be assumed, those who guided his policies. Spies and informers were everywhere. Of this period Tacitus wrote at the very beginning of the *Annals*: "What has been transmitted to us concerning Tiberius, Caligula, Claudius and Nero, cannot be received without great distrust." He further wrote in *The Histories*: "But when the battle of Actium had been fought and the interests of peace demanded the concentration of power in the hands of one man, this great line of classical historians came to an end. Truth suffered in more ways than one. To an understandable ignorance of policy, which now lay outside public control, was in due course added a passion for flattery or else a hatred

seen the value of finding and extolling true virtue in the character of the slave king, whether such virtue was there or not.

However, if Servius actually did exist, and there seems to be a school of thought amongst the scholars that questions his existence, then it would be more likely as one who had raised himself up in a similar manner to Gyges of Lydia,[274] having at the same time a special backing by local money power; possibly in opposition to that money power emigrant from Corinth to Tarquinii in Etruria, which, according to Livy, was the Tarquin family.

The establishment of a silver standard as a base for monetary issuance might very well have been their reward for their assistance towards raising Servius to the throne. The Census, supposedly established by Servius, while being the foundation of the organization of the whole state for defence or aggression, would give that money power a complete picture of the people it was their intention, one way or another, to exploit. In the same manner the doomsday books of the Middle Ages, while recording for the reference of the king, all that in the kingdom was, also made valuable record for the money creative power, which had kings, nobles, ecclesiastics, and the common people, groaning under a burden of debt quite impossible to

---

for autocrats. Adulation bears the ugly taint of subservience, but malice gives the false impression of being independent." (*The Histories*, I.I.; Tr. K. Wellesley; London; 1964.)

[274] It is to be noted that the seal to the establishment of Gyges on the throne of Candaules, otherwise known as Myrsilus last king of Hittite descent on the throne of Lydia, and who he had cuckolded and destroyed, apparently with the ready assistance of Candaules' wife, was the pronouncement of the Pythian Oracle (Herodotus, Book I). Clearly the Oracles would be one of the most important instruments of the international money creative power towards the furtherance of its purposes; and it would have sought, as much as possible, to keep them under its control.

meet (which certainly was one of the main causes of the mood of the English that gave rise to Magna Carta, and of those events which followed until 1290 A.D. when the tax-collecting and money-lending classes, such as had followed the "Conqueror" across the English Channel, were finally evicted).[275]

In a similar manner some 2500 years later, William III of England, owing his throne to the intrigues of the international bullion brokers at Amsterdam, granted them as reward that which they wanted more than anything on earth, which was the establishment of the legality of an undeterminable amount of abstract money, ledger credit page entry, or paper notes, to be based on their gold loans to the state, and the creation of a "Bank" at London from which they might issue this money known as "Credit" as loan against real collateral throughout the whole kingdom. This bank was to be given the appearance of a state department. In this case such status was obtained by permitting it to be named: "The Bank of England."[276]

Considering the above known instance of reward to international money powers for their services, far reaching in its consequences, and many other instances of which there is neither time nor place to write herewith, conjecture in respect to the establishment of a silver standard at Rome by Servius, may not be too far afield. That Romans later rejected this standard as a base for their money, and the calamity and loss of sovereignty it brought them also is clear, for there is no further reference to silver money until that period when Rome was drifting towards the all-out struggle with Carthage: the year of the establishment of the board of Moneyers for the striking of

---

[275] John Richard Green: *A Short History of the English Peoples*, p. 205; London; 1936.

[276] A. Andreades: *History of the Bank of England*, p. 73; London; 1966.

bronze, silver and gold money (289 B.C.): *tresviri aere argento auro flando feriurado*;²⁷⁷ thereby no doubt yielding to the importunities of the International Bullion brokers, with the ensuing outbreak of war thus being made a certainty.

One of the main purposes of those extensive public works which almost invariably followed the establishment of a tyranny, would be towards the establishment of some kind of National Debt, in which is, and was in that day too, most control and profit to those manipulating international finance. That there is no evidence of the existence of such state indebtedness in those days does not necessarily mean that such did not exist. Excavation, or other methods, 2500 years from now would not reveal this indebtedness for instance in the case of England, so far as its relation to the Bank of England was concerned, for, unbelievable though it may seem, there is "remarkable absence of official records" for the first hundred years of the bank's existence!²⁷⁸ In the time of the tyrants, failure to keep books or records would be even more of a certainty.

Valuable by-products of their extensive public works programmes would be:

1. The peasants would leave the land enticed by the money wages offered for work on these projects, and the

---

²⁷⁷ R.A.G. Carson: *Coins, Ancient, Medieval, and Modern*, p. 106.

²⁷⁸ A. Andreades: *History of the Bank of England*, p. xxvii. In the words of H.S. Foxwell who wrote the preface to this work in giving the reasons why no adequate history of the Bank of England appears to have been written previous to Andreades: " The first is the remarkable absence of official records in connection with the Bank, especially for the first century of its activity. It has often been observed that the English are peculiarly fortunate in this matter of records;. The Bank of England stands out as a striking exception to the rule. It never seems to have published any reports or even to have preserved its own minutes and accounts."

pleasures and excitement that could be bought in the city with such money wages. There, once the construction boom was over, they formed a leaderless, hungry, and easily embittered "Proletariat."

2. The same "Proletariat" could be manipulated by the agents of Money Power as a mob, towards such political purposes as such Money Power might desire; including, besides removal of the natural nobility, removal of the so-called tyrant when his purpose was served.

Professor Ure, author of *The Origins of Tyranny*, ventures as close to the truth in respect to the meaning of a tyranny as any others who have written on the subject. Although attributing the rise of the tyrants to Money Power he does not define what this Money Power may be; whether money creative power, or just those of considerable possession and treasure. In this omission he cannot be blamed. Professor Ure for instance traces the source of the power of Peisistratus, Tyrant of Athens 561-527 B.C. according to Herodotus,[279] as being partly from those silver mines in the district in Thrace through which flows the Strymon river, and partly from the Laurion mines in Attica.

However, it must be pointed out that a man who apparently was a mining man and lived therefore within that restriction, would be unlikely to understand the finer shades of monetary emission. It seems quite reasonable to suppose that the class of persons hidden within the Aramaic speaking middle classes that permeated the whole Levant and Near East during the first Millennium B.C., and whose business was money and all that stemmed therefrom, in that they were interfering with that which clearly was a power to be exercised only by the very gods themselves, were scarcely likely to instruct their instrument, Peisistratus, therein. Therefore, it may be concluded, the tyrant rose because he was the one who had found favour with the

---

[279] Herodotus: *The Histories*, Book I.

all-pervading money power of the day. He was not money power itself!

In that most of the great public works of the Greek cities had been carried forward by the tyrants is the evidence; for as the secretive money power of today, world-wide in scope, thrives primarily upon government loans directed to purposes of war and the enormous spending that wars involve in order to strengthen their outrageous claims against the nations, in ancient days similar heavy spending had to be devised. In that day, as previously pointed out, a great Acropolis or some other such magnificent public work with whose construction and financial organization Money Power was fully conversant, sufficed equally well with war; which, all said and done, with hardy aggressive peoples could also prove considerable danger to themselves, or their purposes.

So, with the tyrant, we see the force by which Greece, previously living in natural order, was moulded to an instrument more suitable to those bankers: private money creative power, who, lurking in the shade as needs they had to, burned with rancour at the natural rulers who but treated them as stewards, although the essence of power for all that, lay in their hands for more than such rulers understood.

Thus were the simple and industrious and brave Greeks now raised up to be the new vehicle through which the final and destructive purposes of those controlling international bullion and slave trades would be achieved, as they shepherd the peoples of the world further down that road of no hope for themselves or the rest of mankind.

PERGAMUM AND PITANE

Aristotle, author of some lucid thinking on the subject of money, if not ruthlessly penetrative, was himself married to the niece of a banker installed as co-tyrant (or "Front Man") with another such tyrant-banker. "(Hermias the Tyrant of Assos and Atarneus) was a eunuch slave of a certain banker: he went to Athens and attended the lectures of Plato and Aristotle, and returning, he shared the tyranny of his master who had previously secured the places around Atarneus and Assos. Subsequently he succeeded him and sent for Aristotle and married his niece to him."[280]

.In this slave, banker, philosopher and despot Leaf[281] sees a tyrant who owed his position to his wealth. He quotes Euaion, the pupil of Plato, who, not far to the North at Lampsacus "lent money to the city on security of the Acropolis, and when the city defaulted, wanted to become a tyrant."[282]

While bankers in the present dream of entrapping the whole world via their "United Nations," in the past they contented themselves with the entrapping of a city! Just as in the present they create an entirely false picture of the nature of their operations and carefully promote the legend they are lending

---

[280] P.N. Ure, M.A.: *The Origins of Tyranny*, p. 280; New York; 1922.

[281] Walter Leaf: *The Journal of Hellenic Studies*. p. 167.

[282] *The Origins of Tyranny*, p. 281. In his footnote Dr. Ure remarks that Leaf might have gone on to quote the case of Timaeus the Cyzicene, who, like Euaion, and perhaps Hermias, had been a pupil of Plato: "Timaeus the Cyzicene having granted bonuses of money and corn to the citizens and having on that account won credit among the Cyzicenes as being a worthy man, after a short while made an attempt on the city by means of Aridias. *Athens* XI. 509a. footnote p. 281, *Origins of Tyranny*.

the public's money, so they did in antiquity, we may rest assured. No doubt they spread exactly the same story in the time of the tyrants, and people in that day, understanding no more about money than they do today, believed it.[283] The following may be accepted as instance of their activities in ancient times.

.Pergamum, that city that arose in South West Asia Minor, lasting as independent from 283-133 B.C., was originally founded as the fortified treasury of Lysimachus, successor to Alexander in Thrace. This fort and the treasure therein amounting to 9000 talents, was in the charge of a eunuch steward named Philetairos who justified the trust reposed in him in so far as the management of this treasure was concerned. During the quarrels of the *Diadochoi* or Successors to Alexander, presumably at the strategic moment, he transferred his allegiance from Lysimachus to Seleucus, doubtless on condition he be guaranteed his continued position as Master of the Treasury.

Despite the murder of Seleucus by Ptolemy Keraunus, the wily Philetairos clung to the fortunes of the Seleucids, probably understanding in their particular case, the political purposes of the International Money Power of Babylonia and Alexandria in these respects, and ingratiated himself with Antiochus, son of Seleucus, by buying the body of Seleucus from Ptolemy for return to Antiochus,[284] thus, through it all maintaining his position at Pergamum.

---

[283] "if the praetor gave the money as it is set down, he drew it from the qoaestor, the quaestor from the public bank, the public bank derived it either from revenue or tribute.". Which does not suggest that the great Cicero also had too much of an understanding of money: this was said over 2000 years ago. *Orationes*. Cicero. Book XIX, *Pro Flaccus*, p. 445. Vol. II, C.D. Yonge, B.A., Bell, London, 1883.

[284] P.N. Ure, M.A.: The Origins of Tyranny, p. 285.

Philetairos proceeded to use the treasure to which he had so masterfully established almost total right, with a skill which could only suggest training in the money shops of Babylonia, or Alexandria, or as close advisor, one so trained. The conception of the 9000 talents of treasure in itself being the sole maintaining force behind the extended power of Pergamum, would be quaint to say the least; as quaint indeed as the story of the 6000 talents of silver held in reserve in the Acropolis at Athens as the sole finances with which the Peloponnesian war was fought; or in a later day of the gold supposedly existing in the vaults of the Bank of England or its predecessor, and its parent bank, the Bank of Amsterdam (the vaults of the latter on inspection by Napoleon[285] after occupation of Holland, proving absolutely bare!). 9000 talents drawn on for military and civilian expenditures, extensive bribes, etc., would not go very far.

Returning again to Professor Andreades, in his *Finances De Guerre d'alexandre le grand*,[286] the annual expenditures of Alexander during the earlier years of his campaigning were 5000-7000 talents, which would, in the first year or two, certainly until the battle of Issus (Oct. 333 B.C.), have been in hard cash for the most part, to use the terminology of today's banker; that is, coined money or silver bullion, or the gold bullion of which the mines at Phillipi had made steady yield. In the later years of campaigning, Andreades estimated the annual expenditures of Alexander at 15,000 talents. If the money for this expenditure derived from coined precious metal plunder, it would go even less far, for in newly occupied territories, the exploitation of the miseries of the people usual to these circumstances would exist, and there would be a collapse of "Credit" or abstract money, until reorganization set in. There would be total disturbance of the revenues deriving from taxes.

---

[285] A. Andreades: *A History of the Bank of England*, p. 80; London; 1966.

[286] A. Andreades: *Annales D'histoire economique et sociale*, p. 330; Paris; 1929.

Silver, particularly, would either move eastward against luxury trading, which seems to continue as much as ever in such times, or would disappear into hoards.

During the first Millennium B.C., the ratio of silver to gold never went below 10:1, being usually 13:1 in Europe and the so-called Middle East. In farther Bactria, India and China, it was rarely more than 6:1 and in some parts as low as 1:1.[287] Therefore, once precious metal coinage was spent, particularly silver coinage, and passed into the hands of merchants, contractors, etc., finally returning to the bankers or money changers, with that field for assured profit by settlement of oriental trade balances with coined silver or silver bullion such as clearly existed, as according to Gresham's law,[288] its local circulating volume might be assumed to decrease rapidly, and without a doubt *did* so decrease.

It might safely be said that the money power which enabled Pergamum to secure controlling interest over the cities of Pitane and Cyzicus,[289] was not drawn from what might be left of that store of 9000 talents (the loan in the case of Pitane, probably a very minor transaction, was sufficient to substantially ease the burden of a debt of 380 talents). It would have been part of a credit inflation which would have used the 9000 talents, or the legend in respect thereto, as its base, and more than likely those interests holding the debt of the city of Pitane were themselves indebted by another ledger entry transaction to Pergamum. Thus that "Credit Money" transaction whereby pitane was loaned money would be no

---

[287] A. del Mar: *A History of Monetary Systems*, p. 505: Ratios.

[288] A. del Mar: *A History of Monetary Systems*. p. 355; New York; 1969. In the Maxims of Theognis (line 21) is stated: " nor will anyone take in exchange worse when better is to be had."

[289] P.N. Ure, M.A.: *The Origins of Tyranny*, p. 285; New York; 1922.

more than an entry in the books of pergamum as a credit to pitane, automatically being thence debited and transferred to the credit column of the holder of the loan as previously existing against pitane, and thus returning him to solvency.

In other words, Pergamum, at cost of pen, ink, vellum,[290] and slave scribe or perhaps (and more likely) cost of clay tablet and stylus book entry, was now in a position to dictate the political affairs of Pitane. Perhaps the agent for the Babylonian bankers or their Alexandrian counterparts, as the previous holder of the Pitane loan may have been, consequently recovered his liquid position so far as Pergamum was concerned, and was now able to look around again for more profitable investments.

The extent of the semi-military operations of the Attalid Money Power of Pergamum was shown above all by their purchase of the island of Aegina for thirty talents.[291] This island they most likely set up as a centre for entre-pôt trade and a financial outpost, i.e., "Branch Bank": which had to be in opposition to the decaying athenian money power which at that time did not have the silver resources of its earlier days on which to base its money power, and the legend of its great wealth.

The Laurion mines were petering out, and those markets in South Russia,[292] Thrace, etc., formerly supplied by Athenian manufactured products, were fast failing at the time of Pergamum and the Attalids; having set up their own local manufacturies. Athens, no longer centre of an Empire, neither military, or financial power, with fewer markets ready to settle debit trade balances with those slaves so much required for

---

[290] A. del Mar: *A History of the Precious Metals*, p. 105; New York; 1966.

[291] P.N. Ure, M.A.: *The Origins of Tyranny*, p. 285.

[292] Mikhail I. Rostovtsev: *A Social and Economic History of the Hellenistic World*, Page 108; Oxford; 1941.

silver mining, as had been South Russia, was likely just a pleasant place to live in; the storms brewed by settlement of International Money Power as in days gone by, passed over.

As Pergamum marks the beginning of that period when Delos and Rhodes were leading money and slave markets of the world, it would seem that some kind of agreement must have existed between those who controlled trade and finance at all these points.

Considering the essential secrecy that necessarily attends the corrupt operations of so-called bankers, it may be quite reasonable to suppose, that in Pergamum itself, in Aegina, Delos, Rhodes and for that matter, a dozen other trade centres, there was a class of persons who very well understood each other's interests, who very likely were related by racial and religious custom, and whose supra-nationalism transcended all city boundaries and borders of states.

Money was their trade, and they married only amongst their own group as the best protection towards maintaining inviolable the secret of that financial hegemony they had established internationally, and which in a way had put them above kingship; no doubt in the fevered imagination of some of them, one with the gods. Through the illusion of the establishment of silver as the standard of value internationally or nationally, and whose supply they totally controlled, it is true, they actually did wield that power which formerly had been the sole prerogative of the gods in the cities of ancient Sumeria, through their sons upon earth, the Priest-Kings; even if only as the venal and self-interested men that they were.

The activities of this group towards the instigation of wars, and disturbances never ceased. Out of the needs of peoples in despair came their advantage and strengthened control; and because they controlled the fiscal affairs of the temples, whose very existence became completely intertwined with their activities,[293] it may safely be said that they controlled the oracular pronouncements which so often could decide yea or nay to war. Out of rumour generally they guided the moods of the peoples. Such wars were necessary, as much as today, towards the maintenance of their great arms industry and their continued control through the sale of the best and newest of weapons to that new "conqueror" who promised most of all to serve their purposes in the renewal of their stocks of treasure, so necessary to maintain "confidence," and their stocks of mine slaves. war also revived that feverish and competitive demand for that treasure; and in the hurly-burly it created, merchants gladly accepted as money anything offered from seemingly reputable sources including that abstract money denoted by ledger credit page entry; the loan of which but cost the lender the entry by slave scribe on the clay tablet, though immense real wealth might be offered as "collateral" as against failure to repay such alleged loan by the date stipulated.

The far-flung activities of Apollonius, economic manager to Ptolemy Philadelphus, as recorded by Professor Rostovtsev,[294] give but a glimpse of this interlocking control by an Aramaic speaking middle class, within which the Hebrew may also have been an interwoven thread. Perhaps the weft, although not the weft and the warp.

For indeed there is no evidence that he was all, and that such magnates that controlled the economy of the ancient world were many of them Jews. Nevertheless the claim by the Universal Jewish Encyclopedia[295] that the Hebrews, as a people

---

[293] Oskar Seffert: *A Dictionary of Classical Antiquities*, p. 91; (Trans. a Nettleship, M.A., New York; 1904.)

[294] Mikhail I. Rostovtaev: *A Social and Economic History of the Hellenistic World*, p. 227, Vol. I.

[295] *Universal Jewish Encyclopedia*, p. 172, Vol. I.

who absorbed foreign cultures, yet rigidly maintain their national identity caused them to be most appreciated by the brilliant and ambitious Alexander, should not be lightly dismissed. Alexander was trainee of Aristotle, who, as husband of the niece of Hermias, Banker-Tyrant of Assos and Atameus, certainly should have come to learn something of the true meaning of Money Power. Alexander therefore, presumably had substantial understanding of the meaning of money relative to Kingship.

The Hebrew, as equally skilled in money and trade as the Aramean and equally fluent in Aramaic, since he was established in most of the important cities of the ancient world, from the Pillars of Hercules to India in which Aramaic, certainly existed as *lingua franca*, at least in those cities between India and the Levant, could very well have been a major part of that vehicle constructed by Alexander to spread his dream of Pan-Hellenism. His special concessions to Jaddua, High Priest in Jerusalem in 333 B.C. in respect to those Jews of both Judea and Babylon, and also in respect to the foundation of Alexandria,[296] certainly suggest deference to a power far beyond that power visibly represented by that relatively small group of people who dwelt at Jerusalem and on the highlands by which it was surrounded. According to the Universal Jewish Encyclopedia: during the siege of Tyre by Alexander, Jaddua, High Priest of Jerusalem, not wishing to offend Persia and Darius, had refused Alexander the troops and provisions he sought.[297] After the fall of Tyre, Alexander advanced on Jerusalem, ancient ally of Tyre as the assistance of Hiram, King of Tyre towards the building of the Temple of Solomon will

---

[296] *Ibid.*

[297] *Ibid.*

call to mind;[298] undoubtedly with the intention of reducing that city should no satisfactory settlement be reached.

As Alexander neared the Temple, so the story goes, the High Priest clothed in full vestments of gold and purple, and the Priests in their sacerdotal robes, and a great multitude dressed in white, went out to meet him, the decision having no doubt been arrived at that discretion was the better part of valour. Alexander, seeing the High Priest and his mitre on which was written the Name of God, reverenced the Name and saluted the High Priest. He said he had seen a figure such as the High Priest in a dream, who had told him he would give him Lordship over the Persian Hosts.

Then Alexander entered the city, and, as was his usual custom with submissive cities, he sacrificed to their God.

The fact that he gave the Jews of Palestine such special concessions as a years remission of taxes which was also extended to the Jews of Babylonia, and specially invited any Jew to settle in his city of Alexandria, would suggest that the visible help refused him by Jaddua had been more than made up for by assistance of a less visible nature such as, it might reasonably be expected, had helped to secure the fall of Babylon, to Cyrus, ancestor of Darius, and founder of the Achaemenid Dynasty of Persia.[299]

---

[298] *Chronicles*, Book II. Chapter 2.

[299] On this matter *The Universal Jewish Encyclopedia* reads: "The objection that alexander could have no interest in the Jews is answered by his own life and subsequent actions. An astute statesman of penetrating vision, alexander was quick to grasp the indispensable value of the Jews in the cultural, political and intellectual sphere of his world empire. Alexander's aim was the synthesis of Occidental and Oriental cultures into the mould of Hellenism; undoubtedly he appreciated the capacity of the Jews to absorb foreign culture, while rigidly maintaining their national identity thus making them an

The stress on the Aramaic speaking middle class of all those "Empires" from the assyrian, until the successors to alexander, and perhaps beyond, is more than justified in view of the results of the studies of various scholars. if aramaic was the language of officialdom under the achaemenid rulers of the persian empire, and remained so under alexander and the successors, it may reasonably be supposed that the official and merchant classes that used aramaic as their everyday language, had gone far beyond the borders of the persian empire, both to the east and to the west. as has been previously pointed out, with that aramaic interstratum moved also to the east and west, the agents of that money power centred in mesopotamia, heir to the secrets, not only of the sumerian priesthood, but of the priesthood of much more ancient times, selling as they went along the idea of the use of precious metal money.

No sooner had short sighted rulers instituted the use of precious metal money, than the agents of such money power, to whom by now the ruler was beholden for supplies of bullion, were setting up "modern" banking houses. in short order the various practices of dubious legality that are the foundations of such money power would be instituted; firstly that of the creation, relatively without limit, of abstract units of exchange as through the institution of ledger credit page entry money, under whatever cover to create legality, and which the banker claimed was backed by his "Credit"!--(As if he could have more "Credit" than any sovereign people and their ruler!)-

---

ideal vehicle for his civilizing enterprise. As Jews were already an International commercial power, numbers of them being found in most countries of Alexander's domain, he granted them many political privileges when he founded Alexandria, and even gave them a portion of Samaria with exemption from taxes in order to gain their support. It is even possible that alexander had first heard of the jews from his teacher, aristotle who, according to the report of josephus, had met a jew who was a veritable philosopher and a "Greek" not only in language but in soul." *Universal Jewish Encyclopedia*, p. 172. Vol. I.

-and which was usually backed in final analysis by little or nothing other than the sanction of a foolish prince. Secondly, from the point of view of maintenance of "confidence" so far as lesser trade was concerned, was the issue of intrinsically valueless facsimiles of existing precious metal coinage, for every one of which a customer who accepted them in the exchanges, thought that there was a precious metal original lodged in the local temple or acropolis.

To our Lord Jesus Christ, Aramaic was the everyday language that would have enabled Him to travel, and converse freely with scholar, poet, priest, and merchant, certainly as far East as Peshawar. Aramaic is used in the Syrian Christian Church, in the Jewish liturgy, and still lives in the villages of the Anti-Lebanon, in South East Anatolia, and on the Eastern shores of Lake Urmia in Armenia.[300]

Thus the opinion of Emil G.H. Kraeling[301] that the Aramean was the vehicle by which the so called eternal values of Hellas and Israel were communicated throughout the Orient, in a way concurs with the Opinion of the Jewish Encyclopedia referred to above.[302] That those values denoted by Hellas withered and almost disappeared, while those as denoted by Israel through Christianity, flourished until relatively recently, is merely further proof that money power must destroy the body on which it feeds, and is nourished, and the body it fed on at the time herein recorded, that is, immediately after Alexander, was Hellas, and indeed, Israel itself. It cannot flourish alongside blind belief and simple faith which instinctively tear off its impudent claims as they gnaw their way into the very heart of the Tree of Life.

---

[300] Peter Bamm: *Alexander the Great; Power as Destiny.* p. 72. London; 1968.

[301] Emil G.H Kraeling: *Aram and Israel*, p. 1.

[302] Present work.

Nevertheless, out of Babylonian money power itself, oblivious it seems to its own real self interest, carrying Christianity as far as those limits unto which its total hegemony prevailed, Christianity itself rose as an island of love and goodness in an ocean of hatred, confusion, greed, and depravity that had come to exist as the ultimate result of at least three thousand years of the depredations of such private money creative power. With one convulsive shrug it threw off the snake like coils, reestablishing thereafter the natural order of life, of god, priest-king and priesthood and the people, all living as was ordained, with faith, piety, and sure belief. Thereafter, for a thousand years, International Money Power can only be faintly discerned, as a smouldering ember; a fire not entirely extinguished; evidence thereof being an occasional wisp of smoke as it waited for a day when a certain evil wind might blow, and flames come forth again to deal man total woe.

VOICES FROM THE DUST

Before ever the lust seized the Greeks for the precious metal pieces on which were recorded their laws in respect to the unit of exchange; that is, before Greece became completely thrall to the international bullion and slave interests, money had existed among them in various forms for a long time previously.[303] Little knowledge remains of such systems of exchange as existed prior to the assumption of international bullion and slave interests of total hegemony over a great deal of Greece, but exist such systems did, and the significance of its monetary units issued against state expenses, and as opposed to issue by private persons as against collateral security, was understood, as the evidence of the Sparta of Lycurgus indicates.

On this subject Babelon, French Numismatist of the 19th Century says: "Having established the existence of these salmons or spits of iron that were the circulating money of the Pewloponnese, it will be easy for us to define clearly the part played by this prince (Pheidon). He was not inventor of money, but the same as Servius Tullius, a reformer. He introduced into the Peloponnese a definite system of weights and measures, instead of the numerous systems that had thrown confusion and disorder into commercial relations; he adapted the weight of the new money to the new system of weights, and he officially abolished the old and cumbersome iron money, of which he consecrated several samples in the Temple at Argos."[304]

---

[303] See present work..

[304] Après avoir bien constaté l'existence avant Pheidon, de ces saumons ou broches de fer qui était la monnaie courant de Peloponnes, il nous sera facile

Numismatists airily dismiss the suggestions of the symbols of money as being indicated in ancient times on leather, wood, or baked clay, which are found in both Cedrenus, Suidas, and Seneca,[305] but study of so-called primitive currencies of today, such as the shell moneys of Oceania, leave little doubt that our forefathers, fully understanding of the true philosophy of money, may very well have used such intrinsically valueless materials to record the values of their tangible money, prior to the commencement of precious metal coinage; in the same way as the Melanesians and Micronesians have used shells for such purpose, from time immemorial.[306]

There can be no doubt that those social organizations such as existed prior to the establishment of precious metals as a standard by which values were assessed, were often, in the case of the Northern Mediterranean and Anatolia, erected on a structure, of which integral part was system of exchange constructed according to the teachings of such philosophy.

However, that the numismatists dismiss the significance of such money and question it as having ever existed, is not surprising considering that they merely record the money towards the creation of which the controllers of bullion

---

de définir nettement le rôle de ce prince. Il ne fut pas l'inventeur de la monnaie mais seulement, comme servius tullius, un réformateur. il introduisit dans le péloponnèse un système fixé des poids et mesures, a la place des systèmes multiples qui jetaient la confusion et la désordre dans les relations commerciales; il adapta le poids des nouvelles monnaie au systèmes pondéral nouveau; il demoneta et aboli officiellement la vieille et encombrante monnaie de fer dont il consacra quelques échantillons dans le temple d'Argos". *Les Origines de la Monnaie*, p. 211, Ernest Babelon, Paris, 1897.

[305] François Lenormant: *La Monnaie dans l'antiquité*, pp. 215-216, Book II, Tome I.

[306] Kingston-Higgins & Paul Einzig: *A Survey of Primitive Money* and *Primitive Money*, respectively.

supplied the material; thus in a way controlling its issue and such order of society as it gave rise to, and therefore the numismatists themselves. Consequently the dismissal by the numismatists of other materials for money and its symbols, not internationally desirable or controllable by their masters might be expected.

According to Professor Fritz Heichelheim in his *Ancient Economic History*, Suidas ascribes the monetary use of leather and "ostrakina" (pieces of shell and pottery) to the romans previous to numa pompilius. shells appear on the coins of magna graecia, especially those of tarentum, which may be an indication that shell money was known in the italy[307] of historical memory, at that time. Oyster shells discovered by Heinrich Schlieman in the Royal graves at Mycenae together with obsidian weapons, indicate that in an age when obsidian weapons were still in use, also remained respect for certain shells that in former times had been evincement of stored wealth.[308] But equally as any other, such a currency only had value insomuch as it carried with it the will of the ruler.

In the Hittite language there are many words almost identical to their counterpart in Latin:[309]

Troy fell to the Greeks under Agamemnon in 1250 B.C. according to the modern dating and the opinion of Herodotus. That Troy was the outpost of the Hittite empire that controlled the Dardanelles, and that the rulers of Troy spoke a Hittite language, is reasonable supposition.[310] The destruction of Bog-

---

[307] Fritz Heichelheim: *An Ancient Economic History*, p. 478, Vol. I.

[308] Robert Payne: *The Gold of Troy*, p. 199.

[309] Christopher Dawson: *The Age of the Gods*, p. 255.

[310] The kings of the dynasty ruling in Lydia until 689 B.C., or Phrygia as it may then have been, of which Myrsilus (or Candaules) was the last, mostly

Haz Koi, the Hittite capital is now accepted as being 1225 B.C. This event, which could only have taken place as the result of investment by experienced, disciplined, and well organized forces, with an excellent engineering corps, considering that so many well walled cities had fallen before them, brought the Hittite world to fragmentation.[311]

Therefore during the years from the time of the crossing of the Dardanelles and the sack of Troy, to the time of the total collapse that must have followed the destruction of Bog-Haz Koi, refugees would have sought freedom by sailing westward, which direction it seems was the only way to go. To the North and North-West were the "Peoples of the Sea," to the south-east was Assyria, obviously ally of the same "Peoples of the Sea," and to the south, Ugarit and Alalakh were empty ruins, and the coast to the sinai border occupied by the enemies of the hittites.

Therefore it seems reasonable that the legend of the settlement of Aeneas, refugee from Troy in the territory of Latinus as recorded by Livy[312] the same as most legends, had a basis of fact. This is further shown by the close resemblance between

---

bore Hittite names. According to Del Mar in his *History of Monetary Systems*, p. 41, the Phrygian (or Lydian) chronicles extend back to 1300 B.C. (when Bog-Haz Koi and Troy still existed). According to Professor W.F. Albright (*The Amarna Letters from Palestine, Cambridge Ancient History*, Vol. II; p. 43.), "The Hittites had established several vassal states in northern Syria." "At least two of them, Carchemish and Aleppo, were ruled by princes of the imperial Hittite dynasty. In a third state, Khattina, the reigning princes still bore names derived from imperial Hittite history as late as the ninth century B.C."

[311] Although the fall of Bog-Haz Koi undoubtedly ended forever the system of empire over which the kings of the Kheta presided, fragments established local autonomy thereafter. Such fragments were the state of Khattina above mentioned and the cities of Marqasi, and Carchemish.

[312] Livy; Book I.

the Hittite, Trojan, Latin languages as pointed out above. According to Dawson[313] the production of leather in the Hittite world was a state monopoly. Such monopoly of leather production would suggest the possibility, if not the likelihood of leather as the material on which the symbols of their money were recorded.

For any state to be as strong as indeed was the Hittite state for a relatively long period of time, and, moreover, stable, it had to control, not merely the issue of the unit of exchange, but also the material of which its visible symbols were made; which, of course had to be total monopoly. The fact that the Hittite state appears to have been one constructed to the same order as those early Mesopotamian cities, that is, of God, Priest-King and priesthood and the devoted living in natural order, makes this deduction the more likely.

The similarity of language, together with the legend relative to Troy would certainly suggest the forefathers of the patricians of Rome derived from Northern Anatolia, and therefore from within the Hittite (or Bog-Haz Koi) sphere of influence. If so, would it not be natural for them to reinstitute the same monetary system amongst themselves as they had known in their homelands?

The numismatists and historians date the *Aes Grave*, considered by them to be the first true metallic currency of Rome, from 338 B.C.[314] accepting the opinion of Professor Haeberlin.[315] What then did Rome use for money prior to that date considering the relatively exact property valuations and taxes of

---

[313] Christopher Dawson: *Age of the Gods*, p. 304; London; 1928.

[314] E.J. Haeberlin: *Aes Grave*; Frankfurt; 1910.

[315] Accepting the opinion of Mommsen however, the *Aes Grave* dates from 454 B.C.-430 B.C. *Manuel Des Antiquités Romaines*. Tome X. Paris; 1888.

Servius? That they used rough lumps of copper (*Aes Rude*) as everyday money, cannot be accepted. There is no vestige of a doubt that a refined system existed by no means unrelated to the exchange systems definitely known to have existed in Greece, and in which a form of "Credit," too often a privately created abstract money, was made use of. This system may have been no more related to silver bullion, than it may have been to any other commodity, and international silver bullion interests would exercise no definite control therein.

There would be no reason whatsoever to discredit Suidas' remarks in respect to leather and clay money previous to Numa Pompilius. The clay "scarabs" still being unearthed in Etruria may very well represent evidence of the clay units. Leather money of course would long since have perished. nor is there reason to think that the fiduciary money of clay undoubtedly issued by the bankers of athens in the 5th Century B.C.,[316] was in anyway a new idea. As throughout the Near East clay was the principal medium for the keeping of records, the use of clay money follows naturally, and might well be expected in Etruria or wherever the agents of the Babylonian or Greek bankers traded; the clay coin itself also being record; a tangible evincement of the creation of a unit of exchange, or divisible or multiple thereof.

According to Livy, relative to the financing of the cavalry of Rome of the Kings: "Each century had a grant from the treasury of 10.000 *aeses* for the purchase of horses, with a further grant levied on rich widows of 2000 a year for their feeding and maintenance."[317]

---

[316] François Lenormant: *La Monnaie dans l'Antiquité*, p. 66, Book II, Tome I.

[317] Livy: Book I; (Aubrey de Selincourt: *An Early History of Rome*, p. 66; London; 1960).

If then there was neither minted silver or copper at the time of Servius, are we to understand that the rich widows came to the treasury with bags of pieces of rough copper?[318]

Where taxes withdraw units of exchange from circulation, there must be a force which injects such units of exchange into the circulation. What therefore was the source of such units of exchange or moneys as were injected into the circulation in order that the people of Rome of the kings might estimate their *worth* with some exactitude and according to a certain standard? Clearly there is no reason to doubt this record of Livy.

In the Panadects of Justinian, Tenth Book, occurs this remarkable passage from Julius Paulus, jurisconsul of the third century of our era:

"The origin of buying and selling began with exchange. Anciently money was unknown and there existed no terms by which merchandise could be precisely valued but everyone according to the times and circumstances, exchanged things useless to him against things which were useful; for it commonly happens that one is in need of what another has in excess. But as it seldom coincided in time that what one possessed, the other one wanted, or conversely, a device was chosen whose legal and permanent value remedied by its homogeneity the difficulties of barter. This device being officially promulgated, circulated, and maintained its purchasing power, not so much from its substance as from its quantity. Since that time only one consideration in an exchange was called merchandise, the other was called price."

Whether those devices such as governed the exchanges of early Rome and Etruria were clay or leather or wood does not really

---

[318] The *Aes Rude*.

matter. As such they were true money being intrinsically valueless, and only of value because of that law which ordered their acceptance in the exchanges and that they be of value as according to their scarcity or otherwise relative to the goods and services for sale. What would above all matter would be the ease with which they could be counterfeited, no doubt the source of their ultimate failure, and whether they were loaned into circulation by private persons against so-called collateral, or paid into circulation as against government expenses, as were the *Aes Grave* at a later date.

This fragment from Paulus repeating the words of a commonwealth scholar of whose work even then little remained, did no more than express the opinions of all the philosophers-scholars of antiquity, at least, those of whom record exists. Almost all of them wrote of numerical or fiduciary systems of money as being the only natural systems. None of them, however entered into discussion as to whether issuance should be as against state indebtedness. It was so obviously a necessity for good order and well-being in life, that such discussion never seems to have occurred to them. The success of private monetary emission in this day and its boldness now that its former criminal activities are recognized and accepted as inevitable, such men could not even imagine, not even Aristotle, who it is certain by reason of his family connections, must have known something of the undercurrents of the financial world as it existed at that time.

Aristotle, Plato, Socrates, Zeno, all seemed to have been clear on the subject, and all lived at a time when fiduciary systems were still in existence, both in the Greek states although there is little record, and elsewhere.[319] Plato was most clear on the subject and no doubt had studied the numerical system that

---

[319] Augustus Boeckh: *The Public Economy of Athens*, Vol. I; p. 43; London; 1828.

had obtained at Sparta not long before when he was a young man. Living between 429 B.C. and 347 B.C., he must have been at Athens during the Peloponnesian War when such system certainly must still have existed in Sparta, or have been a recent memory; even if, as seems most likely, as a result of the war, it had been replaced by the Athenian system of private money issue based on the fiction of precious metals or valuables in reserve. As Aeschines, also pupil of Plato was conversant with that fiduciary system of Carthage,[320] it is more than likely that Plato was so instructed. As no coinage in precious metal was struck at Carthage itself until 340 B.C.,[321] it may reasonably be supposed that at the time of writing *The Laws*, either 348 B.C. or 349 B.C., there would have been Carthaginian agents at Athens, well able to explain their monetary system to enquirers. On the subject Plato wrote:

"Further the Law (of the ideal Republic) enjoins that no private individual shall possess or hoard gold and silver bullion, but have money only for domestic use, such as is necessary for dealing with artisans and servants, sojourners and slaves. Wherefore our citizens should have a money current amongst themselves but not acceptable to the rest of mankind. For foreign expeditions, journeys, embassies, the expense of heralds (abroad) and such matters, the government must also possess a fund of coins in other states. When an individual needs to go abroad, let him obtain the consent of the Archon and go; but

---

[320] According to Aeschines: "The Carthaginians make use of the following kind of money; in a small piece of leather a substance is wrapped of the size of a piece of 4 drachmae (3s); but what this substance is no one knows except the maker. After this is sealed and issued for circulation; and he who possesses the most of this is regarded as having the most money, and as being the wealthiest man. But if any one amongst us had ever as much, he would be no richer than if he possessed a quantity of pebbles." (A.J. Church: *Carthage*, pp. 122-123; New York; 1914.)

[321] R.A.G. Carson: *Coins, Ancient, Medieval, and Modern*, p. 75; London; 1962.

on his return if he has any such money remaining let him deposit it in the treasury and receive an equivalent sum in local money. If he is discovered to have concealed it, let it be confiscated, and let him who knows and does not inform, be subject to anathema and dishonour equally with him who brought the money, and also to a fine not less in amount than that of the universal money which had been brought back."[322]

Gathering together further fragments of evidence we see that Aristotle less than 400 years after Pheidon of Argos, made comment: "Numisma (Money) by itself is a mere device which has value only by law (Nomos) and not by nature; so that a change of convention between those who use it, is sufficient to deprive it of value and its power to satisfy our wants."[323]

In *The Ethics*, Aristotle states further: "By virtue of voluntary convention, Nomisma has become the media of exchange. We call it Nomisma because its efficacy is due, not to nature but to Nomos (Law) and because it is always in our power to control it."[324]

Thus despite at least four hundred years of control of trade by the masters of precious metal bullion, the scholars still clearly understood the actuality of money and that it was an evincement of the law. They still understood it was but so many numbers injected into a circulation amongst the people relating value to value, and not in any way influenced by the material on which these numbers as laws were recorded. The scholars must, however, have been aware that in the case of these laws being recorded on precious metal, if the convention in respect to the value of the unit of exchange was changed, so

---

[322] Plato: *The Laws*, Book V.

[323] Aristotle: *The Politics*, I, 9.

[324] Aristotle: *The Ethics*, V, 5.

far as financial houses with facilities for smelting and export of bullion were concerned, there was no loss. If the change in convention was disadvantageous to such holder of precious metal coin, such coin could be reduced to bullion and quietly exported to that country offering the most advantage to holders of such bullion.

To say that money as such began with the striking of precious metal coinage is therefore incorrect. The statement that an international control over money came about as a result of a certain group of private persons, members of which were located in all major states of the world, creating a monopoly of those precious metals of which its symbols were coming to be made, or, better put, on which they were imprinted, would be more to the point.

The evidence that the earliest coinages in Greece had essentially a local circulation in no way alters the picture previously outlined of silver money as being part of an international conspiracy. All Greek states apart from Athens and Samos, Siphnos and Corcyra, and possibly one or two others, had to obtain silver bullion for their coinage from abroad, which necessarily obliged them to deal with those traders who specialized in dealing in bullion. Such trade in bullion had to be in the hands of a small and highly secretive group, as much on account of the sources of supply being relatively few and scattered as it were out to the ends of the earth, as on account of the fact that it would be only such a group that could also control those supplies of slave labour and their purchase from triumphant peoples whose warlike activities, as likely as not, they had instigated themselves; slave labour so necessary to the success of their mining operations.

For example, the fact that the Carthaginian mines of Spain show no signs of even the use of the ordinary propping and shoring associated with mining,[325] cannot but indicate that the miners were most likely captives of war from distant parts, purchased for a song from a victorious general, and driven under threat of the lash.

At that period it would appear, such labour was so plentiful that the cost of purchase of new slaves, would have been less than the cost of ordinary safety precautions. The silver mines of Spain as worked by the Romans, show interestingly enough an entirely different story.[326] All safety methods, including the use of concrete, were used; which also agrees with the fact that Rome, even when silver money was in use, particularly in foreign trade, so far as internal exchanges were concerned, had a relatively ample supply of money for the details of day to day organization in the overvalued bronze fiduciaries, the most grandiose *aes* and its parts or multiples.[327]

History has proven over and over again that a precious metal coinage will move one way or another to where it might realize the most profit either as coin or bullion. The so-called law of the economists known as Gresham's law states just that: "Bad money drives out the good." which means that the silver in circulating would be replaced by that less intrinsically valuable money, if such also circulated, and which the economists described as "the bad," (the question of course being bad for whom?); such silver being hoarded and exported to whatever market offered the best price or advantage.

---

[325] A. del Mar: *A History of Money in Ancient Countries*, p. 323; London; 1885.

[326] Ibid.

[327] According to Harold Mattingly, (*Roman Coins*, p. 53): "The bronze coinage of rome was the original coinage of the land; it always served the home market and played little part in rome's expansion abroad. It is perhaps not surprising then that it resisted change more persistently than the *world currency* of the denarius." (Italics by present author.)

Cases of wider application of this so-called law are without number, and as much as of application to a lesser degree. A few outstanding ones are:

a. The disappearance of silver from Athens and its replacement by baked clay facsimiles during the 5th Century B.C. and by yellowish copper (or orichalcum) at the end of the same century.

b. The drain of silver from Rome during the late commonwealth and the early Empire, particularly to the Orient,[328] where the ratio varied around 6:1 to gold as compared to that established by Caesar of 12:1, and its replacement by bronze or orichalcum fiduciaries.

c. The drain of English silver coinage to India after the act of 1666.[329] Such silver being replaced by the "Bad" money of the goldsmith's receipts and the Bank of England notes and ledger credit page entries.

d. The disappearance of the silver roubles in Russia[330] during the 18th Century almost as soon as they left the mint, their place being taken by the "Bad" money of the copper roubles, and, later, after catherine, by the "Bad" money of the paper roubles (assignats).

e. The almost complete disappearance from the circulation between the years 1967-1973 of silver coins of our own country of Canada: such silver being replaced by coins fabricated from base metal alloys, relative to the silver coins, without intrinsic value.

---

[328] Both Cicero (*Pro Flaccus; Orationes*; Book XXVIII), and Pliny (*Naturalis Historia*, xii, c.18), make mention of this flow of silver Eastward.

Cicero says that gold moved Eastward to the temple at Jerusalem. This may also have been so.

[329] A. del Mar: *Barbara Williers or a History of Monetary Crimes*; pp. 8-44.

[330] A. del Mar: *Money and Civilization*, p. 303; London; 1886.

Returning to Ancient Greece, Professor Heichelheim states: "Such hoards as found previous to 560 B.C. are found in the areas in which they were minted and never in other countries."[331] Which fact indicates that prior to 560 B.C. it is probable that laws governing the export of coin were strictly enforced in Greece. Any silver that left a state would do so covertly as bullion. The following Athenian Edict is evidence that such laws existed: "Let no Athenian or sojourner lend money to be exported unless (to pay) for corn or some such commodity allowed by Law."[332]

By the time of Plato, something less than two hundred years later the real weaknesses of precious metal systems of coinage were beginning to show, hence the increasing discussion of the matter of money in the schools of philosophy, although such discussion does not seem to have given rise to any vigorous action by the Grecian States. The establishment of the *Aes Grave* system at Rome may have been a direct result of such discussion, and the establishment of this numerical coinage of bronze certainly bears close resemblance to that internal coinage as recommended by Plato for the ideal Republic.[333] By the date generally accepted as the commencement of the *Aes Grave* system, that is 338 B.C., Roman scholars would have been fully aware of the teachings of Plato. This city state, already stirred by consciousness of its world destiny, would have neglected no instrument towards the maintenance of morale and strength in the structure of its internal life. Such an instrument was the *Aes Grave* system in which the national money was paid into circulation by the state, and only of value insomuch as the symbols on which its numbers were recorded, were scarce or otherwise.

---

[331] Fritz Heichelheim: *An Ancient Economic History*, p. 251; Vol. I.

[332] Potter: *Antiquities of Greece*.

[333] Plato: *The Laws*, Book V.

The weaknesses inherent in precious metal coinage systems as becoming apparent in the time of Plato were as follows:

    a. The coins wore out or were hoarded out of circulation.

    b. Hard rock mining was never profitable without slave labour so far as the Master Miner was concerned.[334]

    c. The mine slaves died and sometimes, there being no wars, they could not be replaced so easily.

    d. The mines themselves became exhausted.

    e. In a time of national calamity, when coinage was most of all needed, it disappeared into hoards, largely held by foreigners, members of that secret class of persons to whom wars were but opportunity to drive harder bargains yet again, with mankind and his states and peoples.

    f. Even in time of peace, captains and merchants, if permitted, were ever seeking a cargo for their return trip. If such cargo was not available, they would take away their balances in precious metals or slaves.

A country such as Greece, by no means rich agriculturally as was the Egyptian Delta, yet having a relatively large population to feed, in its declining days would usually have an unfavourable balance of trade; which further, despite laws to the contrary, drained away its precious metal coinage or bullion. At the time of Plato, this condition must have been really showing and its significance.

The Laureion mines were petering out despite the agitation by Xenophon for the Government of Athens to purchase ten

---

[334] W. Jacob: *An Historical Enquiry into the Production and Consumption Metals*. Del Mar, quoting from this book, gives a most reasonable analysis of the apparent loss associated with the working of the silver mines of New Carthage in Spain, by the Carthaginians. (A. del Mar: *History of the Precious Metals*, p. 68.)

thousand slaves to lease to mine owners,[335] (presumably to be obtained from his financial sponsors), and where in days gone by there had been considerable silver circulating at Athens particularly, now it had become scarce and there was an insufficiency.

The numerous clay facsimiles of Eastern Mediterranean coinages, still being found at Athens,[336] show that the foreign bankers, in accordance with Gresham's so-called law, were quietly filling the void now appearing with issues of a fiduciary character such as our paper money, exemplified in their case by the baked clay facsimiles mentioned by lenormant which the bankers clearly were injecting into circulation to their own private account, and, of course, that of their most useful greek agents. This would be effected by pointing out to a customer to whom the banker was prepared to make a loan, how much safer the actual silver would be if left with the banker's reserve in the Acropolis where it would be guarded by the gods themselves, and how these clay facsimiles which all the customers were accepting, could always be redeemed in silver if really necessary. (!)[337]

---

[335] Xenophon: *A Discourse upon improving the Revenues of the State of Athens*, (Pages 317-322, *The Political and Commercial Works of Charles Davenant LLD*; 1771)

[336] François Lenormant: *La Monnaie dans l'Antiquité*, pp. 215-216, Book II, Tome I. Several Athenian and Corinthian residents have these clay coins in their possession (N. Boucara of Corinth).

[337] In London 2000 years later, when the goldsmiths operated exactly the same "racket," the confidence of the public was gained through the connivance, witting or unwitting, of the Royal House, and the storage of the goldsmiths reserves in the Tower of London. The fact of their being in the Tower offered the same sanctity to the goldsmith's practice of issuing receipts as against non-existing reserves, i.e., fraudulent receipts, as had been offered to similar practice in ancient times by the undoubted storage of the reserves of the *trapezitae* in the Acropolis. In either case to encourage the

Seltsman in *Greek Coins*[338] says that about this period, following the complete collapse of the Athenian Empire, Athens resumed its previous financial activities through the growth of powerful "Banks," such as that of pasion which operated in all major Greek cities, providing a money market for all of the Greek world. however, seltsman makes no mention of abstract expansions of the monetary unit, nor of the clay facsimiles which were the tangible evincement of such expansion, and whose power to inspire confidence was the main source of that renewed financial activity, and whose existence and purpose was defined by françois lenormant, even if somewhat diffidently. (p. 27, present work.)

What Seltsman really points out to us in stressing that Athens resumed its previous financial activities with powerful banks such as that of Pasion operating in all major Greek cities, is the correctness of our previous conjecture that the real underlying purposes of the "Great" peloponnesian war was to establish private common money market across the greek world totally controlled by the *trapezitae* or bankers in modern terminology. Banks, too, could not thrive and realize full potential except that government was become their instrument, and that Government, the creator of the laws of the land, was in their debt, as according to these same laws of the land, as much as private citizens. The foundation of this god-power, to which, as a result of the utter exhaustion of Athens and Sparta, and the death of their noblest, there were none to offer resistance, was government borrowing of the banker's fictitious "Credit" money; and although there may be little evidence of such in athens at that time, it is clear that this situation had been brought about. the frantic efforts of the athenian government

---

circulation of his receipts, he could plead the difficulties and the dangers of the formalities attached to withdrawal of the metal itself for the purpose of settlement of an account.

[338] Charles Seltsman, M.A.: *Greek Coins*, p. 179; London; 1933.

after the war to devise methods to stimulate increase of government spending, such as the donatives and the theorica, while at the same time devising methods to withdraw money from the public circulation, such as by sales tax,[339] reveal that Athenian Government was now more firmly than ever in the hands of International Money Power, if Sparta was but now rearrived there after absence of three hundred years or so.[340]

Both Athens and Sparta were in no better a position than they were before the war. Neither one had won and neither one had lost. Both lay exhausted, and over their prostrate bodies the servants of this same sardonic Money Power drew the chains of their slavery.

Although Seltsman says the source of the renewal of the prosperity of Athens was the new markets in Cyrene, Chalcidice, and South Russia, Rostovtsev points out that the South Russian market, the most important of all, was closing due to local manufactures, and in the fourth century, Attic and Ionian imports disappear entirely in South Russia,[341] where, in the sixth and fifth centuries they had been extensive.[342] According to Rostovtsev, at Athens during the fourth century B.C., both population and unemployment increased, prices rose, and there was so-called "class struggle" and discontent.[343]

Increase in prices is usually indicative of increase of the number of monetary units in circulation, that is, of the money supply relative to goods and services for sale. Unemployment would

---

[339] Royal Ontario Museum Display.

[340] From the time of the Institution of the Financial Reforms of Lycurgus.

[341] Mikhail I. Rostovtsev: *A Social and Economic History of the Hellenistic World*, p. 108; Vol I, Oxford; 1941.

[342] *Ibid.* p. 106.

[343] *Ibid.* p. 108.

not cancel out such increase in the money supply; for money had to be created for the Donatives and *theorica* which belong to this time. Herein is further proof of some artificial and invisible growth of the monetary unit. So while the markets for Greek agricultural and industrial products had shrunk considerably, and were no more able to absorb the goods that were being offered to them by Greece,[344] money was still being created, in Athens particularly, and being put into circulation as against "Free Bread and Circuses," such as indeed were the donatives and theorica; consequently causing inflation and the rise of prices of record. considering the findings of professor rostovtsev as being more likely than those of seltsman, it is clear that what athens exported, and possible some other cities in greece where such as pasion had branches, was, after the "Great" peloponnesian war, privately created capital.[345] Thus in what we know of as Antiquity, the full meaning of the unit of exchange as a purely abstract conception, regardless of what material it was recorded on for the purposes of day to day exchanges, was clearly understood; and without a doubt this

---

[344] *Ibid.* p. 104.

[345] Perhaps an internationally functioning unit like the Euro-Dollar, originating from that form of ledger entry money known as the "swap" deposit. While doing the world's business, relative to the work it does, it bears little relationship to the workings of the originating financial system. Such "swap" deposit money, although it will buy a loaf of bread or, at the other end of the scale, a ship, and therefore is money as much as any other kind of money, originates free of control of governments or central banks. Such Euro-currencies "can expand by the process of money creation without infusions from oil nations or payments deficits." Clearly they largely exist more as a special convenience to a certain group of people whose "business" is manipulating world currencies, and therefore prices, for their own needs and profit without reference to the good or authority of the state that permits the generating of such externally circulating monetary units, or to the good of its peoples. For a detailed explanation of the Euro-Dollar see *Report of the Royal Commission on Banking and Finance*. pp. 138-140; Ottawa; 1964.

knowledge was inheritance from ancient days, long before the advent of exchanges based on silver by weight.

Judging by Sparta, perhaps some of the Greek states mentioned by Boeckh,[346] and later by Rome itself, it seems that in ancient times there was some considerable understanding of the power inherent in precious metal money to destroy, by lending itself to manipulation, the *status quo* of any race or state. The tremendous possibilities inherent in its use as the material on which the visible units of money were recorded towards the manipulation of prices and the consequent monopolization of wealth which always derived therefrom, through the process of loan against collateral security inflating the money supply, and giving rise to the seeming prosperity of great activity, followed by the "calling" of such loans, under one excuse or another, when the resultant prosperity was at its height, was well understood by the "Bankers." Also was known how to create periods of "lack of confidence," during which prices fell to less than the previous cost of manufacture, and when consequently manufacturers became disheartened, and were glad to sell out to anyone to whom the banker directed them for whatever they could get. That is, if they were lucky. If they were not quite so lucky, then their stock and factory would be seized as against the supposed debt, and sold at auction. No doubt such auctions were rigged in ancient times, just as much as they often are today.

Those states previously mentioned, understanding therefore the evils of private emission of precious metal money, and that precious metal money must always be private money emission, except the state owns the mines, and takes absolutely total precaution to prevent the export of its metal except by its own decision as against its own needs, clearly, when all other states

---

[346] Augustus Boeckh: *The Public Economy of Athens*, Vol. I; p. 43; London; 1828.

and princes were succumbing to the world drive of the international bankers, rejected banking as such, and the bullion brokers its founders. It was not until the 4th Century B.C. that they finally gave in, to what was undoubtedly an unremitting pressure, and this more likely as a result of the conquests of, firstly, the Achaemenid Princes of Persia, and secondly, the conquests of Alexander.

After Alexander there do not seem many states left in which precious metal money did not constitute the circulating medium, and therefore could not be influenced by the activities of that secret and international group of people who made the so-called Gresham's Law very much of a reality to the undoing of rulers and their peoples.

The sequence of "Boom" and "Bust" just as in today, can be traced as follows:

In the first place bankers and their agents no doubt worked together to cause this money, which it may safely be said, originally cost them no more than entry by slave scribe on the clay tablet, to be seemingly plentiful. As a result, business flourished, wages increased and prices rose. This rise in prices ultimately caused a situation in which foreign merchandise sold competitively on the home market. In consequence some home manufacturers, unable to compete, went into bankruptcy. The panic thus created amongst manufacturers beholden to the banks, prepared them for the inevitability of the likelihood of demand by their bank for repayment of loans outstanding. By now the bankers were telling everyone that Times were bad. "There was a freeze in Credit." and "No Money about". so when such loans were "Called," the manufacturers dutifully hunted up all the silver they could find, and if they were able, paid off the banker. when this collapse of industry, and consequently prices, reached a certain point, it became no longer profitable for foreign merchandise to sell on their home market, creating the opportunity for resumption of their own industries. the bankers, satisfied that the "Depression" had yielded sufficient rewards, and with a new crop of industrialists now directly under their thumbs, or in control of their trusted agents, industry would be resumed. loans again were forthcoming from the banker's overflowing strong rooms, or simply the same place as that from which originated the previous loans, his ledger; being therein merely a creation of stylus and clay tablet. Thus were the foundations laid for a new steady rise in prices.

Herein, in this everlasting "Boom" and "Bust" of the so called "Empires" and "Civilizations" of the last few thousand years is the root cause of the desperate situation in which the indo-european peoples now find themselves, and, in which, seemingly having everything, in reality they have nothing except total exhaustion and the spectre of total anarchy and destruction looming ever more clearly before them, for they no longer have the will to be.

With planned miscegenation and what could very well prove to be planned race self-extermination through the promotion of the use of conception aborting "medicines," and of abortion itself by "operation" involving the tearing of the living fetus from the womb, the so-called indo-european peoples, who writhe in torment as a result of these incredible plans undoubtedly originating in the first place from the muddled minds of the money masters or their agents, fast dwindle to a fraction of the world's population; soon, as may very well come to pass, to be entirely obliterated by those other races of the world who watch with glee this self-destruction of those who they had so recently believed to be one with the gods, such was their seeming superiority. International Money Power, whatever it really is, or whoever they really are, could not care less! Herein was its own design.

But one thing such designers of all this forget. In the magnitude of the total disaster that looms so threateningly in these last days over the path of life, is also final disaster to the planners of this evil; whether this they had expected or otherwise; their own complete obliteration for sure along with the rest.

For if God's kingdom on earth is to arise, it is to arise in a world where little of the sicknesses that trouble us today, will be left, and the binding threads of incompetent thinking, and of evil itself, will be totally unwound. it will arise where the humble and the meek, such as remain, bow down in total acceptance of that natural order as was ordained: of god, which is the self-conscious everlasting itself: of priest-king in whom is the voice of god reigning in earthly glory understandable to men: of priesthood trained to total understanding of all the forces which mould men, and the devoted themselves, those who go about their affairs trusting in the sincerity and ability of their rulers, and who seek no more in life than the glory of their eternal master, and that they themselves always walk in the ways of righteousness.

Thus, returning to Athens and its money in ancient days: the emission by the bankers of Athens of the baked clay facsimiles of the silver coinage they were reputed to have in storage in the vaults of the Acropolis, would have exactly the same effect on prices as the emission of silver coin; it would cause them to rise. Conversely, contraction of that clay coinage by calling of loans, would similarly cause prices to fall; and thus, as in today, "when the depression is over," that is when prices are at rock bottom without totally wrecking the state, the "Banker" merely enters a few figures in his ledger to the credit of one of his agents, so it was in athens in that day. did the so-called customer require ready money over and above the money required for settlement of balances owing, such as could be met by debit, and transfer, and recredit, i.e., by cheque, then the so-called bankers at athens or the piraeus, merely set slaves to work to cast and bake clay coins as fast as they could go! Admittedly the baking of clay coins was a little more expensive than the pen and ink required for ledger entry money, or than the high speed printing press necessary for the paper facsimiles of today.

Hence the enormous potential for the accumulation of wealth by a banker in a city state engaged in manufacture, and whose merchants and captains depended on him alone for their finances, especially when their business was largely with foreign parts. According to Professor Ure,[347] the tyrants of the city states derived their power from the *new* form of capital known as money.

While in agreement with the general idea of Professor Ure, it must be asked: Why *new* form of capital? Metal money as capital, or what? It may be assumed that those references to baked clay, leather and wooden money in ancient Rome previous to Numa Pompilius, the first by Suidas, the second by Seneca, and the third by Cedrenus, also applied to ancient Greece; especially if the conjecture in respect to the leather monopoly of the Hittite state is correct. Suidas makes reference to leather money at Lacedaemon. There is no reason why other Greek city states should not have availed themselves of such readily obtainable material[348] (and cheap at that!) in those days before the augmentation of bullion supplies internationally by the new methods of mining, and the massive wars which gave rise to plentiful supplies of expendable labour.

It seems to be reasonable that the money that enabled those industries that grew up in early Greece to get off the ground, as it were, was of such relatively intrinsically valueless material.

---

[347] P.N. Ure, M.A.: *The Origins of Tyranny*, p. 2; New York; 1922.

[348] "The Smithsonian report for 1876, p. 399, mentions clay stamps for printing cotton cloths (in ancient times). These could scarcely have failed to suggest baked clay coins such as were used in China, Chaldea, und Egypt." *History of Money in America*, p. 44. A. del Mar (in reference to Mexican money).

Behind every industrialist was a banker, and the banker had to be the secret heart of the city. The early use of precious metal coinage in Greece had to have been similar to its use in Babylonia a thousand years before, or as gold in Britain 2000 years later, a standard on which to base prices and establish confidence in the "Great Banker" as being a wealthy man; a base on which a pyramid of ledger credit page money might be erected, represented in the circulation by leather notes, clay tokens, etc.

As Stanley Jevons remarked in our era in 1914: "Gold already acts in England only as small change for notes."[349] In a similar manner with money based on a silver standard, yet relatively little silver in circulation, such silver would have acted as small change in those ancient times. For evidence of greater wealth, leather notes, or clay tokens, or documents denoting cattle, which indeed may have been currency in large scale transactions, seem more likely to have served, at least amongst the Indo-Europeans.

Thus right from the start it is safe to say that silver functioned as a balancing factor in oral and written agreements of merchandise exchange in Greece, actually functioning as a circulating medium itself only after King Pheidon of Argos. Although some authorities[350] say that the silver coinage was of state issuance, whether it was or was not, would make little difference. In so-called democracies, money power cannot but be the force behind the scenes. For that matter, anyone finding the paper notes of the British Empire three thousand years from now, because of the myth of the Queen's Head and the

---

[349] He might have added, pursuing the matter further, that the paper note of today merely act as small change for that abstract money created by the mass of cheques in transit, and behind which exists no more than the misappropriated will of the gods themselves.

[350] C.M Kraay & Max Hirmer: *Greek Coins*, Preface. London; 1968.

Coat of Arms, would assume it too was state issue. They would of course be entirely wrong. Ever since the establishment of that ever changing mirage of the precious metal money system, states and rulers that became corrupted and undermined by the extraordinary deceptions to which such system loaned itself, wittingly or unwittingly, have fronted for those persons, often of criminal background, sometimes designated bankers, who under their very noses, have operated the most unbelievable swindles. It is hard to believe that states and rulers have been aware of the magnitude of the folly they commit in permitting private persons to exercise that power which is theirs as being representative of their peoples before God. Assuming ruler and temple lend their sanction, it is not long before the so-called banker, now able to finance an opposition to any power it is in his interest to destroy, or indeed, to withdraw financing from such power whose destruction he seeks, can literally laugh at those people, foolish, corrupt, or naïve, who, in lack of understanding of the meaning and source of that which was their strength and power, raised him up in the first place.

Once the power of monetary emission is yielded by a ruler or state to private or external interests, it is rare that it can be recovered except as the result of all consuming cataclysm. Immense monopolies and vastly unequal money fortunes are neither gained nor saved by lawful labour or trade. Of necessity they are the natural outcome of the exercise of the power to discriminate, the power to reject or prefer that follows as inevitable consequence, when, in any state, private persons are permitted to create and issue the unit of exchange, whether tangible or abstract; and by whatever device of law such as may be needed to create appearance of legality.

So far as the future of mankind is concerned, out of the deceit it practises on the simple, kind, and trusting, this instrument will be responsible for the complete enslavement and ultimate destruction of most, if not all, of this world. The hands that guide it are declared by themselves to be malevolent, and wittingly function and exert themselves in defiance of the natural order of life with their hearts full of pride and prejudice as for themselves as being some special breed, when merely they are but unfaithful stewards. Contempt for those who front for them in their secret conspiracy or are destroyed by it, shows equally in the arrogance of their manner.

In the words of W. Cleon Skousen reviewing the great and compendious work of Dr. Carroll Quigley *Tragedy and Hope*, according to Dr. Skousen the most authentic and detailed account of the modern day conspiracy:

"As I see it, the great contribution which Dr. Carroll Quigley unintentionally made by writing *Tragedy and Hope* was to help the ordinary American realize the utter contempt which the network leaders have for ordinary peoples. Human beings are treated *en masse* as helpless puppets on an international chessboard where giants of economic and political power subject them to wars, revolution, civil strife, confiscation, subversion, indoctrination, manipulation and outright deception as it suits their fancy and their concocted schemes for world domination."[351]

.For the original Rothschild (Amschel) who uttered that now famous line: "Let me issue and control a Nation's money, and i care not who writes its laws,"[352] one cannot but have some grudging admiration, rogue though he was and should have been dealt with as such; but for those place-seeking persons, cynical or merely naïve, who nowadays prostrate themselves before the doors of the international bankers, as members of the societies dedicated to One World Government, such as The Council on Foreign Relations, The Canadian Institute of

---

[351] W. Cleon Skousen: *The Naked Capitalist*, p. 112.

[352] John R. Elsom: *Lightning over the Treasury Building*, p. 78.

International Affairs, The Royal Institute of International Affairs, etc. one can have little respect.

The first requisite for a man to be truly honoured amongst the people is that he bestow honour. Amongst these to whom the paths of meaningless ambition come first before any concern for their own, for they are largely drawn from that class of dead souls that is international in this, that every race and people on this earth is afflicted by them in more or less degree, the word honour too often will be meaningless. According to another recent writer: "James P. Warburg is one of the most ardent propagandists and financiers of the World Government Movement in the U.S.A. today. This same James Warburg had the audacity and arrogance to proclaim before the U.S. Senate (2-17-50): 'We shall have world government whether or not we like it. The only question is, whether world government will be achieved by conquest or consent.'"[353]

World Government is total government world-wide in which no independent race or people shall be except the rulers, who necessarily will have to be an exclusive caste. Total consent of all presumptuous, if not imaginative, bankers will never be; but out of the weakness and confusion created by them amongst us towards these their own vain purposes, the world Government they mutter about, may come through conquest, though it is not they who will be the conquerors, though indeed, they will be the principal instrument. There would be no way of bringing about that total monopoly of money, industry and empire, which is world government, save through the manipulation of the credulity of man-kind, and the pathetic trust he still maintains that his rulers are the voice of God on earth for him, as he blindly stumbles on, except it be by armed conquest. Armed conquest in its turn in these latter days, cannot be effected without the connivance of conspiratorial money

---

[353] W.B. Vennard: *Conquest or Consent*, p. 12.

power, although such conspiratorial money power in its virtually insane search for paths towards its own establishment towards World Rule *forever and ever*, has now become an institution, which in the horror of the weapons of total destruction and obliteration leading to final subjection that it has called into being, and, in its blindness, has also given to our enemies, can only be described as a juggernaut completely out of control, an all-engulfing Terror, as much for its creators, as he, who, in its original conception, such Terror was supposed to engulf.

Sparta, the Pelanors, Wealth, and Women

Sparta, of all the Greek States, is one that resisted most of all, in ancient times, the encroachments of international money power, and the circulation of precious metals, and all those demoralizing factors deriving therefrom. However, from those laws promulgated by Lycurgus in Sparta, reputedly during the ninth Century B.C., but, as according to the archaeologists, the early sixth century B.C.,[354] it would seem that all those evils deriving from giving such international money power free rein, had already been experienced, and had brought about that reaction amongst the people generally that enabled Lycurgus to take those measures by which he expunged forever the main causes of the sickness of greed and self-interest which ate at the heart of the Doric overlord class of the Peloponnese. To him[355] are ascribed those laws directed towards this purpose such as are described by Plutarch:

---

[354] Humphrey Michell, M A: *Sparta*, p. 27; (Cambridge University Press; 1952.)

[355] Further than the findings of archaeology, the deductions of some of the classical scholars also attribute the so-called reforms of Lycurgus to the sixth century B.C., being therein the so-called *Eunomia*, c 610 B.C.; clearly, therefore, either inspiring the events at Athens brought about by Solon, or being inspired thereby. According to the writer on this subject in the *Encyclopedia of World History*. (p. 50)." By the so-called *Eunomia*, the Spartans, fearing further revolts (of the Messenians) completely reorganized the State to make it more severely military. Youths from the age of 7 were taken for continual military training. Men of military age lived in barracks and ate at common messes (*syssitia, phiditia*). Five local tribes replaced the three Dorian hereditary ones and the army was correspondingly divided, creating the *Dorian Phalanx*. In the tribes were enrolled as citizens many non-citizens. The *gerousia*, comprising 28 elders and the two kings, had the initiative in legislation though the *apella* of all citizens had the final decision. The chief

"Not contented with this (redistribution of land) he resolved to make a division of their movables too, that there might be no odious distinction or inequality left among them; but finding it would be very dangerous to go about it openly, he took another course and defeated their avarice by the following stratagem: he commanded that all gold and silver coin should be called in, and that only a sort of money of iron should be current, a great weight and quantity of which was very little worth. So that to lay up twenty or thirty pounds, there was required a pretty large closet, and to remove it, nothing less than a yoke of oxen.

With the diffusion of this money, at once a number of vices were banished from Lacedaemon for who would rob another of such coin? Who would unjustly detain or take by force or accept as a bribe, a thing which was not easy to hide or a credit to have, or indeed of any use to cut in pieces. For when it was red-hot they quenched it in vinegar, and by that means spoilt it and made it almost incapable of being worked.

In the next place he declared an outlawry of all superfluous arts; but here he might have spared his proclamation; for they of themselves would have gone after the gold and silver, the money which remained being not so proper payment for curious work, for being iron it was scarcely portable, neither if they should take the means to export it, would it pass among the other Greeks who ridiculed it. So now there was no means of purchasing foreign goods and small wares, no itinerate fortune teller, no harlot monger, or gold or silver smith, engraver or jeweller set foot in a country which had no money; so that luxury deprived little by little of that which fed and

---

magistrates, *ephors* were increased to five, with wider powers especially after the ephorate of Cheilon (556 B.C.). Later ages attributed the reforms (the financial sector of which is ignored by this writer) to the hero Lycurgus in the ninth century, perhaps because the new laws were put under his protection."

fomented it, wasted to nothing, and died away of itself. For the rich had no advantage here over the poor as their wealth and abundance had no road to come abroad by, but were shut up at home doing nothing."[356]

Plutarch, of course, lived in a city and in an age when all wealth was assessed in terms of precious metals by weight. Needless to say, in order to have the cooperation of the real ruler, local money creative power, towards the publication of his works, he wisely followed that trend which undoubtedly had been instigated in Athens of making a mockery of Spartan customs, a trend which is still followed to this day by many so called scholars. Sparta, early in the Millennium had come to understand the real significance of precious metal money, as being part of an international confidence game. Sparta also realized the destructive forces inherent in the activities of its controllers and the foreign luxury traders they encouraged and financed in order to debilitate the people, and so make absolute their own secret hegemony, such as destroyed all racial pride in that people on whom they were battening, and thus destroying their will to resist through creating obsession with pleasure. The evidence is in the findings of the British School at Athens from their excavations at the site of the city of Sparta:

"The excavations of the British School at Athens at the site of the city of Sparta reveal a flourishing state of the arts and manufactures in Laconia carried on, if not wholly by Laconian workmen themselves, at least by foreign artists who were welcome and encouraged to ply their crafts without any of the dark suspicion of strangers that was so marked in latter times."[357]

---

[356] Plutarch: *Lycurgus* (*The Lives*: Dryden Translation).

[357] Humphrey Michell, M.A: *Sparta*; p. 12.

The so-called Spartan way of life derived from the necessity of the Spartans to always be prepared for total war from abroad, as their final rejection of international money power made certain would come, and to be always prepared for war from within; i.e., insurrection; an equal certainty deriving from the same causes.

The first Messenian War (736-716 B.C.) was entered into by King Theopompus of Sparta for the usual reasons for any war in a state indicated by archaeological findings as being under the thumb of international money power: instigation by that money power in favour of its arms industry and its other long range purposes. The long drawn out character of the war indicated that the Messenians had equal access to international arms industry with Sparta. Armies are not raised and maintained in long drawn out wars without finances acceptable in international trade and ready access to the best of weapons and equipment; and it is clear the Messenians were not short of such. This war served that purpose most desirable to money power of reducing the power of kings: "The first and second Messenian wars were both followed by constitutional crises. The first settlement was a victory of the Spartan peers over the kings and a curbing of royal prerogatives and powers."[358] Such would have been typical of the progress of international money power in its usual insidious takeover of any state or civilization. "The crisis after the second Messenian war was at least within the ranks of the Spartans themselves, a democratic one, if that very dubious word can be used."[359] The long drawn out character of the second Messenian War indicated the same underlying factor of the original war of conquest: international money-power extending its favours to both sides, to the insurgents and to Sparta. The final edicts of Lycurgus as a result

---

[358] *Ibid.* p. 23.

[359] Humphrey Michell, M.A.: *Sparta*, p. 23.

of the constitutional crisis that followed the second Messenian war, certainly indicate he was aware of the loss of sovereignty that came to any state that based its money system on the product of the international bullion brokers, and which meant dependence on their good graces; the more especially if such state had no mines of its own.

The Second Messenian war which was doubtless to have established total "Democracy," that is, total rule of the international banking fraternity, failed so far as such purpose was concerned. Lycurgus's answer to a man who insisted he create a democracy in the state was "First create a democracy in your own house." Certainly an apt answer!

The complaint of Theognis, admirer of Sparta, visitor from Megara, whos e political aim was directed towards the prevention of the recurrence of a Tyranny at Megara, should not be forgotten, and bore light on the conditions at Sparta, as well, and that gave rise to Lycurgus:

"Tradesmen reign supreme, the bad lord it over their betters, This is the lesson that all must thoroughly master."[360]

Of the reforms of Lycurgus, their cause, and those forces they were directed against, there is no doubt whatsoever, and verification through the findings of archaeology such as the work of Dr. Blakeway in Laconia reestablishes the time as being, as remarked above, after the second Messenian war, namely between 600 B.C. and 550 B.C.

"He has demonstrated from archaeological evidence that between 600 B.C. and 550 B.C., foreign imports into Sparta practically ceased. Corinthian pottery which had been common

---

[360] P.N. Ure, M.A.: *The Origins of Tyranny*, p. 8.

in Sparta in the early or Proto-Corinthian period is exceedingly rare after c.600 B.C. Ivory, amber, Egyptian scarabs, and Phoenician goods likewise cease before 550 B.C. and the same is true of gold and silver jewellery."[361]

There is no doubt that early in the sixth century B.C., the Spartans totally excluded the international money market, such as controlled the rest of Greece through silver and gold money, and the banker's practices relating thereto. They also excluded foreign trade as being equally destructive of the order of life they wished to preserve.

The notion created by Plutarch of that national currency of iron as being something ridiculous and requiring also an ox-cart may be dismissed as part of the steady stream of propaganda no doubt being created in Athens against everything of ancient days, particularly the customs special to Sparta. If it is true that the *pelanors* were of such weight as ruled out their being readily passed from hand to hand, then it may reasonably be assumed that they denoted wealth in much the same manner as the stone rings of Uap and the ancient Indus Valley civilization;[362] more in the nature of a reserve, the circulating money being the leather notes referred to by Suidas as circulating in Lacedaemon, just as the circulating money of Uap was shell strings, similar to *Tekaroro* of the Gilbert Islands.[363] It may equally have been a system whose origins were lost in remote ages; perhaps bearing relationship to that system existing in Europe during the 4th Millennium B.C.,[364] when it is clear that the *spondylus* shell had greater significance than that ascribed to

---

[361] Humphrey Michell: *Sparta*, p. 27.

[362] Paul Einzig: *Primitive Money*, pp. 36-40; also see E.J.C. McKay in *Further Excavations at Mohanjo-Daro*, p. 582.

[363] Kingston-Higgins: *A Survey of Primitive Money*, p. 140. London; 1949.

[364] Colin Renfrew: *The Emergence of Civilization*; pp. 483-544; London; 1972.

it as "Prestige Possession," and was part of a world wide use of shells as money.

Sparta was indeed fortunate to possess considerable reserves of iron ore, the principal deposits being at the Malean Cape and the Taenarian Promontory.[365] Thus, both for her money and for her arms, she was therefore independent, and needed no assistance from abroad. The Laws of Lycurgus excluding international money and trade, directly continued the fomentation of that warlike spirit and racial and national pride bred in the Spartans out of the trials of the long drawn out Messenian wars; and which brought them in as saviours at Thermopylae, and, indeed, of Carthage at the end of the first Punic War (255 B.C.) when the army of Regulus encamped before the city was destroyed by Xantippus the Spartan.

The very fact that the power of the kings had been undermined by the first Messenian War, although their position as absolute leaders of the people in war still existed, became a blessing in disguise. History has shown that the point to which international money power immediately gravitates when penetrating any people living in natural order, is the top, the king himself, either directly, or through the priesthood. Given his sanction and connivance in respect to their schemes, then peoples whose very souls have leaned towards the king as to the Lord's anointed, are easily subdued, and their minds filled with arithmetical calculations and obsession with their animal needs, instead of that great glory of a oneness with the Deity, a oneness with the harmony of the universe, and their being lords of their own world with dominion over all other life.

One of the first steps of such money power towards total assumption of rule has been the eradication of kings and kingly power. Even though a king might be lead into connivance with

---

[365] Paul Einzig: *Primitive Money*, p. 224; London; 1949.

the banker's schemes, through lack of understanding, he always could still awaken and discover his mistake, and realizing the sword was still in his hand, take measures to regain his prerogative. Therefore he had to be disposed of, or reduced to paid and willing servant.

In Sparta there seems to have been another obstacle to the promoters of that "Phony" democracy advocated by international money power, namely the Ephorate whose existence was undoubtedly linked to that national money power of Sparta as instituted, or reinstituted under the protection of Lycurgus. Of the Ephors it may be said their main objectives were: "First the maintenance of home defence and limiting of Spartan dominion to Messenia and Laconia (i.e. no imperial entanglements).[366] Second, the fostering of a steady policy which lead to intervention in the struggle at Athens with the Peisistratids, and the expulsion of the family; third an unrelenting hostility to the pretensions of royal power in the state." "The Ephorate was a profoundly democratic institution that feared and fought against tyranny both within and without the borders of Lacedaemon."[367]

Accepting the tyrant as front man of those alien agents of international money power, the *trapezitae*, in which category the Peisistratids certainly fell, then the meaning of the policies of the Ephorate becomes clear; with the limiting of Spartan dominion to Messenia and Laconia, was the establishment of an area from which Spartans could derive total economic freedom, sufficient to maintain themselves, and that which above all maintained their way of life and its source, their national monetary system.

---

[366] Bracketed comment by present author.

[367] Humphrey Michell, M.A.: *Sparta*, p. 30.

The intervention at Athens and the total opposition to the Peisistratids was obvious policy in view of the unrelenting pressure of Athenian money power as a branch of International Money Power, against Sparta, city that had made mockery of the power of the counting houses of the world financial centres, and had set up example in the world which would become inspiration to others.

The hostility to kingly power by the Ephorate, would be guided by what they doubtless saw was the need, if their national life was to be maintained, of making sure that kings in no way had the power to surrender themselves, and the people they represented, to the blandishments of international money power, whose opportunity, alas! has always been a weak and ill-instructed king.

However the remark of Archidamos, King of Sparta at the commencement of the "Great" Peloponnesian war reveals, even at that day, 428 B.C. how the corruptive forces outpouring from Babylonia, with its immediate agents, had certainly reentered Sparta to some degree.

"And war is not so much a matter of armaments as of the money that makes armaments effective."[368]

In his speech to his own people Archidamos also warns them of the 6000 talents war chest supposedly held by the Athenians in the Acropolis. Both of these statements show no understanding of that in which a king should above all be instructed, National Monetary Emission, and prove how right were the Ephors in the controls with which they surrounded kingship. Archidamos privately was close friend of Pericles, scion of the Alkmeonidae, whose destiny, Greek history shows,

---

[368] Thucydides: *The Peloponnesian War*, Book I, Ch. 6.

to have always been closely linked to that of international money power.

During the period when the national currency of Sparta maintained its integrity, it might be safe to say that the Spartan, in so far as it is possible for true freedom to exist, was a free man. Indeed the helots were more than likely more free by a long way than are the labouring classes of this day; and certainly more free than those classes of the semi-mass production lines of the other Greek Cities, whose monetary systems were almost all, whether fiduciary and of state issue or not, at the mercy of the bankers, and therefore the manipulators of the value of bullion and slaves, wherever it was they maintained their centre; generally assumed to be Babylonia and its outposts, Lydia, and Naucratis in the Nile Delta, and Phoenicia, and Athens, and Cyzicus and Colchis and many other cities in key positions to trade with the world beyond.

A monetary system, simple, inviting neither peddlers of luxury, panders or pornographers to make mockery of the lives of the people, issued and regulated by a benevolent state, and undoubtedly with its units paid into circulation with care and attention to the result on the national well-being and strength, bred a sturdy independent people completely contemptuous of the gold madness raging elsewhere. They were an example by which other great peoples came to profit, outstandingly the Romans. They lived with a feeling of great superiority to the Athenians, who, while having a plentiful currency, except during the periods of exhaustion of the Laureion silver mines, were exposed to all the evils of control over their political life by alien money power through the *trapezitae*.

History gives much information about the means whereby money was collected and raised and spent, but nothing as to those shadowy figures who institute its units in the first place, and, as in the case of the banker's "democracies," inject them into the circulation.

As to when international money power reentered Sparta, there is little enough evidence. But the outlook of King Archidamos suggested it had made quite some progress by the date of the commencement of the Peloponnesian war, and it may be safely said that to win that war, out of which could come nothing but gain to international money power, Sparta had to make almost total concession. The final victory over Athens and her Empire, which ended the war, achieved the purposes of the international bullion and slave traders as surely as final defeat would so have done. As it will be remembered, the relaxation and luxury that inundated Rome after the second Punic war, as a result of the concessions that had been made to international bullion and slave traders in order to be able to re-arm after Cannae, and ultimately drive Hannibal out of Italy, and defeat him in his own territory, within 25 years dragged the Romans down[369] to a debauched money mad mob, though still mighty through the employment at arms of the defeated peoples.

Similarly, after the Peloponnesian War, like causes had done the same for Sparta, and it was but 25 years later, in 371 B.C., the Spartan Phalanx, softened to the core, crumbled into bloody

---

[369] Sallust who lived from 86 B.C. to 35 B.C. drew the following picture of the state of society at that time: "When freed from the fear of Carthage, the Romans had leisure to give themselves up to their dissensions, then there sprang up on all sides troubles, seditions, and at last civil wars. A small number of powerful men, whose favour most of the citizens sought by base means, exercised a veritable despotism under the imposing name, sometimes of the Senate, at other times of the 'People.' The title of good or bad citizen was no longer the reward of what he did for or against his country for all were equally corrupt; but the more anyone was rich, and in condition to do evil with impunity, provided he supported the present order of things, the more he passed for a man of worth. From this moment the ancient manners no longer became corrupted gradually as before; but the depravation spread with the rapidity of a torrent and youth was to such a degree infected by the poison of luxury and avarice, that there came a generation of people of which it was just to say, that they could neither have patrimony nor suffer others to have it." Sallust: Fragm. I.12-13.

ruin at Leuctra, to Epaminondas the Theban and never again recovered the *élan* that had made it the victor of a hundred battles, for the Spartans now, more than any, were consumed by the corrupting diseases of money madness and its attendant liberalism.

That by 360 B.C., the ancient money system that had been the factor behind the morale of the Spartan of Thermopylae was little more than a memory, is revealed by the following quotation taken from Alexander Del Mar:

"The crime of Gylipus, B.C. 360 and the decree offered upon its exposure, viz. 'That no coin of gold or silver be admitted into Sparta, but that they should use the money that had formerly obtained,' shows that as this decay of the state and weakening of credit went on, gold or silver coins, at or near their bullion value, gradually crept into circulation as money. The failure of the decree to pass is conclusive that the iron numerical system was no longer practicable."[370]

In other words, the damage to that which had been Sparta and its people done by the ruler who first of all turned a blind eye to dealings in the precious metals, the regrowth of international trade, and no doubt the holding of deposits in Athenian Banks, and who failed to deal with ferocity with those who interfered with the *pelanors* either by counterfeiting or speculation, was irreparable. It seemed this time the clock could not be turned back.

Thus while Sparta finally collapsed before the unremitting pressure of the Athenian, or better put, the international money market, seeming to yield its ancient strength and the sources of its independence, the Athens that carried on, as well, partly for

---

[370] A. del Mar: *A History of Money in Antiquity*, p. 165.

reasons as elsewhere given, was but a shadow of itself with the approach of the exhaustion of the mines, and thence the failure of the base of its money power and the "confidence" essential to its maintenance. Moreover, still in the hands of the bankers as a centre of trade for trade's sake, Athens was become but a name. As with Rome by the time of the Civil Wars, its original people had disappeared into that mass of freed slaves, and immigrants from elsewhere, the "sojourners," who were now a large part of the Athenian population, and for whose leaders Xenophon the journalist obviously fronted when he proposed that special taxes should be lifted from foreigners who at the same time were not to be required to do military service.[371] (Here it might be remarked that it is perhaps unfortunate that should still survive the writings of a paid propagandist, so similar to the writings of some of his brethren today, when so little remains of Greek literature relative to the total output.)

Of Spartan money as reinstituted under the patronage of Lycurgus, Ernest Babelon, famous French Numismatist of the 19th Century, wrote:

"A long time after the use of money had been spread throughout the Hellenic world, Sparta continued as through tradition, to make use of ingots of iron as a means of exchange. These bars were known under the description of (gâteau de pâtisserie).

Each one weighed an Aeginetic Mina, and to carry only six of them, that is to say about 536 Kg., a wagon drawn by two oxen was required. This information supplied to us by Xenophon and Plutarch agrees with that from central Italy where cumbersome bars of bronze were carried in carts; '*Aes Grave* plaustris quidam convehentes,' said Titus Vivius. All kinds of

---

[371] Xenophon: *A Discourse upon improving the Revenues of the State of Athens*, pp. 311-13; (Trans. Charles Davenant, London, 1771).

stories circulated on the subject of the famous *Pelanors* of Sparta that seem to have remained in use until the Persian Wars. It was said, for instance that the iron used in the manufacture of this money was unsuitable for any other purpose and was rendered brittle by an operation consisting of heating it until red-hot, then quenching it in vinegar. In the conservative capital of Laconia it appears that these ingots of iron were the sole money in use and all citizens were forbidden under penalty of death to possess any other money. When Epaminondas died he was so poor that nothing was found in his house in the way of wealth other than an old iron. At Thebes the native land of Epaminondas where money was known and struck at an early date, found in the residence of the hero could have no more than a superstitious character."

This surprises us less especially as since the 7th century, Pheidon, King of Argos, when he struck the first silver money of Aegina, and introduced a standard system of weights and measures into the Peloponnese, withdrew the former iron spits from circulation that had served as money until then, and consecrated a certain number of samples, "in Ex-voto," in the sanctuary of Hera at Argos. At the time of Aristotle they could still be seen in the Temple."[372]

---

[372] "Longtemps après que l'usage de la monnaie eut été partout répandu dans le monde Hellénique, Sparte continuait par tradition, a se servir de lingots de fer comme intermédiaires des échange. Ces lingots était connu sous le nom de (gâteau de Pâtisserie). Ils pesaient chacun une mine éginétique et pour en transporter six seulement, c'est a dire environs 4536 Kg il fallait un chariot attelé de deux boeufs. Ce renseignement qui nous fournissent Xenophon et Plutarch, est conforme a ce qui se passait dans l'Italie centrale où les encombrantes lingots de bronze étaient transporté sur des chariots: "*aes grave* plaustris quidam convehentes," dit Titus Vivius. Il circulait toutes sortes de fables au sujet du fameux Pelanor de Sparte, qui parait être rester en usage jusqu'a l'époque des guerres médiques: on disait par exemple que le fer destiné a fabriquer cette monnaie était impropre à tout autre usage et rendu cassant par une opération qui consistait à la faire

Babelon, most learned scholar as he was, however reflects the complacent attitude of the bankers of the end of the last century, which was founded on the idea, such had been their luck during the previous century, that their millennium had finally come. With him, money was precious metal, and precious metal was money. Although of interest, his information, a repetition of Xenophon the journalist and Plutarch, offers not much more light. Though over two thousand years had gone by, precious metal money and its promoters still ruled, despite a dozen great kingdoms and empires having risen at its behest and having fallen at its behest Did Babelon see the shadow which lurked behind the throne, he closed his eyes and turned his head away!

Lycurgus was without doubt inspired to reestablish this national monetary system by the clear understanding he must have come to have of the evil effects of this gold and silver madness, and its disastrous effects as a result of the operations of the *trapezitae* or bankers, relative to the destruction of national morale and being. Precious metal coinage was currency whose total circulation the state could in no way control because of the desirability of its material internationally. In the common money market of the silver bullion brokers it was material,

---

rougir au feu et a la tremper ensuite de fer était, parait-il exclusif, et défense sous peine de morte, fur faite à tout citoyen de posséder une autre monnaie.

Quand Epaminondas mourut il était si pauvre qu'on ne trouva dans sa maison, pour toute fortune, qu'un vieil en fer. A Thèbes, la patrie d'Epaminondas ou la monnaie fut connu et frappée de bonne heure, trouve dans la demeure du héros ne pouvait avoir qu'un caractère superstitieux. Ceci nous surprendra d'autant moins que dès le septième siècle, Phidon, roi d'Argos, lorsqu'il fit frappés un système régulier de poids et mesures, retira de la circulation les vieilles broches de fer qui auraient servit de monnaie jusqu'à là, et en consacra un certain nombres d'exemplaires en "ex-voto" dans la sanctuaire de Héra à Argos En temps de Aristotle on voyait encore dans le Temple." (Ernest Babelon: *Les Origines de la Monnaie*. p. 79; Paris; 1897.)

which, whether minted into money by state authority or otherwise, produced a money always of value regardless of local convention. Its value was dictated by the arbitrary decision of that international fraternity who controlled its mining, and the slaves that mined it, and out of manipulation of that pyramid of abstract money they created thereon, controlled the political affairs of states.

The money that had been established in Sparta was of value to Spartans alone. Although no record exists of such matter, it may be safely assumed that the *Pelanors* and the leather multiples or divisibles of Suidas, entered the circulation as against state indebtedness; thus reducing taxation, that vicious destroyer of peoples, to relatively negligible amounts. Their pitted and otherwise worthless appearance deriving from their being immersed in vinegar when red hot, made them of no value for any other purpose than that for which they were intended. The use of this national money was the force that gave Sparta the leadership of Hellas until the end of the Peloponnesian War, even if decline had commenced with the execution of the great General Pausanias[373] by the Ephors in 479 B.C., and was that which necessarily dictated the policy of the extirpation of the tyrannies; the tyrant always being representative for the agent of international money creative power through precious metal control. There might be temptation to assume the *pelanors* were a system of "Iron Greenbacks." But while they resembled the "Greenbacks" in

---

[373] Pausanias was the commander of the fleet of the Greek allies. After his success against the Persians on land at Plataea, in the same year, 479 B.C., he reduced both Cyprus and Byzantium. According to the record, he was executed by the Ephors by being starved to death in the temple of Athena of the Brazen House, having been found guilty of (kingly) domineering which was supposed to have alienated Ionia. The real reason of his disgrace and execution would have been buried amongst the secrets of National or International money power. He had most likely entered into secret dealings with the latter. (Thucydides: *The Peloponnesian War*; Book I; Ch. 10.)

this that they were the total will to be of the Spartans,[374] assuming the truth of their great weight, as pointed out above, they may have been more in the character of that monetary system of very ancient days of which the stone rings of Uap are a last remaining evincement.

A healthy wholesome people who controlled totally their state and existence would have little reason to accumulate money fortunes, and wealth as distinct from the land which was their patrimony; and as such money fortunes begin and end as little more than figures in the banker's ledger, nor could they be guided into becoming mouthpieces for the policies of the bankers. Meals were eaten in common amongst men as in Carthage of earlier days, and a genuine contempt for luxury existed. A simple life was not sought after, so much as it came of its own accord as a natural outcome of such monetary system created for their better and right living, and which preserved them from the encroachments of that liberalizing, demoralizing, and debt creating force of international trade, and its destructive effect on the *esprit de corps* of any particular race or people who are foolish enough to permit its proponents to have their way.

Although it was said of the early days of the Laws of Lycurgus and his monetary reforms that precious metals seized in War were deposited with the Arcadians, of later days Augustus Boeckh wrote of gold and silver in Sparta:

---

[374] According to A. del Mar, the iron currency of the pelanors was strictly a numerical system; confined to Sparta, it was a national system having no relationship to International Standards or ratios with other metals; thus being identical in character to the "Greenback" paper money issued by President Abraham Lincoln, during the American Civil War, and by which means the schemes of the international bullion braking fraternity were temporarily frustrated.

"Sparta during a period of several generations, swallowed up large quantities of the precious metals; as in *Aesop's Fables*, the footsteps of the animals which went in were to be seen, but never of those which came out. The principal cause of this stagnation was that the state kept the gold and silver in store, and only reissued them for war and foreign enterprise; although there were instances of individuals who amassed treasures according to the law."[375]

Xenophon stated that Lycurgus made the privilege of citizenship equally available to all who observed what was enjoined by laws, without taking any account of weakness of body, or scantiness of means; which would mean that no Spartan suffered in respect to the mess or *syssition* to which he was entitled to belong, on account of economic condition. Xenophon had lived in Sparta and was writing before the loss of Messenia. Aristotle who declared failure to pay dues entailed political disenfranchisement, wrote after the loss of Messenia in 370 B.C., and the certain penetration by the bankers of the Piraeus, and the assumption of control of Spartan fiscal affairs which it may safely be said, they were already conceded by an already corrupted Sparta, ready to accept any humiliation to save itself from total ruin. The final military collapse at Leuctra rose from that weakened condition that followed the apparent victory of the "Great" Peloponnesian War, and those concessions that already would have been made to the international bankers, now in the Persian court, as a result of the desperate need of the Spartans for ships. The loan of 5000 talents towards the building of ships which was granted to Sparta by Persia as a result of the Treaty of Miletus, 412 B.C., would not have been granted without major concessions being exacted; most likely abrogation of those Spartan edicts forbidding the sojourn of foreign traders etc. on Spartan territory. It would not take long, once such traders had been

---

[375] Augustus Boeckh: *The Public Economy of Athens*, p. 43, Vol. I.

admitted, for them to undermine the morale of that which had been Sparta, by spreading the money madness, and the promotion of luxury[376] and the creation of unnatural concern with sex, and body needs. Of this situation Polybius, as quoted by Humphrey Michell wrote the following:

"As long as they aspired to rule over their neighbours or over the Peloponnesians alone, they found the supplies and resources furnished by Laconia itself, adequate as they had all they required ready to hand and quickly returned home whether by land or by sea. But once they began to undertake naval expeditions and to make military campaigns outside the Peloponnese, it was evident that neither their iron currency nor the exchange of their crops for commodities which they lacked, as permitted by the laws of Lycurgus, would suffice for their needs. These enterprises demanded a currency in universal circulation and supplies drawn from abroad, and so they were compelled to beg from the Persians, to impose tribute on the islanders, and exact taxes from all the Greeks. For they recognized that under the legislation of Lycurgus, it was impossible to aspire, I will not say to supremacy in Greece, but to any position of influence."[377]

The fact is however, Sparta, while following the Laws of Lycurgus had dominated Greece in more or less degree. As soon as she lost sight of the meaning and purpose of such laws, she became just another petty state; an agency for the subterranean control by international banking through manipulation of the silver and gold bullion basis of her currency; each man, concerned with his own need and greed, aimlessly following the pretty bubble which was the illusion of

---

[376] Aristotle: *The Politics*, Book II, Ch. 9.

[377] Polybius VI. 49. (Humphrey Michell: *Sparta*, p. 305.) François Lenormant: *La Monnaie dans L'Antiquité*, p. 215-216; Book II, Tome I.

the banker's "wealth." The old order, and that which had given them strength and national morale, was soon destroyed through the promotion of foreigners and the lower castes, and the helots, who merely took the name but not the meaning; also by the stirring up of women towards rejection of their subordinate place in life, and therefore instituting insidious attack on the natural order of the home, out of which is bred the natural order of life itself.

The later age of Aristotle, with its hard and realistic facts as referred to by some writers, was no more realistic than the earlier age of Xenophon. Rather it was less so. It was the age of the triumph of those international interests whose arming and instigation of the Messenian helots in an earlier age had decided Spartans to accept that structure of law as advocated by Lycurgus, which meant surrender of so much ease of living, rather than become the same as most other Greek states, an alien money manipulators paradise, with, as Theognis of Megara put it: *"Tradesmen reigning supreme and the bad lording it over their betters."*

As the earliest finds of the clay facsimiles of precious metal coinage at Athens, seem to date around the middle of the fifth century B.C.,[378] it may be assumed that one way or the other, either through Spartans permitted to reside at Athens, or through those Spartan mercenaries who travelled the world seeking employment for their skill at arms, the lust for having, one man more than his neighbour, slowly became injected into them. Perhaps Spartan mercenaries, who always required to be paid in those international currencies of silver and gold, returning from abroad via Athens, had been inveigled into depositing their pay in such gold or silver, with the bankers of the Piraeus, with whom it might "grow" from interest; taking

---

[378] François Lenormant: *La Monnaie dans L'Antiquité*, p. 215-216; Book II, Tome I.

home the baked clay coins as evidence of their account, and thus evading contravention of the Spartan laws in respect to possession of gold and silver.

With the resumption of the rule of international money power in later Spartan history, one of the most outstanding instances of that sickness rotting the fibres of their racial morale, was the tale of those *Homoioi* who seemed to have fallen in the social scale and were no longer able to take their places in those great messes, the *syssitiones*, the breeding places of that *esprit de corps* that was Sparta. Scholars give various reasons for these "disenfranchised" Spartans apparently known as the *hypomeiones*. The reason for their coming to be is however more than clear. They are the direct result of the power to discriminate, which is the natural outcome in favour of the banker, of that actual god-power he exercises once installed as local money creator.

More than likely after the Peloponnesian War, and certainly after the battle of Leuctra in 371 B.C., the reestablished bankers, following usual policy, would have taken care that certain families, who this caste of men instinctively realized might yet create opposition to them, were dispossessed by one means or another. With that banker created money as being now the necessary qualification for membership to the syssitiones, it was a small matter to make sure that such persons whose disenfranchisement they planned, never had enough.[379] Clearly in such later day, the *syssition* or mess charges, being assessed in silver money whose issue the bankers controlled, those to whom such alien bankers extended no favours, and

---

[379] By corollary, those prepared to promote the bankers' policies, however subversive or destructive, would be amply provided for. Of this period Professor A.H.M. Jones (Sparta, p. 39; Oxford; 1967) makes comment: "After Aegospotami there was such an influx of gold and silver that the conservatives tried to revive the Lycurgan ban, and it was decided that the treasury might hold gold and silver but not individuals. *Nevertheless part of the Spartiate's mess contribution was in Aeginetan Obols.*" (Italics present author's.)

therefore ultimately dispossessed through mortgage and foreclosure, not having any longer the wherewithal to pay, no longer belonged. Further, seeing their former helots raised up to place of honour and riches by bankers created wealth, and certainly by the reign of King Cleomenes III (228-219 B.C.),[380] actually sitting in their place in the *syssition*, little desire to retrieve such a distinctly lost cause remained.

The Spartan, whether poor or whether rich (in land), in the days of the national currency had been the social equal of any other Spartan; however, as much as anything, the slow decay of the Spartan principle derived from a most outstanding omission in the constitution which was total lack of provision for the redistribution of wealth at certain definite intervals, and the cancellation of debt as in the Hebrew custom of the 49th year.[381]

Needless to say, even in the days of the national currency, there must have been tendency towards economic inequality resulting from such omission;[382] but the rapid increase of such economic inequality after the return of the bankers, that certainly followed the "Great" Peloponnesian War, additional to furthering the breakup of the caste system that previously had obtained in Sparta in some degree, and wherein each man had known his place in the order of society, also caused a further breakup in the natural order of life of Spartan man as master of home and family.

In that Spartan society wherein women had always known considerable freedom relative, say, to their Athenian sisters, the control of wealth however designated, passed substantially into

---

[380] Humphrey Michell, M.A.: *Sparta*, p. 78.

[381] *Leviticus*, Ch. 25: (King James Version).

[382] Aristotle: *The Politics*, Book II, Ch. 9.

the hands of women.[383] Concern for the growth of "Money," no doubt, just as in this day, replaced care for their men, and concern for themselves as mothers of the race, and concern for the growth of their children.

"Two fifths of the land and wealth had come into their hands, simply because lack of men left them as heiresses, and this wealth they used extravagantly, maintaining race horses which they exhibited at the Olympic games, costly equipages and fine clothes. They meddled in the affairs of state and brought undue influence upon the conduct of the government."[384]

In such society, this stratum of wealthy women have no respect for men as such, too often. While perhaps not classified as *hetaerae*, who all said and done, had served some useful purpose to men, they clearly lived public lives very much the same as the *hetaerae*.

Such women, their heads full of figures and pride, would have served most usefully those alien money powers who ever have sought to further their purposes through corrupt and malleable persons. Women, rarely corrupt in the sense that a man may be corrupt, because of their natural need to shelter behind what seems to be strength, as arrogant Money Power would appear to them, are malleable. Their own Spartan men, either dead, and if not dead, completely confused with the new liberalization programme of the returned bankers, were virtually enslaved; therefore they turned for the protection they needed to what seemed to be the new strength, pudgy and gross though it may have been.

---

[383] *Ibid.*

[384] Humphrey Michell: *Sparta*, p. 50.

MONEY CREATORS AND THE POLITICAL CONTROL

In their inception, so-called political parties were other expression of the principle of rule of tyrant or dictator. Though apparently instituted in opposition to each other, such societies, or groups, or even persons, representing such seemingly conflicting political interests, were the very natural outcome of complete usurpation of the essence of sovereign power, the god-force from on high that gave life to a people or state, through conspiracy in respect to interference with the issue of the unit of exchange. Such front organizations are the natural result of the existence in any such state or people, of semi-secret societies in one form or the other, religious or racial, alien by origin or otherwise, arrogating to themselves that privilege which formerly belonged to the god alone, of the creation of exchange units, abstract or otherwise. The only limit to the amount of such private issue, especially if abstract, i.e., as by transferable ledger credit page entry (indicated by the use of assignments or cheques) would be the limit dictated by caution against over-saturation of that money market, national or international being interfered with. Naturally it was usually born in mind that the (silly)goose that laid the golden eggs, must not be altogether destroyed, and care was taken that the real meaning of these activities[385] was deeply concealed for fear that

---

[385] Further support is given to the opinions of the present author in respect to money creation and issuance by the remarks of Dr. Paul B. Trescott in his work: *Money, Banking, & Economic Welfare* (Page 55), in which the process of deposit creation in modern times (which would be known as money creation if more direct language were used), is briefly, but aptly summarized.

According to Dr. Trescott, in order to make a loan of $1000.00 to a customer, "a bank needs only to credit his account with $1000.00 in its books by a stroke of the pen." The following words of Dr. Trescott

ruler and people might come to realize the true nature of the forces at work in their midst. Each of these groups of persons in the case of so called political parties, or each of these persons in the case of tyrants or dictators, could not but be instrument for private money creative power.

Such establishment of conflicting groups, each claiming to have the answer towards perfect government, and, in the case of a constitutional monarchy, each swearing allegiance to the monarch, now but paid servant of money power, or in the case of a republic, each swearing allegiance to a president, in reality an elective king raised up from the "People," was a very efficient device of such private money creative power towards the maintenance of its own hegemony. Herein was venality and corruption enthroned. Such "Politicians" as turned to look a little too closely at the hand that fed them, promptly found their "Perks,"[386] or "Political Rewards," cut off.

Should any government begin to be restless, and unwilling to accept the axiom that it should have no real say in that most serious matter of all, monetary emission, the line of

---

certainly convey the impression that, despite the fact that nothing has been given by the bank in question that will cause any decrease in its assets, the customer will give the bank something of real value "in exchange for the deposit credit," his IOU, "or an interest bearing security." According to Dr. Trescott, this process by which deposits are created, consequently causes increase in the total money supply. Dr. Trescott further remarks: "The process of creating deposits is obviously a simple and painless one for the banks."

[386] In days gone by it was customary for most who did business with ships, to make a gift, usually money, to both Master and First Mate. These gifts were known as "Perks". The "Perks" of the Master were unknown to the First Mate; in some degree they took the place of commissions that shipmasters had formerly received on cargo bookings in the days before the advent of telegraphs etc., when they truly were kings of the sea in many senses of the word.

communication from the god in heaven to the people, then it would be but a short time before private money creative power transferred its favours to the so-called opposition. Funds would be made available sufficient to guarantee under normal circumstances their winning the "Election" and their consequent assumption of the government. At the same time funds would be withdrawn from the "Political Party" previously in control of the "government"; which would very likely mean that, in the following confusion, men more "suitable" and "pliable" would force their way to the top; so that even if that particular government was reelected, private money creative power would have no further fears. The price was always continuance of those policies most needed by such private money creative power necessary for its own real purposes, and therefore the continuance of its hegemony.

The greater part of the units of exchange as emitted by private money creative power are of no intrinsic value other, perhaps, than those denoted by precious metal symbols, and with which the confidence of peoples and rulers was gained. Therefore the cost of instituting that total control of any state so "captured" by private money creative power, i.e., the bankers, was virtually nil, since clearly such state financed its own lamentable condition!

It is clear that each unit issued into circulation, of fraudulent origin or otherwise, reduced by an exact valuation, the worth of previous units as worked in the exchanges; transferring such loss of worth to the holder of the new unit. If later, with growth of industry deriving from the creation of such unit, all circulating units increased in worth, such increase in worth rarely caught up with the original decline in worth, or purchasing power of those previously existing units.

The steady decline in worth or purchasing power, of the unit of exchange at any place and in any period of history, will be sufficient proof in itself of the existence of secret creation and manipulation of abstract units of exchange by a relatively invisible force. Only under most unusual circumstances would even a sharp rise in the number of precious metal units circulating, cause distinct and disturbing inflation of values, without an accompanying fraudulent, and secret expansion of the total number of working units, through issuance of false receipts against non-existing valuables or non-existing warehoused goods, or by creation of transferable ledger credit page entry money against assignment of "collateral". Precious metal units in themselves soon wear out, disappear for purposes of speculation abroad, or are hoarded.

Thus the creation and issuance of money constitutes free gift to the issuer when such issuer be private person. It automatically and immediately despoils he who thinks himself to have money or to be a person of worth. It is an indirect and hidden form of taxation no less than any other such indirect or hidden tax.[387]

---

[387] Hence the existing situation in what is left of Anglo-Saxon governments: As their (unnecessary) expenditure beyond tax income is financed by the creation of debt directly to private persons, which indeed are the Banks (that everyone so unquestioningly accepts these days as an established feature in living) under incredible conditions,* units of exchange in circulation automatically suffer increase, and consequently there is a steady fall in their purchasing power.

Such fall in purchasing power immediately and arbitrarily constitutes a hidden tax on all who hold monetary units in one way or another. Levied in an unseen manner by those private persons who supposedly make the so-called loan to the government, its effects are not understood by the people, nor its origin.

*For a clear statement of the workings of this unbelievable system in Canada, see Brief submitted to the Royal Commission on Banking and Finance by Mel Rowatt, Ottawa, 1964.

Further than this hidden tax imposed with dubious legality, there is the absurdity of an interest rate, which, parallel to that of previous so called loans, creates a yearly interest bill which in itself necessitates further such borrowing, without ever thinking of paying off the principal; such system

If, continuing to speak of ancient times, such units of money, fraudulent or otherwise, were accepted by the simple folk as money, and seemed to serve equally well as had served that lawful money of earlier times yet again, which had been an order on the treasury or warehouses of the god of the city, then indeed, such units were money to all intents and purposes of the immediate needs of exchange. The fact of their legal issuance as a loan at interest against goods and services as collateral pledges, placed in the hands of their creator and issuer the power of total discrimination, formerly recognized as being the sole and absolute prerogative of the god, through his servants the priest-kings of ancient times; those who were the carriers of the breath of Life Eternal from God to Man. As time went on, the fact of their creation, issue, acceptance, and effectiveness in the exchanges, once the people had resigned themselves to slow inflation of values, placed in the hand of this private creator of these originally fraudulent exchange units, *All-Power*!

Whatever the material on which the units of exchange or their divisibles or multiples were recorded, the customer still thought in terms of silver, as even today most still think in terms of gold though none to speak of has circulated for thirty five years or so. So long as the ruler concurred in the first place in the conspiracy to denominate these exchange units as being as acceptable as those previously issued by the god and his people, and between whom the king had been the connecting link, then the power of preferment or rejection was soon in the hands of

---

necessarily compels a government that has been trained to unquestioned acceptance of its financial liabilities to be servant in some considerable degree, of those private persons, its supposed benefactors.

For the opinions of orthodox Political Economy see: James M. Buchanan: *The Public Finances*; pp. 359-69. Homewood; Illinois; 1965. Reuben A. Kessel and Armen A. Alchian: *Effects of Inflation, Journal of Political Economy*, Vol. LXX, pp. 521-37, December, 1962.

the banker as agent for what corresponded in that day to the international bankers of today totally in opposition to that natural order of life in which the unit of exchange represents the will of the benevolent god.

Needless to say, this person would not extend his preferment to those who instinct told him might be able to come to understand the real truth of the emptiness of those shadowed vaults from which his hand reached forth. It might safely be assumed that discrimination would be exercised against those whose obliteration was included in the overall plans of those mystic, if not satanic figures that lurked in the inner sanctuaries of temple, mint, or counting house; in which secret places were formulated those policies that decided the promotion or otherwise of kings, tyrants, dictators, or political parties.

The extraordinary wealth and power according to the standards of the day of this secretive, and apparently humble money power, is shown clearly by the following extract from Babelon:[388]

"We know that the Greek bankers were money changers; all the more important financial transactions were negotiated through their agency. Their counters were the meeting place of businessman and the stock market. They controlled at the same time the sea-borne trade, and the affairs of the caravans, above all, in Asia Minor. The exploitation of mines was often in their hands. These guardians of treasure received the precious metal deposits belonging to private persons or traders, keeping open account for their clients, thus accumulating enormous amounts; they hoarded, they loaned to Princes as well as private individuals. Listen then to the story of Nicholas of Damascus more eloquent than any commentary:

---

[388] Ernest Babelon: *Les Origines de la Monnaie*, p. 106.

'Wishing to carry the war into Caria, Alyatte, King of Lydia (610-561 B.C.) gave the order to his commanders to bring him their contingents at Sardis, by a certain day. Amongst the generals chosen was Croesus, the oldest son of the King, at that time Governor of Adramyttium and of the plain of Thebes. Negligent and prodigal, ill regarded by his father on account of his dissipations, very desirous of being received back into his father's good graces, and of confounding his calumniators, but not having the wherewithal to raise and hire mercenaries, the young Prince, in order to overcome his embarrassment, resolved to contract a loan. With this purpose in mind he sought out Sadyattes, the richest merchant of Lydia. This person, occupied with his ablutions, firstly let Croesus wait impatiently at his door. Then he agreed to receive him, but this was only to refuse him money; 'If I must lend to all the sons of Alyattes,' he cried, 'there will not be enough!'

Rebuffed, Croesus proceeded to Ephesus. There, an Ionian friend, Pamphaes, learning the reason of his visit, obtained a sum of a thousand gold staters from his father, Theocharides, who was possessed of considerable fortune, and which he hastened to bring to the necessitous prince. Thanks to these subsidies, Croesus, furnished with troops, was the first of all at the rendez-vous, and regained the favour of his father who took him in as partner in this expedition.'

Croesus later on revenged himself on Sadyattes who had turned him away, confiscating his treasure to the endowment of the temple of Artemis at Ephesus. The plunder taken from the unhappy banker was large enough to make two pillars of gold and the golden calves, with which the temple of the Goddess was adorned.

Later we see a banker of Caelenae, Pythias, of Lydian extraction, make a gift to King Darius of a plane tree in gold and a vine in gold. Some while afterwards, doubtless in fear that his immense fortune might only come to excite the covetousness of the prince, Pythias made up his mind to ward off the danger by making a concession. Spontaneously he offered Xerxes subsidies for the war. As the Great King was questioning him in kindly curiosity as to the extent of his wealth, the banker confessed, not without misgivings that he possessed in his coffers two thousand talents of silver, and that he was short of four million darics, by only seven thousand darics.

Sadyattes, Theocharides, Pamphaes, Pythias, wealthy guardians of treasure, possessing the confidence of the public who as well as princes, envied their riches, struck monetary ingots in the doorway of their counting houses."

The above excerpt from Babelon and Nicholas of Damascus illustrates a clear cut case in ancient days of effort by money power to control political succession; for the real reason of the refusal by Sadyattes of the loan to Croesus, although not recorded by Babelon, was that Sadyattes had already pledged himself to the support of Panteleon, Croesus' half-brother[389] and probably was also the source of the rumours in regard to the "unsuitability" of Croesus for succession to the throne, and the unsatisfactory reports to Alyattes. Panteleon was clearly more "suitable," and more "pliable" than the strong minded Croesus, who, Sadyattes probably knew via his spies, would be his enemy; although his offensive conduct towards a royal son would suggest he considered his position inviolable. The surly arrogance of this Sadyattes in causing the young Croesus to wait at the door, and then refusing him his request in no pleasant manner, so typical of this class of person today, as much as in Croesus' day, undoubtedly caused Croesus to enquire a little more deeply into this precious metal money "Racket" when he finally did become king, a "racket" which allowed low and unsavoury persons to make a mockery of

---

[389] Herodotus; *The Histories*; Book I.

kingship. The results of his enquiries undoubtedly showed him that above all, for his kingship to be meaningful, monetary emission had to be removed from the control of private persons.

Further evidence of history would suggest, in Lydia at least, Croesus destroyed the arrogance and power to subversion of this class of persons, not the most noble amongst his subjects, by the institution of the issue of equal weights of precious metal or coin, as state prerogative; thus, he thought, returning to himself as representative of the god on earth, that essential power so necessary towards the maintenance of true order in life, the total control of monetary emission. That the reputed fate of Croesus after conquest by Cyrus, the new Persian Monarch, founder of the Achaemenid Dynasty somewhat later on, was influenced by the longing for revenge of those leaders of finance in Babylon City, in one way or another the main force behind Cyrus and his conquests and for whom Sadyattes would very likely have been important agent or co-conspirator, as previously pointed out, seems reasonable supposition.

Hence the real source of the so rapid decay of all relatively recent civilizations and so called empires of the last 6000 years, whose establishment was so often due to the behind the scenes activities of bankers as agents for what was necessarily an internationally spread network of bullion interests, was the complete dearth in the later days of such civilizations or empires, of dean and noble men in places of control and power.

Such natural and truly dedicated leadership had been destroyed, either by the planned discriminatory activities of the bankers, or by the never dying fires of war that maintained these so-called "Empires". Their places had been taken by the progeny of their slaves, or, as in Sparta, by their women.

Clearly in that day almost all money in circulation arrived there created and issued by private persons of a class stranger to the whole world, and whose only guide was never more than their indifference to the miseries of mankind. Today, despite the continuance of the naïve belief of those who toil from day to day, that this money is created and injected into the circulation by the presumably benevolent will of the state, it is the same as in the days of the corruption and crumbling of the god-given distribution systems of the Ancient Orient, in the face of the attack on their integrity, by the privately issued commodity currencies of silver.

This attack later having been intensified when, as a result of the stripping of the ornamentation from tomb and temple, both in Egypt, and right across the ancient oriental world, that silver apex to the inverted pyramid of abstract money by which the great banking houses were manipulating the exchanges, became further augmented by gold, the magic metal so long dedicated to ornament for the god-kings, in life as in death, or to holy ritual. That burning metal, almost a god in itself, now falling into the greasy hands of the money-changers, exchanged with silver in the ratio, so far as the middle East was concerned, of about 13:1.[390]

So far as ancient Persian and Greek history is concerned, it will be quite safe to say that the apparent beneficiaries of such system were front men for a wider and more international system extending from China to Britain, of which evidence in China may have been that strange Hebrew community whose decaying fragments were found south of Pekin by the Jesuits who entered China in the 17th Century; a community that knew nothing of the Talmud, or of Jesus Christ, and who consequently thought in terms of Christians as in terms of a

---

[390] A. del Mar: *A History of Monetary Systems in Various States*, p. 29, and pp. 35-53.

sect of themselves, and who undoubtedly were the descendants of the agents of a most ancient trading community.[391] The evidence of this world wide financial system in Britain exists in the gold staters of the Iceni, Cassivellauni, Brigantes etc. still existing,[392] and which circulated there long before Julius Caesar. Although gold was obtained in Wales and in Ireland, its use as money could only have been inspired and organized from that central point where the original staters were minted, the Near East and the cities wherein dwelt the controllers of international trade and mining.

Amongst other principles of political control by money power, certainly one of the most important of all, used in ancient times, just as much as today, was that which is known as liberalism. Liberalism in simplified language meaning that he who hath shall give to him who hath not; not so much out of proper charity, but so that he who hath not may come to put his foot on the neck of him who (formerly) had, and who now foolishly gives him his own strength. Thus money power, by injecting liberalism along the very arteries of society through those underground channels under its control, made sure that what might be described in the language of today as "Permanent Revolution," would prevent any power group from having control long enough to see the true source of that which is the power of the ruler, if he is to truly be in the saddle, namely, monetary emission. Money Power, then as today, fully understood the necessity towards the continuance of its hegemony, of the promotion amongst the leading families of the states of corrupt persons who took pleasure in destroying their own; persons basically corrupt who had deeply drunk of the poison of liberalism, persons possessed of the wealth of kings because so pleasing to the central designing force, though

---

[391] William C. White: *Jews in Kaifeng*; Toronto; 1966.

[392] R.A.G. Carson: *Coins, Ancient Medieval, and Modern*, p. 70. London; 1962.

at the same time having the natural outlook of the slave. truly strange combination!

One such family identified in ancient times with the promotion of liberalism and its attendant sister, welfarism, both equally beneficial to money power, was that Athenian family known as the Alkmeonidae, who, although suspected at the time of the Battle of Marathon (490 B.C.) as being the source of the heliograph that sent information across the bay of Marathon to the Persian commanders,[393] strangely enough continued to maintain power and place at Athens. Equally strange had been the awarding of the contract for the rebuilding of the Temple at Delphi after it had been burned down (548 B.C.), to this same family in exile from Athens.

As previously surmised, International Money Power above all must have sought control of the great temples and oracles. Delphi was such, and the oracle at Delphi was highly regarded over the ancient world. The building of a major temple was a gift which must have been arranged by those interests who were best of all served by the family policies of the Alkmeonidae. It might safely be said that if this same family had been rejected by Athens, the gift came from that financial force whose favour they had clearly enjoyed from generation to generation: namely the money power that guided the policies of the Achaemenid Rulers of Persia and Babylonia.

Pericles, scion of this notorious family, while being the front man for those forces driving Athens into war with Sparta, was the instigator of the Donatives and later, of *theorica*,[394]

---

[393] A.R. Burns: *Pericles and Athens*, p. 11; London; 1948.

[394] According to Augustus Boeckh in *The Public Economy of Athens* (Vol. II; p. 289): "The Public donations or distributions amongst the peoples were of frequent occurrence. To these belong the distributions of corn which have been mentioned before, the *cleruchiae* and the revenues from the mines,

outstandingly undermining factor to Athenian self-esteem and national morale. *Theorica* allowed two oboli per person to the lessee of the Oratorium[395] and thus two corrupt purposes were served:

1. It made sure all or at least a great part of the citizenry attended the plays, thus keeping their minds off more serious matters as do cinema and television particularly in this day; more especially keeping their minds off that most serious matter of all which is true understanding of politics; in other words, understanding of the meaning of the essential forces that guided their existence.
2. It assured the lessee of the Oratorium (and that politician who most promoted his interests), a certain profit.

A third purpose would also have been served, although there is absolutely no record that says so: the maintenance of an unbalanced budget and consequent stimulation of government indebtedness to private money creative power, i.e. the bankers. If the sophistication of Sales Tax was known to Periclean Athens,[396] it may safely be assumed were also known the sophisticated practices in relation to government indebtedness as practised particularly in Anglo-Saxon countries today.[397] Officially *theorica* was drawn from the fund for war preparedness. The only conclusion that can be drawn as to the true meaning therefore of the establishment of *theorica*,[398] so far

---

which, before the time of Themistocles (471 B.C.) were divided amongst the citizens; and lastly the money of the *Theorica* for the introduction of which, Pericles is chargeable."

[395] *Ibid.* p. 290.

[396] Display in the Royal Ontario Museum, 1972.

[397] Bray Hammond and the staff of the Federal Reserve System (1939): *The Federal Reserve System*; Omni, Hawthorne, Calif. 1958.

[398] Augustus Boeckh: *The Public Economy of Athens*, p. 289, Vol. II.

as the bankers were concerned, was to further increase necessity of government borrowing in time of war, and so strengthen the hold of that so called National Debt almost certainly held by themselves.[399]

Thus the principles of the total hegemony of private money creative power were as clearly understood by its masters yesterday, as much as they are today. The limiting factors to the complete destruction with which we are now threatened as a result of the flare-up in this all consuming cancer which began about some three hundred years ago, and now rages on virtually uncontrollable, were, at that time, that kings and councils still ruled, and kings still thought of themselves as the sons of God, the saviours of their peoples. If in any way they had understood the malignance of this growth that had penetrated the substructure of life it would have been short shrift for its

---

[399] *Ibid.* p. 277. Vol. II. Analysis of the remarks of Demosthenes as quoted hereunder leave little doubt in respect to this matter:

"In ancient days" says Demosthenes " everything that belonged to the state was costly and splendid, and no individual distinguished himself from the multitude; and the proof of it is, that if any of you know the houses of Themistocles and Miltiades, and the famous men of that time, he will see that they are not more magnificent than those of other people; but the buildings and construction of the State were of such size and number, that it is not in the power of succeeding generations to surpass them--the Propylaea, the Docks, the Porticoes, the Piraeus, and other works with which you see the city adorned! But now all who are concerned in the management of public affairs have a superfluity of riches, that some have built private houses more magnificent than many public edifices and some of them have purchased more land than all of you who are sitting in the court are together possessed of; but your public buildings and works, it is disgraceful to tell how scanty and contemptible they are. What indeed can be said of your works? What of the parapets we throw up? Of the roads we construct and the fountains and trifles at which we labour? Thus speaks the ardent enthusiast for the happiness and fame of his country; his speeches of admonition might with a few alterations be adapted to the present age, in which such vast sums have been squandered away without producing anything useful or durable."

controllers. Hence the necessity for an absolute secrecy most restrictive in its effects. Clay, the material on which records were kept throughout Babylonia at least, did not have any of the potential of paper so far as went the keeping of records. Parchment and papyrus while not standing up to constant use, were becoming increasingly rare and expensive, and vellum, relatively rare, was not known until the time of Pergamum where the first books written on this material appeared in 198 B.C.[400]

Neither did those states escape a certain international control of their money such as did not adopt the relatively new idea of coined precious metal money, but continued to use copper, bronze orichalcum, or iron, and whose value depended on the scarcity or otherwise of its circulating symbols relative to the need for them; designated a fiduciary money.

For instance, in the case of Greece, the silver bullion brokers who were clearly based at Athens, obviously would be able to control the exchange rates of such cities as used their own fiduciary or national currencies,[401] if, as usually would be the case, such cities sought the good graces of Athens towards obtaining food and raw materials and towards marketing their manufactures.

Thus, through the exchange rates, the bankers and bullion traders would also be able to exercise some control over the political life of such cities. The City of Athens itself, its monetary system based directly on their internationally required products, silver and gold, was clearly under their immediate control. If the state owned the mints, of which there seems to

---

[400] A. del Mar: *History of the Precious Metals*, p. 105; New York; 1968.

[401] Augustus Boeckh: *Public Economy of Athens*, p. 43, Vol. I. London; 1828. Also Michael Grant, p. 3.

be no knowledge, it would make no difference. The states own the mints today for what it means; which is little or nothing so far as goes control of Monetary Emission.[402]

With the end of the bronze age in warfare, from one end of the world to the other, enormous amounts of copper and bronze must have come on to the markets of the world as scrap; much of which would have been obtained at little more than the cost of its removal from national arsenals by the money changers or their agents.

Where copper and bronze fiduciaries, as at Rome, circulated at values many times more than their value by weight of metal on the international bullion markets, relative to their value in silver or gold bullion, clearly such copper and bronze bullion such as came on to the markets as military scrap, would have been more useful towards the counterfeiting of such currencies, than sold at its bullion value. For instance, if the value of one libra of copper as offered on the bullion market (if such could exist) at Rome was one *Aes*, the value of a minted *Aes* of one libra weight in an overvaluation of the minted coin relative to copper bullion prices internationally, would be as the demand for them rose and fell, according to supply and demand.

It appears that at Rome during the middle Commonwealth, the overvaluation of the *Aes* relative to the same weight of bullion was 400-500%; in the countryside and more distant colonies often being far more. If in latter times (during the 18th Century A.D.), the copper rouble of czarist Russia, issued at an overvaluation of up to 800% according to the value of copper

---

[402] *The Royal Commission on Banking and Finance.* Ottawa; 1964. Brief submitted by Mel Rowatt, and page 138 on "Swap" deposits etc.

bullion relative to the price internationally of silver bullion,[403] brought into Russia a very inundation of counterfeits minted in Western Europe,[404] clearly the of *Aes* at substantial overvaluation, made the creation and of counterfeit coin an equally profitable affair in ancient Rome.

Thus international money power would have succeeded in diminishing the beneficial effects of such national currency, continuing to use Rome as the example, by mass counterfeiting, which would have seen rapid increase once gold and silver commenced to circulate alongside the *Aes* after the Second Punic War. Clearly the main purpose of the counterfeiters, then, as agents in some degree of the international silver bullion traders, would be to inject their copper or bronze counterfeits into circulation at the best overvaluation possible, which would be through money-lending in the provinces, at the same time requiring repayment, if possible, in silver and gold. Hence the steady disappearance of the precious metals from the circulation, was either due to the activities of the smaller moneylenders dealing in counterfeit, or due to the activities of the *Argentarii* or *Numularii* making loans in exactly the same manner as the bankers today, loans which never saw light as money, being always cheques in transit, but which, in the final repayment were as often as not, gold, silver, or *Aes*; the later being immediately convertible into gold or silver, which seems largely to have then moved Eastward.

---

[403] During the brief reign of Peter III (1762-1763 A.D.) the pood of copper was coined into 32 roubles, copper bullion itself being approximately 5 roubles per pood.

[404] According to the memoirs of Count Munnich, to his knowledge 6,000,000 counterfeit roubles entered Russia from Western Europe being exchanged as against the silver rouble at a profit of 566%. This amount was known. The unknown amount must have been much greater. A. del Mar: *Money and Civilization*, p. 303; London 1886.

This disappearance of the precious metals from the circulation[405] Eastward seems to have been a factor inspiring the vehemence of Cicero in his *Oration: Pro Flaccus*. The indignation of Cicero as recorded in this *Oration* may be traced to the indifference of certain persons who lived close to the Aurelian steps, to the good of the Roman State wherein they lived and whose solidarity enabled them to arrange to have mobs intimidate the proceedings of the court which heard a person, probably a member of the banking family known as the Lollii,[406] attempt to smear the reputation of Lucius Flaccus, who, as Praetor of Syria, had issued edict forbidding this movement of precious metals Eastward for deposit at the Temple in Jerusalem.[407]

Of Roman banking the great 19th century scholars, Mommsen and Marquardt, wrote:[408]

"The conduct of banking was done for the most part through the intermediary of the *argentarii* and of *nummularii*: these last were known under the name of *collectarii mensularii*. In countries of Greek origin there was a kind of state bank as at Tenos, at Ilium, and at Temnos in Aeolide; they were also in Egypt: in

---

[405] *Naturalis Historia*, xii, c. 18. Pliny. *Minimaque computatione millies contena millia sesertium annis omnibus India et Seres peninsulaque illa imperio nostro adimunt. Tanto nobis deliciae et feminae constant.* (*History of Monetary Systems*, p. 126. A. del Mar.)

[406] Michael Grant, (*From Imperium to Auctoritas*. p. 57.), makes mention of a banking family known as the Lollii. Cicero speaks of a Laelius; (*Orationes: Pro Flaccus*, Book XVII.). They are more likely members of the same family.

[407] Cicero: *Orationes: Pro Flaccus*, Book XVII. Clearly transfer of the precious metals in the time of Cicero meant transfer of prosperity in the same way as it did in the European controlled world until recently.

[408] *Manuel des Antiquités Romaines*, pp. 78-85; Tome Dixième; De l'Organisation Financière chez les Romaines. Théodore Mommsen, and Joachim Marquardt. Paris. 1888.

every Nome was found a beneath the direction of a royal employee, and through him as intermediary it was customary to make certain contracts and payments. Among the Romans, on the contrary, it was only in the most extraordinary circumstances that public banks were organized under the direction of state functionaries (*mensa publica*); thus amongst others, in 402-352 (B.C.) under the direction of *quinqui viri mensarii*, in order to facilitate the liquidation of debts, by advances made against guarantees, with state funds, and during the period 538 to 543-216 to 211 B.C. for different reasons, and finally to carry out the collection of funds loaned free to the state.

It was about that time that the *tabernae argentariae* were established of which the first indications are in 443-399 B.C.; often occurring later on.

It is through the intermediary of the *argentarii* that most payments were made, as also they were entrusted with the collection of moneys due, the placing of capitals at interest, the sale of merchandise, and particularly the liquidation of estates by way of auction sales and finally investments of all kinds; exchange transactions, notably the changing of foreign moneys and the sale of Roman money appear originally to have been reserved to the *nummularii*.

Under this heading we must first of all take a look at the dealers in exchange, who had to check the qualifications of new money; as such they seem to have had a *mensa* from which they put new money into circulation, taking in the course of their business old money as well as foreign money, and it was their custom to set the rates of exchange; outside of Rome the *publicae mensae nummulariorum* appeared to have existed. In second place this description applied to private persons whose business was dealing in the precious metals. Concurrently with the *argentarii*, they conducted all the activities that go with banking business; they accepted capitals for deposit, they made payments for the account of other people, they placed capitals at interest and for exchange transactions they levied a charge or bonus. these bankers, the *argentarii*, the same as the *nummularii*, were placed under the surveillance of state functionaries, *praefectus urbi*, at Rome during the empire, and in the provinces under the surveillance of the governor. They were probably the subject of the granting of a franchise, or investiture, that was only accorded to a very limited number of people; in the case of dispute they were obliged to produce their books (*rationes edere*), which were evidence of payments made and transactions entered into. For their franchise they were subjected to legal regimentation.

These books were of three kinds: in the first place was a cash book, *codex accepti et expensi* in which in order of date were recorded the deposits and withdrawals of the *argentarius* with mention of the nature of the business and the names of the persons interested. In second place, a running account (*rationes, liber rationum*) in which the banking operations of the *argentarius* with every person involved were kept by debit and credit; thanks to which, it could be known at a moments notice how much the merchant was owed by every one of his clients, and how much he had to pay out to him.

In third place a book was kept, *adversaria*, in which was preserved record of the transactions under way, and even having their designation in code. Amongst these books, that which is peculiar to the *argentarii*, is the running account book, rendered necessary by the great number of transactions; the cash book, on the contrary, in which were entered by order of date the deposits and withdrawals, *expensum ferre, acceptum referre*, was kept by every head of a family until the IIIrd century A.D., in which period this custom fell into disuse.

mensae scripturae: The mensae scripturae served in that which touched the activities of banking, as much to establish contract, as to furnish proof, and the greater part of payments were effected by transcriptions and endorsements recorded in the account books of the *argentarii*; direct payment (*domo ex arca sua*) was rarely made, but it was very often made through the intermediary of bankers (*de mensa scriptura*),whether moneys had been deposited with them for which they were obliged to give account (*rationem reddere*), or whether it had been possible to open a credit with them out of which they made payment following an assignment."

The above excerpt from the works of two scholars of vast learning, is revealing. No doubt will be left with the reader who understands modern day banking practices, that just as in today 95% of all money in circulation, is cheques and assignments in transit, often written against credits granted by bankers where no actual funds previously existed, but however without which the drive and turmoil of this civilization could not have come to be, so it was in Rome and in Greece. Indeed, for all those movements of vast armies, and for all those movements of peoples through the consequent sale and transfer of slaves, and for the erection of all those great works in stone, many of which still stand, from the pillars of Hercules to Parthia and Arabia, the instigative factor was the same as the instigative factor behind all the mighty works and mysteries of today. It was none other than the driving force of that abstract money that none can see, but that functions just the same as that which can be seen, the mysterious "Credit" of the banker; force that once had been the will of a benevolent god, but now was an instrument towards the wilful redesign and enslavement of mankind. In the late Roman Commonwealth and the early Empire, the assignments and cheques in transit may not have equalled 95% of all money in circulation, and it is by no means impossible that they were even more, taking into account the fact that today's high speed printing presses and coining machines, the fount of the 5% of the circulation that can be seen, can create these visible units on which the inverted pyramid of the invisible units is erected, at a hundred thousand or more times the speed of slaves striking and finishing metal units of money by hand.[409]

In *Harpers Dictionary of Classical Literature and Antiquities*, Roman banking is dealt with as follows, in close agreement with Mommsen and Marquardt:. "The *Argentarius* thus did almost the same sort of business as a modern banker. Many persons entrusted all their capital to them (Cicero: Pro. Caec. 6.16) and instances in which the *argentarii* made payments in the name of those whose money they had in hand, are mentioned very frequently. A payment made through a banker was called *per mensam, de mensa* or *per mensae scripturam*, while a payment made by the debtor in person was a payment *ex arca* or *de domo*. An *argentarius* never paid away any person's money without receiving a cheque (*perscriptio*), and the payment was then made either in cash, or, if the person who was to receive it kept an account with the same banker, he had it added in the banker's book, to his deposit. This was likewise called *perscribere* or simply *scribere. we also find that argentarii made payments for persons who had not deposited any money with them: this was equivalent to lending money; which in fact they often did for a certain percentage of interest.*"[410]

Thus banking was carried on in almost the same manner in the Roman world as in our world of today, and to those who understand the significance of the practices of modern day banking, nothing could be clearer. Even the ostentatious display of a metal safety deposit vault is recorded by the

---

[409] According to A. del Mar in *A History of the Precious Metals*, (p. 88). "At that period when the coining press was unknown, the work of coinage was done altogether by the hammer, shears, and file. A workman could scarcely finish more than twenty coins a day."

[410] *Harpers Dictionary of Classical Literature and Antiquities*, p. 1598, Harry T. Peck, Coopers Square Publishers, New York, 1965.

antiquarian, Lanciana,⁴¹¹ of the time of Hadrian; doubtless to encourage people to leave their valuables with the bank and so strengthen their "confidence."

In the earlier days when the senate was truly government in the saddle, that is until the end of the integrity of the numerical currency, with the resumption of the striking of silver money and therefore reentry into the orbit of the silver bullion brokers, mining of the precious metals had been forbidden in Italy,⁴¹² and copper mining had been state monopoly, clearly indicating the futility of any discussion of whether the striking of coinage had been free or otherwise. Where the policy of the state had been to maintain an overvaluation of its bronze coinage relative to bullion prices,⁴¹³ it is quite clear that it could in no way permit private individuals the privilege of the mints, free or otherwise. To do so would be to concede them the right and the power to manipulate price levels, and so, confounding the economy, dismay the rulers. Thus it was not until the time of Cicero that evidence appears of private persons bringing bullion to the mints,⁴¹⁴ significantly coincidental with the general collapse of the ancient manners, and the essential forces that had guided Rome, as is described by Sallust.

Such matters of state finance seem to have been well understood during the middle commonwealth. However, as a

---

⁴¹¹ Alexander del Mar: *A History of the Precious Metals*, p. 105; New York; 1968.

⁴¹² *Ibid.* p. 55. (Pliny, Books iii, xxxiv, 5. and xxiii, 21.)

⁴¹³ According to Harold Mattingly (*Roman Coins*, p. 19): "In the second period c.280-268 B.C., the *aes* and its parts were issued as before, but a coinage of silver was added for the purposes of the war in S. Italy. The chief coin was the Didrachme. the bronze coins of the series are struck at very variable weights and certainly represent *values above their metal.*"

⁴¹⁴ Harold Mattingly: *Roman Coins*; p. 91; London; 1923.

result of the second Punic war and Trasimeno and Cannae[415] and the desperate need to rearm quickly that followed these unfortunate battles, Rome clearly had been obliged to allow the whole currency system to become based on the international valuation of silver as common denominator of values. She also had been obliged to permit the reduction of the value of the *aes* coinage to the value of its weight as bronze bullion relative to the arbitrary value internationally of silver bullion.

It follows that it was only after Rome had thus surrendered much of her sovereign prerogative in money matters to the international silver bullion brokers, reluctantly, as was shown by subsequent events, that growth of liberalism, and consequent undermining of the morale of the people and their government, finally gave rise to the warlords known as the Triumvirate and the beginning of rule which might best be described as complete negation of that which had been government by decree of the senate.

With the reckless abuse of the powers of their *Imperium* through those bankers who supported them, particularly in relation to their right to strike money in the field, the warlords derived virtual independence from the *auctoritas* of an already corrupted senate and when, in 23 B.C., the *aes* coinage which had been the backbone of the Republic, was returned to the senate with S.C. *Senatus Consulto* (by decree of the senate)[416] stamped thereon, it was more in the nature of a concession to a dignity and authority that once had been the reality guiding Roman political life, but now had become a meaningless front, a shadow.

---

[415] 216 B.C.; in this terrible battle, 86,000 Romans and Italians were virtually annihilated and all their equipment lost to Hannibal.

[416] R.A.G. Carson: *Coins, Ancient, Medieval, and Modern*; p. 127; London; 1962.

Thus with the rise of the warlords, who were in effect, would-be tyrants under arms, each with his own Money Power, was the triumph of the empire concept. In the case of Caesar, his supporting bankers appear to have been the L. Cornelius Balba for whom the A. Hirtius of Caesar's *aes* coinage as issued in the country of the Treveri in Gaul, seems to have been agent with H. Clovius, emittor in Cisalpine Gaul of Caesar's *orichalcum* (brass) issues. Also C. Vibius Pansa and Q. Sulpicius Rufus, all of whom are described by Michael Grant as "eminent financiers."[417] Of this period *An Encyclopaedia of World History* says: "If the crossing of the Rubicon marked the final fall of the Republic, the battle of Actium signalized the final triumph of the Empire. The last century of the republic was characterised by the collapse of popular government, because of the wide extension of the citizenship, the considerable adulteration of the citizen body at Rome by the introduction of un-Romanized orientals, chiefly through the manumission of slaves, the growth in Rome of an unemployed proletariat, the rise of demagogues, and the complexity of the problems of government. The increasingly corrupt senate had lost control of the assemblies, the armies and the generals. The financiers as well as the governors, saw in the provinces only a field for exploitation."[418]

Clearly moneyers and bankers reigned supreme as far as it was possible behind some powerful military figure such as had been Caesar or Anthony or Octavian, or in some measure of direct authority as seems to have been the case with Sosius, moneyer and financial organizer to Anthony, who also came from a banking family. The same Sosius when quaestor and governor of Syria and Cilicia, dethroned Antigonus, the last of the Hasmonean kings of Jerusalem in 37 B.C. after six months

---

[417] Michael Grant: *From Imperium to Auctoritas*, p. 19; Cambridge, 1969.

[418] An Encyclopedia of World History, p. 100, Boston, 1948.

siege, replacing him with Herod, later known as "The Great," first of the Idumean line in that city.[419]

Considering how extensive a part the coinage of Sosius had played in the fortune (or lack of fortune) of Anthony, Sosius was lucky to have been spared by Octavian.[420] The absence of Herod from the deciding battle of the civil wars, the battle of Actium (31 B.C.) under the excuse that he was detained more urgently in Arabia fighting the King of Arabia on Anthony's behalf,[421] may be the answer here. No doubt Sosius, in the same way as any good banker in ancient or in modern times, knew how to keep a foot in each camp; equally wise was also his friend Herod. Q. Oppius who emitted the *orichalcum* coinage inaugurated by Anthony, also appears to have belonged to a well known family of bankers.[422]

The name of the bankers behind Augustus does not appear to be known, but the extent of their massive operations is revealed by the widespread circulation of their heavy weight *aes* coinage from their mint at Nemausen, right across the Empire; from Britain, to Portugal, to Pannonia.[423] It may safely be concluded that their coinage circulated without discount and at par value with all other *aes* coinage previous or present, state issued, or otherwise, or by *imperium* or *auctoritas*.

The question would be: was this excellent and adequate coinage which so well met the needs of great military and civil day to

---

[419] William Smith, LLD: The History of the Bible; p. 550; London, Ontario; 1885.

[420] Michael Grant: *From Imperium to Auctoritas*; p. 41; Cambridge; 1969.

[421] *Britannica*, 9th Edn.

[422] Michael Grant: p. 61-69.

[423] *Ibid* pp. 71-72. C.H.V. Sutherland (*Coinage in Imperial Roman Policy*) also makes frequent reference to Nemausen.

day expenditures, and which undoubtedly was the origin of the sure accession to power of Augustus, emitted by an organization of similar character to the Bank of England of recent world power, or more recently again, the Federal Reserve Bank of the United States of America? Both of which, though apparently state departments, in reality were private international organizations set up by the international circle of bullion traders, or, as they are now generally known, the International Bankers.

That which seems to be clear out of the fragments of information existing, is that there was no such thing as a permanent interest bearing state indebtedness until the period which may mark the beginning of the decline of imperial Rome; the significance of which is that no Roman Government ever entirely lost control of that power so essential to the maintenance of its sovereignty, the power to directly inject the unit of exchange into circulation as according to its own needs.

Of this period until the 3rd Century A.D. the most learned Professor Heichelheim wrote: "There were regular lending associations while usury constituted quite an important item in the legal provisions of the Corpus Iuris and the Talmud. *Only State Usury was rare, for the Roman State was still in a supreme position.*[424] At the most, autonomous areas were the only exceptions here. Large interest free loans advanced to the state by individual citizens or chance patrons for reward in the form of honours or other more indirect advantage, were quite frequent up to the 3rd Century A.D."[425]

---

[424] Italics by present author.

[425] Fritz Heichelhiem: *Ancient Economic History*; p. 243, Volume III, Leyden; 1958-1970.

However, it may reasonably be assumed that even during the period of the Commonwealth and the true greatness of the Roman people, though Roman Government had endeavoured to monopolize all sources of the material of its tangible currency, and had prevented as much as possible the circulation of precious metal, which clearly would undermine the integrity of the state issued unit of exchange, the grandiose *aes*, it still could not prevent counterfeits from entering the circulation. It could not prevent the corrupt practices of oriental banking after the extensive reentry of silver into the circulation as a result, clearly, of concessions made to the international bullion traders during the 2nd Punic war, nor thereafter the functioning of Gresham's so-called law which such entailed. "Bad money drives out the good"; which, of course, depends on what is bad and what is good! Nor, therefore, could it control the extent in absolute, right across the Roman Empire, of the activities of that underground that garnered the precious metal from the circulation for more profitable use elsewhere.

As a consequence of the rejection by growing and powerful states such as Rome of the early and middle commonwealth of the claim of silver bullion interests that all tangible money should be founded on their product as base and common denominator of values, and the creation and paying into circulation of their own tangible money, with value deriving from its scarcity or otherwise, using largely copper or bronze as the material on which its numbers were recorded, as previously pointed out, much copper or bronze that came the way of the international bullion brokers would, undoubtedly have been used in what must have been an extensive industry devoted to counterfeiting of these fiduciary currencies. The product of this industry which would have been carried on abroad no doubt, while yielding handsome profit, through disturbance of that mass of abstract money based on the tangible currencies into which such products would have been injected, would also create instability of price in the states concerned.

Thus would be created conditions in which foreign money lenders would be better able to flourish, and secure the establishment of their own peculiar systems of private money emission based usually on the fiction of valuables on deposit for safe-keeping. Under such systems, when fully under way, the next step would be political control through so called political parties that such money power would bring into being, each necessarily dedicated to some "cause" through a so-called "Leader," also chosen through the agency of such money power and by those forces it controlled. Such leaders would be "suitable" men, and would be chosen because pliable and, too often, naturally corrupt. Raised as likely as not from the lower ranks of society, and therefore dazed by the dizzy heights to which fortune had lifted them, such men would be most likely to carry out without question the policies required for the fulfilment of their master's purposes and dreams; principally that of World Government; which should raise such masters, strange thought though it might be, to the position of world rulers, and therefore heirs of the god-kings of ancient days, in their own eyes; although to the eye of any clear-seeing man they might better have been called the anti-god, or in the language of the naïve Christians of a somewhat later time to the god-kings, demons.

David Astle

MAN PROPOSES BUT GOD DISPOSES

So speaking of One World and of World Rule, a vision stirs of a distant past, and of efforts towards World Rule in a smaller world of another day; a past of which so little remains other than shattered columns, cracked vases, a few precious metal coins and baked clay facsimiles thereof, and the writings of relatively a handful of the best of a former day, amongst which, strangely enough, still exist the works of the propagandists for money power such as Xenophon, and, as some say, Thucydides.

Behind these scattered fragments and the unseen but still existing remains of millions of dead that lie beneath land and sea, consumed in the constant wars of those ancient days, is the enigmatic vision of those half-Greek men amongst their records in the counting houses of Athens and the Piraeus, and the clear picture of them and their "Boy," Pericles, scion of that line of the shifty Alkmeonidae, preparing under their guidance, plans for that "Great War" which would extend their financial hegemony across the whole Grecian world. If events proceeded along those lines in which they would see to it that they were guided, then, who knows? perhaps as a consequence, their financial hegemony might in time be brought to spread across the whole world. ONE WORLD might, as a result of the scheming of their fevered brains, be brought to reality.

This empire was now completely controlled by them. After Klearchos, and the edict of 432 B.C. in which the Athenian allies were forbidden to use any standard other than that of Attica, followed by the edict of 415 B.C. in which the minting of silver was altogether forbidden them, the Athenian Empire must have fallen totally under the control of the banks. The edict ordering the subject allies to contribute money instead of ships, meant that they were to be drained of silver. When the silver was gone, they would be obliged to come hat in hand to the Piraeus for that which the "Great" Bankers were now lending as money against real collateral; entries in the credit page of their ledger, or clay facsimiles of silver and gold money which once had been.

This war would give the bankers complete control of Greece and all that such could bring about through their financial guidance. None would flourish from Colchis[426] to Illyria except they so willed it. The instrument which was Athens and its allies would finally and forever destroy that Spartan hegemony in the Peloponnese that had so long denied them entry, and had refused to accept their terms, and permit the circulation of that which they through trade and money. All that proud Dorian aristocracy of the Peloponnese would be exterminated, as these bankers had arranged long since for the aristocracy of so many other states and cities of the world. Their own future as a people destined to be lord over all, would be secure, except those wretched political hacks of Athens could be called their peers. Gone forever would be the iron and leather money of the Lacedaemonians, over whose issues they had no control, no foreign pedlars being permitted, no "Businessmen," nor trade in imported luxuries.

---

[426] Colchis was a district at the Eastern end of the Black Sea, South of the Caucasus and North of Armenia and Pontus. In Greek mythology it was famous as the destination of the Argonauts, and, as abode of Medea, a special headquarters for sorcery. An independent state at the time of Alexander, when that area subject to Mithridates was invaded by Pompey, Colchis was paying nominal homage to Mithridates. On his defeat it was made a Roman province.

The houses of the scarcely ruined streets of its principal sea port which long since sank beneath the sea as a result of some forgotten earth tremor, still stand in ghostly stillness deep below the surface. The Russians have a submarine which travels these streets for tourist purposes.

So with this vision before them, the war would commence, and from that blood and fire that they the bankers would see to it would sweep the land, could come nothing but good for them as they planned in the shadows in the inner chambers of the counting houses of the Piraeus. These men knew that whatever happened, and the result was certain so they estimated, finally their agents would be permitted that which they wanted above all: permanent residence in Sparta, and time consequently to spread the poison amongst the people of Sparta which only they knew the brewing of to such perfection, the poison of moral decay. Under the stress of war, Sparta, through the agency of its ageing king Archidamos, who was privately friend of the banker's "Boy," Pericles, would secretly accept their terms, and permit the circulation of that which they loaned as money, and permit private persons to possess and hoard silver and gold, which, through the "Principles of Banking" would soon be theirs in any case.

However it seemed as if even in that day it could be said: *The best laid schemes of mice and men gang aft a'gley!* A well planned stratagem that should have established forever the banker's dream of world empire through the creation of common money market embracing the whole world, and that would have removed all remaining resistance towards the realization of such dream, could they but settle once and for all the problem of Sparta, was frustrated; and if something approaching such common money market finally came about, it was not out of the original plan. Plague spread in from Egypt having originated in Ethiopia; Athens particularly was stricken and by 427 B.C., three hundred knights, and four thousand, four hundred of the armoured hoplites drawn from the best of the Athenian middle classes, had fallen, not to the enemy, but to the plague. Woe willed from on High! The deaths amongst women, artisans and slaves were much more. Not merely were the formerly magnificent armed forces of the Athenians reduced to virtual ineffectiveness, so far as the original plan was concerned, but so was the civil war machine, economic or otherwise. sickness and death struck all and the rotting bodies of *trapezitae* or his slave were thrown on the mass funeral pyres together with that of hoplite and his wife. With the flames consuming the dead, most of the immediate schemes of the bankers turned into a wisp of smoke and disappeared into the heavens with an accompanying odour of burnt flesh.

Those precious metal pieces, those copper fiduciaries, those clay facsimiles, all those ledger entries, credits against no funds, money created out of the thin air as by the hand of the gods, all these were the secret of that endless urge and turmoil of the city states of Greece, and of the tumult which finally culminated in the dark years of that miniature "World War," out of which could come no winner but the International Money Power. The "Great Peloponnesian War," as it came to be called, saw a whole system of life crumbling to pieces, just as did these last two so-called "Great" world wars of our time; and still in the final ending not being replaced by that system most longed for by those who have guided us so far along this road of hopelessness.

In these brief moments of time since the fall of so much of ancient ways; faintly discernible as beginning about the period of the collapse of the Middle Kingdom in Egypt under the impact of the horses and chariots of the Hyksos, and that period of turmoil and destruction amongst which was the fall of that Ur of Ibi-Sin, the last great ruler of Sumer before it was eclipsed in its day of glory by all those Semitic peoples spreading Southward, so that even its language almost disappeared.[427] God seems to have more and more withdrawn his face from mankind, now moving without guide along the uncertain ways of time.

---

[427] Sir Charles Leonard Woolley: *The Sumerians*, p. 168 *et seq.* (Norton Edn.).

One thing stands out clearly from the fitting transfer of Ledger Credit Page Entry Money, evinced by tattered fragments relating to man and his money in very ancient days, and that is, ONE WORLD! Through the whole web of confusion, this faint design grows clearly more distinguishable, concept of those who by nature of their secret trade, money, standing apart from life, think they know and understand all the paths of men and life; and because of the international character of that which they now control, delude themselves into believing that they, as designers of it all, rising into the firmament as gods, shall be heirs to it all.

These secret classes who live shut in by the four walls of their exclusivity, had originally believed that one more step would place them forever on the now empty thrones of the god-kings who formerly reigned in lordship over all; towards which place of all-power they had so long guided themselves through the devious paths of knowledge of precious metal money creation and emission, and all the deceits against mankind, to which it had loaned itself. With the establishment of the so-called United Nations Banking complex via the International Bank for Reconstruction and Development, otherwise designated "The World Bank," knowing no master on this earth other than God or the Devil, as the case might be, and with advent of the settlement of international trade balances PAPER GOLD, as the final deceit,[428] these secret classes behind it all, well might believe that the total of human activity, whether as towards War or Peace, depended on their instigation alone. With such triumphs resulting from the long years of planning and waiting, well might they have been justified in concluding that the end of a long and weary way towards WORLD RULE had been

---

[428] June Grem: *The Money Manipulators*, pp. 137-178; Enterprise Publications, Inc. Oak Park, Illinois. 1971. Also see *The Toronto Star*, p. C9; "Monetary Experts favour new System"; Fri., June 14th, 1974.

reached; perhaps the only question remaining being: "Who should be the Ruler?"

But for them already is the bitter assurance that this promised land, even if faintly glimpsed, will never be; and that they stand on the same threshold as the rest of the Indo-European peoples, if not mankind. Beyond this threshold, where in the fatuity of their vain imaginings, was to have been a money changer's World Kingdom, and for them and theirs, life everlasting, are in reality the desolate ways of the gulf of time and infinity, no less for them as for all. Those absolute weapons dreamed into existence as instruments towards the final realization of such world kingdom, mainly through the genius of the Indo-European peoples, have also been placed by the unruly agents of these secret classes, in the hands of other races of the world; races who now thrust God-wards, and whose hearts may be an ocean of envy, if not hate itself, for the same Indo-European who now totters towards the grave to which he was being led, sick unto death.

And even should this ONE WORLD come to be, what of INTERNATIONAL MONEY POWER itself and its fatuous dream of a money changer's world dominion? and what will happen to it when the Indo-European who was its unwitting host and protector for so long, is gone? for, except for some unforeseen change in the course of events, gone he surely will be, and one or the other will have taken his place as world leader.

The present day Chinese, for instance, who very well may be strong in the competition for the throne of the gods from whence ONE WORLD would be ruled, in the event of their accession to such throne, either by election, or by force of arms, would not be likely to tolerate this finance core, privately and irresponsibly controlled, and from which has been drawn the threads of evil that have so long tormented the so called Indo-European world; which long since has been totally entrapped in the web that has been woven. No more did the

Chinese of ancient imperial days extend toleration to such activities throughout their long history.

But it may not be doubted; little if anything will be left anyway. Even should this world we know be spared total obliteration, after the pestilence of decay, once again will be just shattered columns, crumbling concrete, paper that turns to dust with the touch and ruin over all. Life's urgent clamour will be followed by the silence of its extinction. The brief and fading evidence of all this turmoil will be but faint shadows on the accumulating dust.

THE END

"And there came one of the seven angels which had the seven vials, and talked with me, saying unto me, Come hither; I will show unto thee the judgement of the great whore that sitteth upon many waters:

With whom the kings have committed fornication.

So he carried me away in the spirit into the wilderness: and I saw a woman sit upon a scarlet beast, full of names of blasphemy.

* * *

And upon her forehead was a name written, a mystery, BABYLON THE GREAT, THE MOTHER OF HARLOTS AND OF ABOMINATIONS OF THE EARTH

* * *

And he saith onto me, The waters which thou sawest where the whore sitteth are peoples, and multitudes, and nations, and tongues.

* * *

And the woman which thou sawest is that great city, which reigneth over the kings of the earth

* * *

And the kings of the earth who have committed fornication and lived deliciously with her, shall bewail her, and lament for her, when they shall see the smoke of her burning.

* * *

For in one hour so great riches is come to nought. And every shipmaster and all the company in ships, and sailors, and as many as trade by the sea stood afar off,

* * *

And they cast dust on their heads and they cried weeping and wailing, saying, Alas, alas that great city wherein were made rich all that had ships in the sea by reason of her costliness! for in one hour is she made desolate."

REVELATION XVII. 1. TO XVIII. 21.

BIBLIOGRAPHY

Albright, W.F. The Amarna Letters from Palestine. 1966.

Allegro, M. The Chosen People. London. 1972.

The Sacred Mushroom and the Cross. 1970.

Anderson, Adam, An Historical and chronological deduction of the Origin of Commerce. Four Vols. London. 1789.

Anderson, Benjamin, The Value of Money. New York. 1926.

Andreades. A. History of Greek Public Finance. 1933.

Annales D'Histoire Economique et Sociale. (Les Finances de Guerre d'Alexandre Le Grand). Paris. 1929.

History of the Bank of England. (reprint) Andrews, A. The Greeks. London. 1967.

Aristotle. The Ethics

Oeconomeia

Arnold, Arthur Z. Banks, Credit, and Money, in Soviet Russia. Columbia.

Arrianus, Flavius, Anabasis Alexandri.

Ashley, William, Economic Organization of England. 1933.

Babelon, Ernest, Les Origines de la Monnaie. Paris. 1897.

Badinel, James, Trade in Slaves (1842). reprint. New York.

Bakewell, Paul, What are we using for Money? 1952.

Bamm, Peter, Alexander the Great, Power as Destiny. 1968.

Banerjee. N.C. Economic Life and Progress in Ancient India.

Baring, Frances, Observations on the Establishment of the Bank of England. New York. 1968.

Boeckh, Augustus, Public Economy of Athens. London, 1828.

Bolin, Sture, State Currency in the Roman Empire. 1958.

Breasted, John, A History of Egypt. New York, 1956.

Bright, John, A History of Israel. London, 1960.

Burns, A.R. Money and Monetary Policy in Early Times. 1927

Pericles and Athens. London, 1948. Burton,

Richard F. The Gold Mines of Midian. 1878.

Bury, J.B. A History of Greece. New York, 1900

Cambridge. Cambridge Ancient History.

Cambridge Economic History.

Canney, M.A. Ancient Conception of Kingship. London. 1933.

Canot, Theodore, Adventures of an African Slaver. 1928.

Carr, Guy, Pawns in the Game. Omni, 1955.

Carson, R.A.G. Coins, Ancient, Medieval, and Modern. 1962.

Cassel, Sir Ernest, Lloyd's Bank in the History of English Banking. 1968. Cassel, Gustav, The Downfall of the Gold Standard. 1968.

Chadwick, John, The Decipherment of Linear "B". 1958.

The Chinese Repository (Memorials to the Emperor; ii, p. 279; xv, p. 211; xx, p. 290; re. money and circulation). Church, A.J. Carthage. New York, 1914.

Cicero, Marcus T. Orationes.

Clapham, John H. History of the Bank of England. 1944.

Concise Economic History of Britain. 1951.

Colbourne, Maurice, The Meaning of Social Credit. 1933.

Unemployment or War. New York, 1928.

Dalseme, Monnaie, Histoire de l'Or, de l'Argent, et du Papier. 1970.

Dawson, Christopher. Age of the Gods. London. 1928.

Del Mar, Alexander, Money and Civilization. London, 1886.

History of Monetary Systems. London, 1886.

History of Money in Ancient Countries. 1885.

The Science of Money. London, 1886.

Barbara Villiers or a History of Monetary Crimes.

The Middle Ages Revisited. New York, 1900.

History of Money in America. London, 1899.

Desroches-Noblecourst, Christiane, Tutankamen. 1963.

Dimont, Max., Jews, God and History. New York, 1962.

Douglas, C.H. The Monopoly of Credit. Omni, 1970.

Driver, G.R. Ancient Codes and Laws of the Near East. 1952.

Dunbar, C.F. Bank of Venice. Quarterly Journal of Economics. 1892.

Theory and History of Banking. New York. 1891.

Einzig, Paul, Primitive Money. London, 1949.

Elsom, John R. Lightning over the Treasury Building. 1941.

Engell, J. Studies in Divine Kingship in the Ancient Near East.

Evans, A. The Palace of Minos IV. 4 Vols. London, 1921.

Fisher, Irving, The Purchasing Power of Money. 1920.

Fisk, Harvey E. English Public Finance. New York, 1920.

Flinders-Petrie. W.M. A History of Egypt. London. 1897.

Fortune, Thomas E.F. History and Charter of the Bank of England. 1805.

Frankfurt, F. Kingship and the Gods. New York, 1948.

Freeman, Kathleen, Work and Life of Solon. London. 1926.

Gadd, C.J. Ideas of Divine Rule in the Ancient Near East.

Gardner. History of Ancient Coinage.

Gaster, T.H. Divine Kingship in the Ancient Near East.

Gordon, Cyrus H. Ugaritic Literature. Rome, 1949.

Goulevitch, Arsene de, Czarism and Revolution. Omni, 1962.

Grant, Michael. From Imperium to Auctoritas. 1969.

Grem, June, The Money Manipulators. Enterprise, 1971.

Green, John R. A Short History of the English People. 1936.

Griffith, G.T. The Mercenaries of the Hellenistic World. 1968.

Groseclose, Elgin, Money, The Human Conflict. 1934.

Money and Man. New York, 1961.

Grote, George, Greece. London. 1846-1856.

Guiseppe, John, The Bank of England. Chicago, 1966.

Guizot, F.P.G. The History of Civilization reprint. 1974.

Histoire de la Revolution d'Angleterre, Paris, 1854.

Haeberlin, E.J. Aes Grave. Frankfurt, 1910.

Hammond, Bray, and the staff of the Board of Governors of the Federal Reserve System, The Federal Reserve System.

Hargreaves, E.L. The National Debt. London, 1965.

Harper. Harpers Dictionary of Classical Literature and Antiquities. 1965.

Hattersley, C.M. Wealth, Want, and War. London, 1933.

Hasebroek, Johannes, Trade and Politics in Ancient Greece.

Hawkes, Jacquetta, Dawn of the Gods. New York, 1968.

Prehistory and the beginnings of Civilization.

Hawtrey, R.G. The Art of Central Banking. London. 1965.

Heichelheim, Fritz, An Ancient Economic History. 1958-1970.

Henderson, Fred, Money Power and Human Life. 1932.

Herodotus. The Histories.

Hirmer, Max. Greek Coins. London. 1968.

Historical sketch of the Paper Money of the American Colonies. 1969.

Hobbs, Franklin, Gold the Real Ruler of the World. 1943.

Homer. The Odyssey.

The Iliad

Humboldt, Alexander, The Fluctuations of Gold. 1900.

Huskinson, Thomas W. The Bank of England's Charters The Cause of Social Distress. London, 1912.

Jacob, William, An Historical Enquiry into the Production and Consumption of the Precious Metals. Philadelphia, 1832

Jain, LC. Indigenous Banking in India. London, 1929.

Jastrow, M. The Civilization of Babylonia and Assyria. 1915.

Jevons, William S. Money and the Mechanism of Exchange.

A serious fall in the price of Gold ascertained and its Social Effects set forth. London, 1863.

Jewish Universal Encyclopedia.

Johns, C.H.W. Assyrian Doomsday Book.

The oldest Code of Laws in the World, Hammurabai. 1903.

Kemp, William, Precious Metals as Money. London, 1923.

Kenan, H.S. Federal Reserve Bank. Ocala, Florida, 1967.

Keynes, John M. General Theory of Employment, Interest and Money.

How to Pay for the War. New York, 1940.

King, Leonard W. A History of Babylon. London, 1915.

Kingston-Higgins, A. A Survey of Primitive Money. 1949.

Knies, Carl, Geld und Kredit Vol. I of "Das Geld". 1888.

Knupfer, George, The Struggle for World Power. 1963.

Kraay, Colin M. Greek Coins. London, 1968.

A reply (to W.P. Wallace) Numismatic Chronicle, p. 417. 1962.

Kraeling, Emil G. Aram and Israel. Columbia, 1918.

Kramer, S.N. Sumerian Mythology. (Translation of the Epic of Enmerkar of Uruk). Philadelphia. 1944.

Laum. B. On the Origins of Money. Jena. 1924.

Lenormant, Francois. La Monnaie dans l'Antiquite. 1878.

Lewis. A.B. Melanesian Shell Money in Field Museum Collections. 1929.

Lichtheim. M. The High Steward Akhamenru. 1948.

Livius. Titus. Early History of Rome. Chicago, 1929.

Locke. John. Several papers relating to Money and Interest and Trade. (1696); Reprint: New York. 1968.

Lot, Ferdinand. End of the Ancient World. New York. 1939.

Macpherson, D. Annals of Commerce. 4 Vols. (contains: The New Fashioned Goldsmiths.). London, 1805.

Madden, F.W. Coins of the Jews. London, 1881.

History of Jewish Coinage. Reprint. New York. 1967.

Mallowan, M.E.L. Kingship and the Gods. London, 1947.

Malthus, Thomas R. Measure of Value. New York, 1968.

On Population.

Mansueli, Guido, Etruria and Early Rome. London, 1966.

Marco Polo. The Travels of Marco Polo. Yule Edn. 1969.

Marquardt, Joachim, Manuel Des Antiquites Romaines, De l'Organization Financiere, Tome X. Paris, 1888.

Marshall, John, Mohenjo-Daro London, 1931.

Maspero, G. The Dawn of Civilization. London, 1894.

Mattingly, Harold, Roman Coins. London, 1923.

McCulloch, John R. Old and scarce tracts on Paper Currency and Banking. London, 1857.

Selection of scarce and valuable tracts on Money and Metallic Currency. Reprint, London, 1933.

McKay, E.J.H. Further Excavations at Mohenjo-Daro. 1939.

McLeod, H.D. Theory and Practice of Banking. 1892.

Mellaart. James, Catal Huyuk. 1960.

Catal Huyuk. London, 1967.

Michell, Humphrey, Sparta. Cambridge, 1952.

The Economics of Ancient Greece. 1946.

Miles, John C. Ancient Codes and Laws of the Near East.

Mises, von, Ludwig, Human Action. Yale, 1949.

Mitchell, Wesley C. A History of the Greenbacks. 1903.

Mommsen, Theodore, Manuel Des Antiquities Romaines.1888

Monroe, A.E. Monetary Theory before Adam Smith. 1923.

Morgan, Victor E. History of Money. London, 1965.

Napoleon III. Julius Caesar. 2 Vols. Translation, 1865.

Necker. Finances of France. Paris, 1785.

Noonan, John T. The Scholastic Analysis of Usury. 1957.

Oesterly and Robinson. A History of Israel. Oxford, 1932.

Oppenheim, A.F. Letters from Mesopotamia. Chicago, 1967.

Oppenheim, A.L.O. The Golden Garments of the Gods. 1949.

Oxford Classical Dictionary.

Payne, Robert, The Gold of Troy. New York, 1959. Pearson, Kenneth, The Dorak Affair. London, 1967.

Penetration of Money Economy in Japan, and its Effects upon Social and Political Institutions. London.

Pigott, Stuart, The Dawn of Civilization. New York. 1961.

Pink, Carl, Triumviri Monetales and the Structure of the Coinage of the Roman Empire. 1952.

Plutarch, The Lives.

Plato, The Republic.

The Laws.

Pliny, Naturalis Historia. Polybius.

Postan, M. M. The Rise of a Money Economy. Economic History Revue.

Postlewaythe. Dictionary of Trade and Commerce. 1759.

Potter's Greek Antiquities. London. Poulsen, F. Delphi. London. 1920.

Quigley, Carroll. Tragedy and Hope. New York. 1966.

Radhakrishnan, Sarvepalli, A Source Book in Indian Philosophy. 1957.

Raynal, Abbé, History of the East and West Indies. 1783.

Reid, Sir Edward J. Japan. London, 1850.

Renfrew, Colin, The Emergence of Civilization. 1972.

Report of a Royal Commission on Banking and Finance. (Brief by Mel Rowatt) Ottawa, 1964.

Ridgeway, William, The Origins of Metallic Currency and Weight Standards. Cambridge. 1892.

Rogers. Thorold, The First Nine Years of the Bank of England. 1887.

Economic Interpretation of History. 1888.

Rostovtsev. Mikhail I. A Social and Economic History of the Hellenistic World. Oxford. 1941.

Rowatt, Mel, Brief submitted to Royal Commission on Banking and Finance. (In respect to sophisticated practices governing creation of so-called National Debt in modern-day Canada.) Ottawa, 1964.

Sandars, N.K. The Epic of Gilgamish. London, 1960.

Schlieman, Heinrich, Mycenae. (reprint) New York, 1967.

Sée, Henri, Les Origines Du Capitalism Moderne. 1928.

Seligrnan, C.C. Egypt and Negro Africa. A Study in Divine Kingship. 1934.

Seltsman, Charles, Greek Coins. London, 1933.

Seffert Oscar, A Dictionary of Classical Antiquities. 1904.

Shaw. Theory and Principles of Banking. London, 1930.

Sinclair, History of the English Revolution. London, 1803.

Skousen, Cleon W. The Naked Capitalist. 1970.

Smith, William, History of the Bible. London, Ontario, 1885.

Soddy, Frederick, Wealth, Virtual Wealth, and Debt. Omni.

Money Versus Man. London, 1931, Strabo. Geography; (Books: Vl, Vll).

Strachey, John, The Coming Struggle for Power. 1933.

Suetonius, The Twelve Caesars.

Sutherland, Carol Humphrey V. Coinage in Roman Imperial Policy. 1951.

Gold. London, 1959.

Sydenham, Edward, Roman Republican Coinage. 1926.

Tacitus, The Histories.

The Annals.

Tamagna, Banking and Finance in China. New York, 1942.

Tawney, R.H. Religion and the Rise of Capitalism. 1926.

Taylour, Lord William, The Mycenaeans. London, 1964.

Thucydides. The Peloponnesian War.

Tooke, Thomas, History of Prices. London. 1838-1857.

Toutain, Jules, Economic Life of the Ancient World. 1930.

Trescott, Paul B. Money, Banking, and Economic Welfare.

Ure, p.N. The Origins of Tyranny. New York. 1922.

Vennard, W. B. Conquest or Consent. Boston, 1963.

Ventris, Michael, Documents in Mycenaean Greek. 1956.

Vickers, Vincent C. Economic Tribulations. Omni. 1965.

Vissering, G. On Chinese Currency. Leyden, 1877.

Wallace, W. p. The Early Coinage of Athens and Euboia (p.23) Numismatic Chronicle. 1962.

Warmington, B. H. Carthage. London, 1960.

Warburg, Paul M. The Federal Reserve System: its Origin and Growth.

Watson, M. O. Class Struggle in Ancient Greece. 1947.

Webster, T.B.L. From Mycenae to Homer. London, 1964.

Westerman, William L. Warehousing and Trapezitae Banking in Antiquity: Journal of Economic and Business History. III, pp. 30-54. 1930.

The Slave Systems of Greek and Roman Antiquity: American Philosophical Society, Philadelphia.

White, William C. Jews In Kaifeng. reprint Toronto. 1966.

Wilson, McNair R. God and the Goldsmiths. Omni. 1961.

Woodhead, Geoffrey, Thucydides on the Nature of Power. Harvard, 1970.

Woolley, Charles L. Abraham. London. 1937.

Excavations at Ur. London. 1954.

Ur of the Chaldees. London. 1950.

A Forgotten Kingdom. London. 1953.

The Sumerians. New York, 1965.

Prehistory and the Beginnings of Civilization. 1963.

Xenophon. A Discourse upon improving the Revenues of the State of Athens. Tr. Charles Davenport. London. 1771.

Captain David Astle,
Colborne, Ontario
September 15th 1993,

Great indeed was my surprise when I opened your small parcel to find therein a translation into Hungarian of "The Babylonian Woe." Please accept my thanks! I esteem your unsolicited work as a great honour, and it is indeed an event in my life. There may be other translations, but I do not know where they are. It is not the easiest type of book to translate. A Greek lady set down to translate it into Greek but she gave up after a chapter or two (so far as I know). She told me that it was as difficult as translating Plato into English! I am the more pleased that you are one of the relatively few who truly understand the theme and its significance in the rise and fall of civilizations. The impression that Hungarians in Toronto have given me is that there is no people more aware generally of this fact. No specially deep thought is required to see that everything we describe as civilization and indeed all of its works, is the derivative of Money Power and its creation as indeed by Sovereign Power or by the activities of an International criminal caste. Law No. 7 of Hammurabai that I quote on page 9 is evidence enough. Also the proscription by Manu of the Goldsmiths who used their trade to deceive: "The most pernicious of all deceivers is a Goldsmith who commits frauds. The Maharajah shall order him to be cut to pieces with razors." The principal fraud being that which has appeared and reappeared throughout history, the issuance of fraudulent receipts as against Gold supposedly on deposit. This knowledge is written deep into the memory of your people for there cannot be much doubt that it was the destroyer of Sumer. If not, why then Hammurabai's Law, a repetition of similar Laws out of much more ancient codes yet again?

Have you produced a finished book? And if so, have you circulated it? If you have not done so, then that is obviously the next step. I myself am at the moment concerned with the

United States. "SPOTLIGHT" in Washington plan a review within a few weeks, which should wake things up thereabouts.

If you do not feel that you want to go further than you have (at the moment) I might try myself. Though it seems to me that you should be better able to so do in North America. But there is also Hungary itself, and this is an understanding they need more than any at this moment when Communism is supposed to have collapsed and the Jackals will be seeking to take over.

I do not remember whether I replied to your last letter and the copy of "The Rise of the Money Power" you sent me. Was it from "The Red Dragon"? And was that the title of the book found in the library at Cincinnati? I am alone here and do not mind admitting that I am not as well organized as I would like to be. Anyway I had some copies of "The Rise of the Money Power" zeroxed and it is doing good work. If I did not reply please accept my apologies.

The fact is I am 77 years of age and Alas! not getting any younger! However, as you see, I keep going. My main effort "The Babylonian Woe" was not finished until I was practically 60 years of age, and then on top of that, it had to be sold and promoted generally.

But nevertheless in the last seventeen years it has trickled all around the world; principally due to my own efforts. When Mrs. Thatcher said to the British Parliament that she would not lead Britain into a COMMON MONEY MARKET, you need have no doubt whose book she had been reading; she had had it for 13 years!

If you decide to publish your translation itself, I can advise you to some extent. However it seems to me there is a wide field open, not only in North America etc., but in Hungary itself.

I vaguely remember Lillooet as a village near the junction of the Thompson River and the Fraser river, not far from Ashcroft and the small town of Merritt with the Douglas lake ranch in between. There used to be good fishing around there. I cannot imagine what it is like now. When I was there some 45 years ago, the road was just a dirt track crawling around the edge of the canyon.

If you come here again [why don't you] immediately look me up. At present I live very much in the country about 83 miles from Toronto — Eastwards. In this letter I am giving you my home address the telephone No. is 416 xxx xxxx. Although I keep box 282, Stn. 'P' going, most of my mail comes here these days.

Thank you once again for the honour your work bestows on me and hoping to hear from you soon

Yours very sincerely

David Astle

PS: "The Red Dragon" is "'Y Draig Coch" in Welsh. As you may know it is their very ancient flag.

Lightning Source UK Ltd.
Milton Keynes UK
UKHW02f1127300718
326492UK00012B/712/P